Keeping Parents Out of Trouble

Also by Dr. Dan Kilev

NOBODY SAID IT WOULD BE EASY
(Published as a Warner paperback under the title
KEEPING KIDS OUT OF TROUBLE)

KEEPING PARENTS OUT OF TROUBLE

A Modern Guide to Old-fashioned Discipline

Dr. Dan Kiley

WARNER BOOKS

A Warner Communications Company

Although he can't answer all your letters,
Dr. Kiley would like to hear from you.
Write him at Box 909, Decatur, IL 62525.

Warner Books, Inc.,
75 Rockefeller Plaza,
New York, N.Y. 10019

 A Warner Communications Company

Book design by Thomas Nozkowski

Distributed in the United States by Random House, Inc.,
and in Canada by Random House of Canada, Ltd.

Printed in the United States of America

First printing: April 1981

10 9 8 7 6 5 4 3 2 1

LIBRARY OF CONGRESS CATALOGING IN PUBLICATION DATA

Kiley, Dan.
    Keeping parents out of trouble.

    Includes index.
    1. Discipline of children. 2. Children—
Management. I. Title.
HQ770.4.K54   649′.64   80-23152
ISBN 0-446-51221-4

To my wife,
Nancy,
who keeps me out of trouble

Preface

A mother struggles with her shopping list as she battles with two youngsters who are unceasingly disruptive. A divorced mother exhausts all alternatives in trying to control a high-spirited six-year-old who bites, screams, and explodes when faced with the mildest frustration. Parents are exasperated when they tell their fifteen-year-old daughter that she may not go out and she replies, "Who asked you?"

Parents who face these and similar situations share one thing in common: Their lack of disciplinary control is getting them into trouble. Although the situations described above may or may not call for professional consultation, there are many troublesome situations that can be solved with my "get-tough" approach to child-rearing. Parents can indeed keep themselves out of trouble by establishing their authority early in a child's life or by reestablishing it once their child demonstrates that he or she is beyond parental control.

My get-tough views are not exactly the hottest item at cocktail parties. It's not popular to admit that raising kids is tough and sometimes you'd like to send your children to Siberia until they've grown up. Whatever your frustration, I hope you give me a chance to persuade you to give your kids the one thing they're crying for—a loving toughness that will help them learn the self-control necessary for survival.

In my first book, *Nobody Said It Would Be Easy* (as a paperback, *Keeping Kids Out of Trouble*), I focused on situations that are troublesome. I gave answers that were specific to the disruption described in the situation. In this book I still deal with many difficult problems. However, my dos and don'ts are more fundamental. They can be applied to many situations, not just after disruption has occurred. My first book described the cure; this one focuses on prevention.

Several reviewers thought my first book was too tough. They noted that my take-charge recommendations would destroy parent-child communication. In fact, no-nonsense discipline enhances, not destroys, communication. One editor thought my advice was that of a harsh dictator and said, "I'll use it on my cats but not my kids."

My reply: "Harsh? *Never!* Dictator? Well, as the old saying goes, "You ain't seen nothing yet." Compared to this effort, my first book was the work of Mr. Nice Guy.

If you're a parent, I have some advice you're going to love. It will take the pressure off you and permit you to control *and* to enjoy your children. If you're an expectant parent or some-day plan to be a parent, my get-tough approach will help you start off on the right foot. If you're not sure whether or not to have kids, this book may convince you that it won't be as easy as you think. If your children are grown and gone and you feel guilty because you were too tough, this book will lighten your burden. You probably were right all along.

Teachers, deans, judges, cops, store managers, and other authority figures will appreciate my get-tough approach. You'll see that I think we've let this "Nurture our poor, weak children" business get out of hand. We're dangerously close to nurturing our children into a state of moral weakness from which they may never escape.

Don't be surprised if much of my advice rings a bell of familiarity. My work is based on common sense and on the everyday headaches of raising kids. I've added just enough modern science to give old-fashioned child-rearing a much-needed shot in the arm. You'll quickly see that if it is applied as recommended, my get-tough approach will keep parents out of the trouble that results when children decide that they can do what they damn well please anytime they want to.

A major problem with my recommendations is that they sound so simple. You'll find yourself saying, "Of course he's right. Everybody knows that. It's just good common sense."

But, be careful. Don't take my words for granted. You'll find that time and again I warn you that talk is cheap. The only redeeming grace of the talk that I've put forth in this book is that if you believe my words, then you'll have to take *action*.

You know the old adage "That game plan looks good on paper; too bad the game isn't played on paper"? Well, my words look good on paper, but this book isn't worth the powder it would take to blow it to hell if you don't put my words into action.

It takes more than mouthing the words of love and discipline to keep parents out of trouble. It takes action that is tough to give as well as to receive. One young man recently confided in me, "The army gives survival training; why can't parents?"

If you want to keep yourself out of trouble by giving your children survival training, then you'll have to follow my favorite one-liner: "If you love them enough, then you gotta get tough."

DAN KILEY, PH.D.

Acknowledgments

Many "warm fuzzies" go to the thousands of parents who have phoned or written to me in the past two years. Your encouragement and suggestions have been very helpful.

A special thanks goes to Jon D. Robinson, attorney, of Decatur, Illinois, for advice and direction on the legal aspects of drug abuse.

Contents

Introduction

Struggle to understand; strive to communicate; work at talking, for talk can cure; avoid the use of power, and downplay your authority; back off any sign of rebellion, for you'll only make matters worse; and, above all, guard against scarring the unconscious psyche.

This collage of recommendations is taken from popular child-rearing advisers. At best, they've overemphasized certain aspects of parenting. At worst, they are dead wrong and have misled us into thinking that parents have all the responsibility and kids have all the rights, when, if anything, the reverse is true.

Modern-day child-rearing must be based on tough-minded discipline. Tough discipline is a key to healthy and happy children. It forms the foundation for self-confidence, frustration tolerance, and impulse control. These three personality traits

1

give children the initiative and strength to attain the "good life"; that is, to build a career, improve their education, form lasting love relationships, and invest in the adult world, reaping the best rewards possible.

Tough discipline helps a child reach a stage at which he or she can say, "I am strong and can survive whatever life throws at me. When life gets tough, I can get tougher!"

Parents have been led to believe that there are serious drawbacks to this hard-nosed attitude. The "Nurture your child at any cost" approach tells parents that discipline could lead to permanent psychological damage. As one mother recently confided to me, "I know my child needs discipline, but I don't want to mar her for life."

Although admonitions about prudent use of discipline are appropriate, I doubt that doomsday is so close at hand. Even I have a sinking feeling of helplessness when I read about the formation of damaging "unconscious attitudes." If you are concerned enough to read this book, then you wouldn't knowingly hurt your children. And since these attitudes are supposedly hidden from conscious awareness, your worrying about them is not going to help in any way. Besides, your child will have his or her own brand of problems to cope with later in life.

The experts who've gone off the deep end in favor of nurturance would have you believe that mistakes in your parenting can form harmful clusters of ghostlike personality quirks that resemble psychic ice crystals, formed in the deep recesses of the child's cloudy mind, swirling in mass confusion, waiting for that rainy day to storm all over the child's sunny disposition. And, to cap it all off, *you* did it without knowing what you did. How do you like that for a guilt trip?

Are parents so powerful that they can actually create these mental monsters? Whatever happened to a child's willpower? Where has the power of self-control gone? It seems to have been trampled by those who would have us believe that our children are nothing more than robotic clones, destined to drone on forever under the programming of unconscious controls. If you believe this, then you've never seen the antics of a five-year-old who is impossible to control even though Mom has reared three other responsible children, or a twelve-year-old who after over a decade of compliant behavior suddenly discovers rebellion.

In case you haven't guessed by now, I think that the pursuit of the phantoms of the unconscious mind is fruitless. It may make for fine literature or a good novel, but it'll never pass for reliable child-rearing. It's a waste of precious time, and it's a waste of valuable parental energy.

Our children aren't fragile pieces of glass that can be destroyed with one or two ill-timed mistakes. They're tougher than that. Children have a drive to bring out the best in themselves. Like it or not, you can't control everything that your child decides to become.

You may contribute to your child's problems. You may pass on severe guilt trips, give little or no moral guidance, or engage in subtle forms of emotional abuse. But these represent your personal problems, not discipline. If you want to avoid marring your child, accentuate no-nonsense discipline and respectful behavior and forget about the unconscious. If you do, you'll have more time to spend with yourself, enjoy warm feelings about raising responsible children, feel good about being alive, and rarely miss an opportunity to share good times with your kids. If there is an unconscious, this would be an excellent way to shape it.

The world our children must learn to adjust to is getting tougher every day. Life is still worth living, but the price is going up. Chances are that our children will not have it as easily as most of us had it. They are going to have to get by on less material goods and services at greater cost. We may have taken our last walk down easy street.

We've gone through the horn of plenty, and now we are on the horns of a dilemma. Life offers more pleasures than ever before, but the acquisition of these pleasures calls for more work, increased sacrifice, and tremendous patience (that is, if we get these things legally). It's not a time to sit back and relax;

we face an age of frustration. Authority figures of every persuasion must balance the warmth of nurturance with the chill of the lessons that nature must teach.

You often hear that we must nurture our children so that they can become the best that they can be. This is true—to a point. We can nurture them so that they will have the self-confidence and courage to face the world on their own. But when our nurturance interferes with the lessons of nature, we have short-changed our kids. Nature has many important things to say to our children. Let's help them hear the messages. When your kids fall down, don't pick them up; *help them to pick themselves up.*

I implore you to reconsider your attitude toward discipline. I ask you to get tough! You'll see that you don't have to take it on the chin from a defiant child. You can be tough and strong, and bend only *after* your child has demonstrated responsibility. You can pass this toughness on to your children. Then, when they look in the mirror, they will see a survivor. They can take pride in their reflection and not be afraid of the challenges that await them outside your front door.

Above all, I ask you to be an authority figure—first, foremost, and always. Don't let someone else teach your children how to behave. Nobody can discipline your children better than you can, because nobody loves your kids more than you do.

1

Grandma and Grandpa Weren't All Wrong

Unlike most of my peers, I grew up in an old-fashioned way. I milked cows by hand, gathered eggs, and worked in the garden to put food on the table. As a toddler, I scraped together grass cuttings as a special treat for the only horsepower we had on our small Illinois farm—two haggard old geldings named Blackie and Brownie. One of the happiest memories of my preteen years was the installation of our indoor plumbing. What a treat! Sears Roebuck catalogues could finally be used as they were intended to be—as kindling for the cook stove.

I didn't have much time to experiment with being a wild child. At or near my seventh birthday, I was told that I had attained the age of reason and self-control. I was directed to enter into an "examination of conscience." I was supposed to

discover the manner in which I had used my reason to violate
the moral code I had been taught. This particular event, complete with religious trappings, was my close encounter with a
"coming of age" ceremony.

I'm not sure why the church and my parents selected seven
as the age at which I was to be held accountable for my
actions. It probably had something to do with the fact that I
had graduated from strictly home-bound care and was adjust-
ing to school. I had entered the outside world, and my parents
wanted to make certain that I didn't destroy myself before I
grew up.

It didn't take long before I realized that being accountable
was different. The basic dos and don'ts hadn't changed. Do
the chores; don't hit your sister. Do eat your vegetables; don't
lie. But suddenly it was *my fault* when I did something wrong.
Putting the blame on my brother, the weather, or an errant
clock didn't work. As it does with most children, the experience of responsibility gave me a new outlook on life.

Accountability and the resultant "growing up" had a double
effect. On the one hand, it frightened me. After all, if I hit my
sister, I was at fault. This was especially serious because Sis was
not yet seven and therefore not totally accountable for her
actions. Even if she hit me first, I was still at fault. I had to be
very careful. On the other hand, I got a thrill from responsibility. Following or breaking the rules gave me a sense of
power. I, a seven year old—with power!

I could make things happen. When I ate my peas (I never
could do it with a knife, like Grandpa), I received extra cob-
bler. When I lied, I got the evil eye of disapproval and had to
do my brother's chores. Day-to-day activities taught me that
my actions could initiate reactions in other people. Looking
back on those experiences, I see that I was learning to exercise
my willpower.

Age seven marked the beginning of my free will—or,
should I say, my awareness of it. I discovered that all people
have the power to *will* things to happen. We can do what we
choose to do. One time I chose to jump off the chicken shed
in order to fly like the birds. Shortly thereafter, I learned that

free will was limited by the power of physical laws, or what might be called "nature power."

At about this time, my parents and teachers were exposing me to another obstacle to my willpower. It was the limit imposed by the words and actions of authority figures. Rather than giving me a nasty bump on the head, my parents and teachers had the ability to back up their words with rewards and punishments that limited my willpower.

If I chose not to eat my veggies, I lost my dessert. When I did the chores without constant reminders, I received approving smiles and an extra slice of home-baked bread. My parents' ability to control what happened to me often influenced *my* ability to control what I chose to do. Occasionally, my willpower clashed with their control power. As in my bout with nature, I usually gave in and modified my willpower. Eventually, my willpower and authority's control power came to coexist. With this coexistence, accountability and responsibility became a part of my willpower. I *wanted* to be responsible. As this developed, my understanding of the difference between right and wrong was sharpened.

There was a fourth power operating in my life throughout these crucial years. I was well into adulthood before I understood what it was and how it worked. I now know that this power was more important than all the rest combined. However, it still defies accurate description. One has to experience it to know that it's there. It operates differently in each person yet is absolutely essential for the survival of all of us. In fact, if it isn't present, then the other forces have no balance or organization. I call this force "love."

By the time I reached adolescence, the four powers—nature, authority, will, and love—sat like members of the board of directors of my life. When a decision was made, each had its say. Nature told me what was rational to attempt. Authority showed me when to restrain myself for the long-term good of myself and others. Will gave me the courage to try what was possible, retaining a dash of healthy defiance. Love created the energy to make the whole thing worth doing in the first place.

I like to think that my willpower, directed by love, was, and still is, the chairman of the board, his vote carrying a little more clout than the others.

As I study today's families, it is clear that many kids are not as fortunate as I. It is also evident that life is more complicated than it used to be. The simple, rural life has regretfully all but disappeared. I also lament the loss of a clear demarcation line signifying the coming of age of the conscience. Even though my experience at age seven was only symbolic (I obviously exercised my willpower much earlier in life), it was good for me to have experienced that day when I said to myself, "Now *you* are in charge!" It is clearly not true that a child wakes up one day and is suddenly struck with the awe-inspiring notion that he or she has been blessed with willpower. We know that it just doesn't happen that way. It's much more complicated.

Today's families are experiencing a monumental clash of forces. Children use whatever means at their disposal to force their will upon authority and, in many cases, upon nature's physical reality. Love becomes lost in the rush as kids believe there is no limit to their will. They know about their rights but don't want to hear about responsibilities.

Parents and teachers face the opposite problem. They are unsure of where their control power fits. They read and hear so many conflicting stories about the pros and cons of discipline that their confidence gets buried beneath an avalanche of uncertainty. They are painfully aware of their responsibilities but have lost sight of their rights.

I had a lady in my office recently who was lamenting the nasty antics of her two children, ages three and five. They fought with each other, constantly defied her, and created havoc with demands to be the center of attention. When I asked her why she didn't take action against them, she replied, "I've been told that if you expect the best from your children, you will get the best."

This belief is common among modern-day parents who've read many of the child-rearing books that have sprung up in the last two decades. These well-intentioned parents honestly believe that talking is sufficient in shaping a child's willpower.

Although talk and expectations are important, they are not enough. The assumption that words and hopes will ensure decent, moral behavior is just unmitigated hogwash. (The belief deserves a much stronger adjective, but this book is rated "G.")

Children's exercise of will is dangerously close to getting out of hand. The disruption, tyranny, and lawlessness we see in our homes, classrooms, and communities reflect this problem. It takes action, not just words, to stop these and other forms of deviance.

Parents and teachers often react to a child's forceful will in one of two equally undesirable ways: Either they put the entire situation out of their mind, too consumed with their own problems to do anything about it, or they overreact, going to one extreme or another, in hopes of finding an immediate answer. When the storm hits, they lose sight of the stability that comes with a healthy balance of love and control.

When teaching parents to keep themselves out of trouble, I first help them to put their authority in proper perspective. I do this by giving them a mental image of how the forces of nature, will, authority, and love should fit together. This is how I see it:

Imagine that your child is a ball, revolving about you as the earth about the sun. Imagine also that when the child first comes into your life, you form two attachments to him or her. One is the emotional attachment made by your heart. This link binds you forever to the child and is a pathway for the two-way flow of compassion, warmth, tenderness, and the multitude of things that come with loving. This attachment is *unconditional,* in that you "hook on to" the child regardless of his or her ability to reciprocate the love. You hope for love in return, but you don't make it a condition of your giving love. Contrary to poetic tradition, the attachment of the heart never breaks, even when faced with death. The second link is best viewed as a rope, attached to the child for the purpose of control. The control rope represents authority and is *conditional,* in that its use depends upon circumstances, the child's behavior, and the day-to-day problems encountered by the controller (parent) and the controllee (child). It is through judicious use of this control rope that parents can teach children right from wrong and thereby shape a child's willpower so that he or she *wants* to be responsible.

As a parent, you stand on a platform at the center of your child's revolutions, spinning slowly with the child, keeping your eye on him or her as much as possible. Each revolution takes a year. Each birthday marks the beginning of a new revolution. The love of your heart creates the movement; the rope modifies and controls the movement.

At birth, the rope is very short—say, an inch or two. Consequently, the child's revolution, or orbit, is confined to a small space, permitting little unfettered contact with the outside "universe." With each year, the child's orbit is increased as you, the controller, give the rope slack. The child's orbit into the universe is controlled by the length of the rope.

During the first five years, it is advisable that the rope have little slack and be lengthened in a slow, deliberate fashion. Keeping the rope taut means that slight movements of the rope have a very direct and immediate effect on the child. The amount of exposure to the outside universe is controlled by the parental rope.

Expect your child to stick close to you during his first few revolutions in space. During this time of close supervision, use the control rope to develop *clout*, that five-letter word that means your kid recognizes you as an authority figure. If you gain clout in the early years, you will have an easier time handling the struggles that result when your teenager thinks he is old enough to be totally independent.

During these first few revolutions, the expression of love in all forms is imperative. It is through gentle words, soft touches, and other gestures of love that the child develops a sense of self-respect and self-control. The child's logic is quite simple: "If I am loved, then I must be loving. If I'm loving, then I must learn to love myself. The best way to love myself is to protect myself from harm, loving others who, in turn, will love me back."

When the child enters school (age five or six), the orbit dramatically increases in circumference. This increase signifies that the child is encountering a larger area of the universe than in earlier orbits. In fact, the volume of the universe encountered doubles and triples within a few months.

The pressures that develop at or near the sixth revolution are tremendous. There are two forces that you must reckon with.

If you can visualize yourself on a spinning platform, doing your best to adjust the control rope attached to your child (or managing two, three, or four ropes of varying lengths), you don't have to be told that you're under constant pressure. The child wants to investigate the universe that lies beyond. That's normal. In fact, you should be pleased that your child has a normal, "nosy" attitude. The constant strain on your psychic muscles results from your attempt to provide the child with consistency in orbital patterns. After all, your common sense tells you that a child's inquisitiveness and exploration must be tempered with authoritative control.

The drain on your parenting energy is caused by two forces, one pulling outward, the other inward. The combination of the drive for self-enhancement and the confidence of self-love pushes the child outward. Your desire to monitor and influence the child's movement into the universe pulls the child toward you.

Attaining *and* maintaining a proper balance of these two forces puts you in a position of constantly flirting with trouble. It is unrealistic to think that these two forces will balance themselves in a smooth, hassle-free manner. More often than not, the orbits reflect a pull-push relationship between the parents' control and the child's will.

In the first few years, when the rope is taut and you have immediate influence over the child's behavior, the orbits take on a choppy appearance akin to that of the blade of a circular saw. The child moves outward, hits a situation in which his exploration is getting out of hand (for example, moving toward a hot stove or throwing food at his sister), and must be pulled back into a proper orbit quickly.

Hence, the young child's orbits have sharp points, reflecting sudden course-correction measures in the form of jerks on the rope. Such actions as slapping a child's hand when he is about to touch the stove, taking a plate of food away from a disruptive child, or standing a child in the corner for failure to comply with a directive are examples of immediate disciplinary measures designed to get the child in line.

In later years, it is imperative that the child be given slack— that is, ample opportunity to use his self-control to modify his own orbit. A shift toward self-determination is taken when you *delay* your reaction to a problem situation (unless it is clearly dangerous). You give the child time to think and to exercise whatever self-control he has developed. If you decide you must take action, you spread out the incentive or punishment over time. Thus, if a kid goofs up, he must live with his mistake for a few days or weeks (grounding, loss of privileges). If he does well, you praise him several times over a time period and give him an extra privilege three or four days later.

The orbits begin to smooth out as the child exercises self-control. The child's will to be responsible begins to replace the control rope. As the child's self-control takes over the job of correcting deviant behavior, you will find it more difficult to manipulate the control rope. As long as the child keeps the orbit within the bounds of your morality, you are well advised to let the world teach the child important lessons. Some would say that the child should be allowed to enroll in the school of hard knocks.

Parents can structure the lessons that reality has to offer by making a major switch in disciplinary emphasis. I characterize this switch in the use of the control rope by suggesting that parents gradually get rid of *inducements* and replace them with *enforcements*.

Inducements are what you say or do to your children to force, remind, or otherwise instruct them to follow your rules. Inducements come *before* errant behavior, and you hope they will encourage the child to do the correct thing. Inducements are the avenues you use to communicate the difference between right and wrong. "Don't forget to take out the garbage," "I want you to keep your room picked up," and

"Remember, your curfew is nine P.M." are inducements. In order to promote self-control, the number of inducements must decrease with each revolution.

Enforcements are actions you take *after* errant behavior. They tell the child how he or she succeeded or failed in doing as told. Enforcements are the rewards and punishments a child "earns" with his or her behavior. Without enforcements, the morality contained in the inducements does not translate into action. "Thank you for remembering the garbage without being told," "You lost your toys for one week because you didn't put them away," and "You lose Friday night because you are forty minutes late" are examples of enforcements.

Once a child reaches the thirteenth revolution, he or she certainly knows what you expect of him or her. The rules have been made very clear. Inducements are no longer needed. Thus, to help the child internalize the morality you've been preaching, decrease your inducements to near zero and maximize your enforcements.

During this period, the power of control is slowly transferred from parent to child. As the hassles mount, many parents mistakenly slack off in expressing love as they let go of controls. After eight, ten, or twelve years of loving, they slip into the common oversight of giving and taking love for granted. If parents knew how much trouble this oversight caused, they'd never let it happen.

During the power-transfer phase, I encourage parents to double and triple their expressions of unconditional love. Out of the blue, they should hug their child. Or, without special circumstances, they should approach the child and say, "You know, Son, I sure do love you," or "Sometimes I forget to tell you, but you're special to me." It's particularly difficult but crucial to express this love to a smart-aleck, independence-seeking sixteen-year-old. Small expressions of genuine, unconditional love, when combined with no-nonsense discipline, will promote self-love and, in the end, self-control.

It is the absence of self-control and spontaneous expressions of love that most concerns me about the future of our children. Without these two things, children are left defenseless in a world that wants to eat them alive. As I often tell parents, today's children don't know when to fear and when to brag. Their self-protection and self-confidence are all mixed up. They must be taught to fear more and brag less.

Two problems of extremes can occur in helping children find the happy medium between the fear that comes with self-protection and the bragging that is part of self-confidence.

First, consider what happens if you, in the name of permissiveness, let the rope dangle and fail to maintain some degree of control. The child is left to experience life in a willy-nilly fashion, guided by the haphazard reactions that occur when his or her will collides with the limits inevitably imposed by the environment.

Uncontrolled children bounce around their universe like a Ping-Pong ball in a windstorm. They go wherever the random influence of impulse takes them. They may suddenly switch directions when hit with peer pressure or a new fad. To continue in this manner spells eventual disaster. As I so often tell parents, if you don't stop your wild child, somebody or something most assuredly will.

The world stops these children in one of two ways. Either an authority figure other than the parent slams the door to opportunity or nature exercises its option, making the children conform to physical laws. Both constitute rude awakenings and trouble for parents as well as for children.

If a teacher, dean, judge, or employer gets sick and tired of a kid's lack of conformity to rules and regulations, he or she can flunk him, kick him out of school, put him in jail, terminate his employment. Many children have been stopped in this manner and in some cases have gone on to make up for that failure. These are the lucky few. Many others end up rebelling their way into deeper trouble.

If a child's poor self-control collides with nature, the outcome is sometimes worse. Nature has a way of working more slowly, but its effect is usually more painful or deadly. Drug overdose, pregnancy, alcoholism, insanity, psychologically induced physical problems (such as ulcers), suicide, and accidental death are just a few ways nature tells an uncontrolled child, "Yes, it can happen to you!"

The other extreme in the struggle to reach a happy medium occurs when parents overcontrol, not allowing the child enough slack to develop self-control. A child who experiences too much parental control remains a tightly controlled satellite, never straying far from the parental influences. In short, the control rope remains too taut, strangling the child's exploration.

These children may be told that they are loved, but they never get the opportunity to practice self-protection. They are smothered in what appears to be concern but is actually an unbridled punitive attitude.

Most children eventually tear loose from this restrictive life-style. When they do, they burst out of the control orbit like a neutron shot out in a nuclear reactor. They usually overshoot the happy medium, ending up at the opposite extreme. Their flight to "freedom" puts them in chains. They are spellbound by the first barnstorming, phony messiah who promises that his or her leadership will yield self-determination. Each year, thousands of soft-minded adults join hysterically minded cults or communes that are obsessed with deliverance but deliver only obsessions. The tragedy that usually results is another powerful argument for my get-tough approach.

The heartache and the turmoil caused by children's running into the world's barriers or being led astray by groundless beliefs are not experienced only by those parents who over- or undercontrolled their children. I've seen families in which children, although blessed with fine parents and surrounded by love and given rational control, ended up at one of the two extremes. It is this unpredictable turn of events that convinces me that the popular view of children as products of the inter-action between their genetic inheritance and their environ-ment is inadequate.

One of these days, the theorists are finally going to recognize that a person's willpower is an entity, an equal partner with heredity and environment. With or without that recognition, all authority figures must remember that any discussion of children's troubles or of potential disruption must include not only heredity and environment but also what children elect to do with what they've got. Thus, when kids take a drug overdose in a blind search for happiness, or commit suicide as their testimony to life, we must not forget that to one degree or another, they *chose* to do it.

When parents accept the role of a child's will, they are relieved that some of the blame is taken off their shoulders. However, they express a fear that even if they do everything "right," there's still a chance the child will choose to make things go wrong. It is at this point that parents tend to get nervous about their authority. When this happens, their common sense drowns in a sea of frustration. When I see parents overcome by uncertainty, I tell them to remember to express their unconditional love, knowing that the things of the heart are always more durable than the things of the world.

I also help them recognize their child's individuality. Different kids with different strengths and weaknesses approach their universe at different speeds. Some kids' orbits are larger than others'; some will move faster than their friends. A ten-year-old might behave as if he were ten going on twenty-five; at other times, the same child will act as if he is ten going on two. The love should always remain constant while the control rope is adjusted to fit the situation.

I will spend most of the later chapters discussing how and when parents can jerk, tug, loosen, and/or tighten the control rope given the specifics of certain situations. If parents maintain a sensible awareness of the child's behavior, they can adjust their power in keeping with how far they believe the child is off the appropriate path of maturation.

Even a fourteen- or fifteen-year-old who orbits away from his parents can be influenced by the control rope. If, for example, a boy begins to experiment with disruption at school or decides to "play" with drugs, his parents can muster a mighty muscle and yank the rope in order to get the kid back in line. This late-arriving yank leads to a crisis period in which you must remind your kid that even though he or she has established a high degree of self-determination, your rules and regulations remain in effect.

If you weather the storms of your child's adolescence, accepting the fact that a kid's orbit will be a little odd from time to time, you can eventually let go of the rope. Thus, at age eighteen or nineteen, give or take a year, spin-off occurs. The child leaves orbit and heads into the universe to find his or her own space in which to establish residency. This spin-off, to be most successful, should occur *after* the child has proved that he or she can maintain a sensible orbit around authority, not before.

Given all the unpredictable factors in a child's orbital behavior, I've seen most kids work their way toward adulthood and a successful spin-off by going through several stages: Four or five closely monitored orbits that are characterized by sudden jerks on the control rope are followed by several orbits in which the child smooths out his or her behavior through initial experiments with self-control. These orbits lead to a dramatic increase in exposure to the universe, resulting in orbits that are difficult to monitor and that give the child ample opportunities to practice self-determination. The orbits that make up the teenage years are highly unpredictable and often call for parents to muster the strength and courage to yank the control rope just about the time everyone thought the rope was no longer needed.

Reminding teenagers that they still must deal with authority figures is usually troublesome to parents, but exercising clout at this late date can stimulate the spinning-off process. When a kid decides to complete his independence by leaving parental rules and regulations behind, he becomes his own authority figure. You might say that he leaves orbit and takes up residency as a self-sustaining planet.

Given this picture, parents can take heart even in the face of erratic behavior. The rocky road between childish defiance and adult compliance is filled with many bumpy experiences, all of which have the potential of teaching the child the difference between right and wrong. If seen in a positive light, problems requiring jerks and tugs on the control rope can be excellent opportunities to teach the child about the dangers of the world.

Throughout maturation, the child must increase his knowledge of the distinction between unconditional love and conditional control. You always love him, but you don't always approve of his behavior. If parents maintain this distinction, children will look at their own behavior and say to themselves, "I am a good person who just did a stupid thing." With this understanding, children have the vehicle with which they can make the most important journey of their life—a visit with their soul and a discovery of the power that lies therein.

Dos and Don'ts of Using the Rope

The following dos and don'ts give parents guidelines for when to pull, tug, jerk, loosen, ignore, and finally let go of the control rope. I will revisit these recommendations from different perspectives throughout the rest of the book. By the time I'm finished, all authority figures should know how to use the control rope so that they can maximize their clout while minimizing the incidence of rope burn.

DON'T think you have to handle every situation like a superstar. Maybe, sometimes, you're just too tired to parent. Don't expect yourself to be all things to your children at all times.

DO give yourself a break now and then. If the child has done well lately, be willing to overlook a mistake. Just make sure that you notify the child loud and clear that *you*, as authority, are *giving* him or her the break.

DON'T think that you have to respond orally to everything, especially when you're angry.

DO take time out from difficult situations. The best get-tough recommendation for some situations is the old-fashioned idea of counting to ten before you do anything. A few moments of silence right in the middle of a storm can do wonders for parental sanity.

DON'T always use punishment when trying to control disruptive behavior. Too many punishments will inevitably work against you.

DO use ignoring once in a while. Reward the child for good behavior by smiling and saying a few kind words. Use the evil eye, preaching, lecturing, and setting examples as alternative styles of discipline.

DON'T permit children to think that if they can create an excellent explanation, they can automatically excuse their misbehavior.

DO give children a chance to present evidence, which you, as the judge and jury, will take under consideration in deciding what to do about disruption.

DON'T try to be "nice" when giving a punishment. Being nice has nothing to do with giving the child something he or she doesn't want. In fact, it probably serves to confuse them.

DO give punishments with an air of aloofness and cold factuality.

DON'T mix your many roles—teacher, friend, confidant, adviser, maid, cook—with that of authority.

DO let your child know that when you warn, admonish, or direct, you are doing something very special. The more clearly you can signal a change in your role, the more clout you'll have when you give direction.

DON'T jump into an authority role without warning.

DO change your facial expression, the warmth in your eyes, and the tone of your voice in an attempt to let your child know that something different is about to happen.

DON'T let your authority be sidetracked by words. Don't let your parenting ego get so big that a word or two can destroy your control.

DO keep your eye on compliance. If the child does as he or she is told, you can be assured that the complaints are designed to upset you and give the child a sense of revenge. If you don't get upset, the child has no reason to sass you and will eventually give it up.

DON'T repeat a warning if you are confident that the child heard you the first time. The more you repeat warnings, the more you tell the child that he or she doesn't have to listen to you in the first place.

DO take action if you don't get compliance after the *first* warning. Put the child in a seat if you said "Sit down." Take her finger out of the cookie jar if you said "Get your hand out of there."

DON'T put yourself in a corner by making absolute statements. In other words, never say "Never!" Avoid iron-clad "deals"; you may end up the loser.

DO establish several issues over which you will *not* negotiate—for example, drugs in the home, sexual promiscuity. Leave other issues open to discussion, change, or renegotiation. This gives the child a sense of security on some issues and permits a spark of creativity on others.

DON'T give your children the idea that you have to live by the same restrictions they do. You can have sex in your home; they can't. You can drink; they can't (if that's how you feel). You can stay out all night; they can't. Obviously, some restrictions must be placed on your activity in order that you can supervise your child's activity.

DO be aware that setting a good example is probably the best of all disciplinary strategies. Although you permit yourself some privileges because you're mature (I hope), do keep yourself in line with the moral code that you expect your children to live by.

DON'T hide your mistakes from children thinking it will undermine your authority if you tell the truth. Admitting mistakes has nothing to do with being an authority; it has to do with being a person.

DO   explain your errors so that your children will see how you blew it and what you are doing to correct it. Setting this example can be an excellent way to tell your children to be honest about their mistakes.

There's one major drawback to these guidelines. Many parents don't want to take control; they are reluctant to be authority figures. They don't like to admit that they have power and must use it. A majority of parents like to think that they can use reason, discussion, and other forms of discourse to shape their children toward self-discipline and law-abiding behavior. I think they are wrong.

When it comes to disciplining children, talk is cheap. Talk may be necessary in some cases, but it isn't enough. Children come into this world biologically determined to *act* defiantly, not to *talk* compliantly. Parents shy away from action because they have been told that tough action destroys good communication and therefore forever violates the sanctity of the parent-child relationship. That is absolute bunk! If you really want good communication with your children, teach them how to behave themselves. Then they will have respect for you and will seek you out when they need help, advice, and guidance.

It may sound old-fashioned, but I believe parents must be more than the ultimate authority in the home; they must be the *only* one. Parents must determine and set the standards for their children's morality inside and outside the home. This means parents have the responsibility *and the right* to establish a code of conduct and to enforce it. Enforcement entails authority, and authority means someone is in charge.

When parents fail to take charge of the home or teachers fail to take charge of the classroom, we hear that kids are in charge. This is not true. Don't fool yourself into thinking that children can ever be in charge. They can't; that's why they're children. When authority fails to take charge, *no one* is in charge.

Children should be allowed to be children. With guidance, they should be encouraged to be foolish and goofy. Under a watchful eye, they can make mistakes, learn how to control their silliness, and grow into adults who can take charge of their own lives. That's how most of us had to do it. And I don't think we turned out all that bad.

Our parents and grandparents taught us a valuable lesson, and in our rush to be modern and "with it," we're losing sight of it. The lesson was built on survival and being needed. Fifty or sixty years ago, children were needed for survival. There was little or no time to worry about going to a rock concert or buying a dress for the junior prom. These matters took a back-seat to putting food on the table.

It's unfortunate that we've become so secure in our afflu-ence that we don't give today's children a similar lesson in the relative importance of work, freedoms, privileges, and sur-vival. I'm not suggesting we sell our homes and move back to the country in order to be closer to poverty. But there's no reason we can't rediscover a spirit of get-tough survival under trying circumstances. (In case you hadn't noticed, we have trying circumstances surrounding us these days.)

Many people criticize this viewpoint as being too "preachy" and old-fashioned. They seem to think that parenting guide-lines that were built on common sense prior to our "age of enlightenment" are, by definition, inadequate to meet today's challenges. Grandma and Grandpa must have done a few things right to get us this far. Just because modern science teaches us new·things doesn't mean we must throw away the things that experience has taught us. Old-fashioned is *not* the same as out-of-date.

2

Get Tough

Joe Decker is not a bad kid. He's a little bit spoiled but has a friendly smile and warm welcome for everyone he meets. He loves peer approval, gets excited with new things, dislikes order and discipline, and often slumps into that "I don't care about anything" attitude. Joe's a typical teenager.

Like all kids, Joe has problems. He hits the panic button when his girl friend talks to other guys. His grades aren't what they should be, and his language often borders on the disrespectful. Four weeks ago, Joe got into a scrape at school. Three girls told the principal that Joe was selling small quantities of marijuana. The principal called Joe's parents and, with them present, confronted Joe with eyewitness evidence. Joe vehemently denied the allegations. Without hesitation, Joe's parents attacked the principal for making accusations based on the testimony of some "silly girls." Joe's father finished his tirade by saying, "I know what my son is doing. Don't you think I could tell if he were selling that crap?"

The pride of Joe's parents made them blind. Their belief that their son could do no wrong contributed to Joe's deviance. Joe had indeed sold marijuana, one or two joints at a time. But his parents were looking the other way. No wonder Joe thought it was no big deal.

Mr. and Mrs. Decker are typical of many parents. They are middle-class people, intensely interested in the welfare of their kids. They were children of poor parents and lived on a shoestring when they were first married. They are proud to give Joe and his brother things they never had. They automatically assume Joe will realize how lucky he is. They are wrong.

Mrs. Decker does an admirable job caring for her children. She enjoys tennis, volunteer work, and reading. She sees herself as a modern-day parent, well informed as to good discipline. She doesn't admit it, but she will back off her authority if the kids start to argue.

Mr. Decker works just as hard. He is an aspiring executive whose life centers on providing a good living for his family and shooting in the low eighties on Wednesdays and Saturdays. He believes in firm discipline and meaning what you say. He will deny it, but Joe can talk him out of anything he wants.

Let's dust off our microscope and take an in-depth look at a string of events that proved to be a fortunate turning point in Joe's life. I consider the following "The coming of age of Joe Decker." Too bad more kids don't share this experience. We start with the anatomy of a crime.

It's nine-thirty on a Sunday evening. Joe is busy studying. The sixteen-year-old isn't happy to be cramming for a test in math. Yet ever since he flunked algebra, he's tried to get better grades in school.

Seven minutes from now, Joe will take the first step toward serious trouble. He won't realize that he is doing anything wrong until it's too late. Joe's encounter with irresponsibility will last about twenty-four hours. During the course of the disruption, Joe has the chance to stop himself several times. But he doesn't have the maturity to do so. This is what happens:

SUNDAY

9:37 P.M.	Joe gets a call on his private line from his friend Kevin. Kevin tells Joe that he is planning to skip school the next day and party with his girl friend. He wants Joe and his girl friend to join them.
9:38 P.M.	Joe starts to worry about skipping school.
5 seconds later	Joe stops worrying and gets excited about the party. He asks for details.
1 hour later	Joe and Kevin have covered the plan thoroughly. Joe gets increasingly excited. He agrees to purchase some marijuana for the party.
10:45 P.M.	Joe hangs up and begins to plan where to get the dope.
10 seconds later	Joe's girl friend calls. He tells her about the party. Amy says she'll get her car, pick up Kevin's girl friend, Joyce, and meet the guys at Kevin's house. Amy and Joe exchange words of love, pledging to make this party a "mind blower."
12:30 A.M.	Joe says good-bye to Amy.
12:32 A.M.	Joe drops off to sleep, visions of a wild time with Amy racing through his head.

MONDAY

6:40 A.M.	Joe's father must shake Joe to wake him.
7:04 A.M.	Joe begins to figure a way to camouflage his activity so that his parents won't suspect anything. He checks his billfold to make certain he has money for the marijuana.

7:20 A.M.   Joe's father tells Joe, "Get a move on; it's time to leave for school."

7:24 A.M.   Joe leaves for school, riding with his father.

              During the ride to school, Joe pretends to doze so that he will have time to think of a way to escape initial detection when his father waits for him to move toward the school's front door. He can't go in the door for fear the principal will watch him leave again.

7:40 A.M.   Joe's father pulls up in front of the school and wishes his son a good day. Joe replies, "Yeah," and gets out of the car. As he moves to shut the door, he "accidentally" drops his notebook, scattering papers all around. He feigns disgust and remarks, "Great way to start the day! Pull away, Dad, so I can collect my things. See you tonight."

7:42 A.M.   With his father safely out of sight and his papers back in hand, Joe moves around the side of the school. He walks across the street into the Burger Palace, which is open early for students to have coffee.

7:44 A.M.   After exchanging pleasantries with some acquaintances, Joe looks around for Stan, a handsome senior who has the reputation for selling the best dope in school. He sees Stan pull up in the parking lot, excuses himself from his fellow students, and slips out to talk with Stan.

7:50 A.M.   Joe, avoiding detection by any kids who might tell somebody, approaches Stan and buys eight joints at a buck apiece. He ducks down a side street and heads for Kevin's house.

              Meanwhile, at Kevin's house, Kevin's parents wish him a good day as they warn him that he will be late for his first class if he doesn't hurry. They leave for their respective jobs as Kevin finishes his orange juice. By the time they are a block away, Kevin has lit up the rest of the joint he was smoking while talking with Joe last night.

8:10 A.M.   Joe arrives at Kevin's house. Kevin is dragging hard on the final little piece of the joint. Joe pulls the joints out of his pocket with obvious self-satisfaction.

8:25 A.M.   As Kevin and Joe discuss the fun they will have that day, Amy and Joyce arrive. Kevin pulls four beers out of the refrigerator and they start the party off by toasting to Kevin's parents, who'll never miss the beer.

8:45 A.M.   The group decide to give the principal excuses for their absences. Each dials the phone, asks for the principal, and, pretending to be a parent, explains that the student is sick. Joe excuses Amy, and Amy vouches that her "son," Joe, has a touch of the flu. Joyce does the same for Kevin, and Kevin reciprocates, pretending to be Joyce's father. They don't worry too much about the principal's running spot checks, because he usually spends the morning talking with kids who were absent or disruptive the day before.

9:10 A.M.   They continue drinking beer and have begun to feel the effects of it and the marijuana. They get rowdy. Joyce pours some beer on Kevin; Kevin screams loudly, jumps away from Joyce, knocks over a lamp, bending the shade. Joe pours some beer into the aquarium, sending the fish into fits. Joe returns to Amy, and they sip each other's beer, giggling uncontrollably.

9:40 A.M.   Kevin suggests that the group needs a few more beers for the day. He pulls a faded ID card from his billfold and tells Joe to drive to a certain liquor store that doesn't check for minors too closely.

10:15 A.M.   The marijuana and the beer are making everyone hazy, dazy, and a bit crazy. They decide to stop in a remote wooded area, near the construction of a new house. Since there are no workmen around, the group moves the party inside.

10:50 A.M.   After drinking more beer and smoking another "j," the couples pair off. Amy and Joe go upstairs while Joyce and Kevin settle down on rolls of insulation.

11:40 A.M.   After extensive and provocative petting, both couples engage in sexual intercourse. Joyce, being uptight, is not enthusiastic about the encounter. She moves away from Kevin, and he gets angry. Amy convinces Joe that he is a terrific lover, and he feels tremendously confident. His high continues to peak as he repeats the sex act.

11:55 A.M.   Kevin's high turns increasingly sour. He becomes agitated and returns to guzzling beer and rapidly inhaling marijuana.

12:10 P.M.   Kevin picks up a two-by-four and wanders around the lower level, hammering on studs. Suddenly, exploding in frustration, Kevin starts smashing the windows that are lined up along the walls, in storage. Frightened, Joyce says nothing. Hearing the racket, Joe quickly pulls on his pants and moves to Kevin's side. He tells him to be cool, offers a beer, and lights up another joint.

12:35 P.M.   Joyce suggests they leave before somebody shows up. Kevin demands to drive. His determination is not challenged, even though he is in no condition to drive a car.

12:55 P.M.   The group regains its spirit of hell-raising. The car is weaving in and out of the white marks in the center of the road.

1:25 P.M.   Kevin sees a farmer's truck in the distance, parked at the side of the road. He slows to thirty-five mph and brags how he will come within inches of the truck. Joe feels hazy enough to dare him to try it.

1:26 P.M.   As Kevin passes the truck, the front bumper rips the side of the truck and spins the car around. Amy screams, Joyce hides her face, and Joe yells, "Oh, shit!" Kevin puts the car back on the road and speeds away. No one notices the farmer working in a nearby field.

1:40 P.M.   Joyce suggests they find another place to park. Shortly thereafter, Kevin pulls into a deserted park. The group recovers from the close call by drinking more beer. Joyce gets sick, but no one seems to care.

2:15 P.M.   After wandering around the park, Joe finds that the rusty lock on the park pavilion is easily broken. Kevin suggests they make a bonfire before they have to go home.

2:25 P.M.   They gather stray boxes and trash, placing them around the picnic table inside the pavilion. Kevin ignites the rubble and secures an instant inferno. The group gather around the fire, smoking joints and finishing the beer.

2:50 P.M.   Frustrated by the lack of a lasting flame, Kevin picks up a smoldering piece of lumber and smashes the windows on one side of the pavilion.

2:55 P.M.   Joe, realizing that school is almost out, suggests going home. They leave the fire to die on its own.

3:25 P.M.   Joe stops the car a block from Joyce's house, and Joyce staggers home.

3:30 P.M.   Joe lets Kevin out two blocks from his house. He then parks the car a short distance from his own house. After five minutes of necking, Joe tells Amy good-bye. He walks slowly home.

4:45 P.M.   Joe's mother gets home and finds Joe asleep on the couch.

5:45 P.M.   Joe eats dinner with the family as usual. When asked about his day, he makes general comments about school's being boring. He then retires to his room to listen to music.

7:50 P.M.   Two city policemen knock on the door at Joe's house. They explain the situation to Joe's parents and ask to talk to Joe.

8:35 P.M.   Joe is taken to the police station, where he is confronted with Joyce, Amy, and Kevin. Identified by the farmer through her license plate and approached by the police, Amy has told the entire story.

9:40 P.M.   After telling his version of the story, Joe is released in the custody of his parents. He is to return to juvenile court at a specified date.

Joe's parents were still in shock when they sat down in my office. Joe sat quietly, hoping for the best. The parents complained and lamented, alternating their comments between how badly they felt and how terrible Joe's behavior had been.

Joe attempted to make light of the situation, saying that he wouldn't be in trouble if Kevin had been more careful. His cocky attitude intensified his parents' distress.

I stopped their bickering in a no-nonsense fashion, explaining that their bitching at one another was a waste of time and money. All three remained quiet. I proceeded with "lecture number 13" (I number my little talks so that kids will realize that other kids have heard the same warning of doom).

"You really had a good time, didn't you, Joe? I'll bet you smoked dope, drank beer, and played around with Amy. Sure beats the hell out of going to school, doesn't it? Sure wish I could play around like that instead of working."

Joe looked a little surprised to hear a "doctor" talk like that. I continued.

"I bet you're sitting there thinking how cool you were the other day. Well, from what I can tell, you were so stupid it's unbelievable." I leaned forward and softened my tone in order to avoid overdoing my fear technique. "You didn't take care of business worth a damn, Joe. You drove a car you shouldn't have, you buddied up with a guy who can't keep his head straight, and you left a trail of illegal behavior that my dumb dog could have followed. If you were trying to be slick, you blew it!

"Do you realize the number of laws you and your little band of gorillas violated? Let me give you a hint: truancy, impersonation, illegal purchase, transportation and consumption of alcohol *and* a controlled substance, contributing to the delinquency of a minor, speeding, hit and run, leaving the scene of an accident, criminal damage to property, arson, breaking and entering, and God knows what other state, federal, and local violations. If that's cool, then I'm Mother Goose!" I gave Joe a hard stare to punctuate my litany.

Not wishing to browbeat Joe and realizing that too much fear was just as bad as his cocky indifference, I changed the pace of the talk. I got Joe a Pepsi and asked his parents to wait outside. Joe settled back, not sure what to expect.

Without warning, I started laughing. I sought not only to relieve some of the tension but also to let Joe know that his antics weren't earth-shattering. After all, he was just behaving like many other normal, impulsive teenagers. His story had its share of comedy as well as tragedy. It was time to let him know that though he had done some stupid things, it certainly wasn't the end of the world.

Joe and I talked for twenty minutes about the details of the wild spree. The more we talked, the more he moved toward a healthy balance of fear and self-confidence. As he began to trust me, he started sharing his feelings, the strongest being a sense of inequity. Finally, he let out his main bitch: "Why me? I didn't do anything worse than other dudes do all the time. Kevin is more guilty than I am, but his parents didn't take him to see a shrink!"

His lousy feeling and sarcastic tone stimulated lecture number 7, or, as it might be called, "You Don't Realize How Lucky You Are, Fella." In contrast to number 13, lecture 7 is easygoing and supportive.

"Hey, man," I said, "don't put me in a category with a guy who works with crazy people. You ain't crazy. If you were, I wouldn't be talking with you. You gotta know by now that a regulation headshrinker is not as cool as I am. Don't tell me that you can't see that I can help you shape up; you know better. I'll tell you what: Just think of me as your friendly neighborhood freak, hanging out on any corner you choose, grooving on some fine tunes, toking on my pipe, just waiting to rap about life to any dude or 'dudette' who comes along."

Joe's giggle broke the ice, and I knew we had arrived. He was ready to learn from me. Number 13 had brushed his cockiness to one side, and number 7 brought him to a trust level at which he could work on his problems. Once Joe got off his high-horse attitude and no longer needed the defense of "You can't tell me anything," he turned out to be a terrific kid. He was just as normal, healthy, and devilish as the next teenager.

Unfortunately, I wasn't quite ready to help him. I was only half finished. I knew I'd have to go through the same disarming procedure with his parents. I couldn't make needed changes in Joe's life without helping his parents to change, too. I dismissed Joe and asked his parents to step back into my office. I started the process all over again. I knew I wouldn't have to repeat lecture 13, since his parents were already scared out of their minds. What was needed was a solid dose of number 7 and a special application of lecture number 3. (Three is my lucky number.)

Number 3 reexamines a forgotten human trait, but must be

applied differently with each family. With Mr. and Mrs. Decker, it went like this:

"Listen, Joe Decker is a neat kid. It may not look like it at this moment, but it's true. You guys have done a fantastic job in raising an independent-minded young man. He just made a big mistake, that's all. If we all help him, he'll be a better kid for having done these things. I know you want to feel guilty about 'going wrong with Joe,' but forget it. I'm sorry to say that you're not that powerful. You didn't *make* Joe screw things up. Joe did. Remember, Joe has a free will and could have chosen to stop himself. He didn't. There is no way you or any parent can step inside of a teenager's head, rip out his free will, and *make* him do anything. I ask you to forget about guilt and think of ways you can contribute to Joe's decency while you still have a chance. You don't have much parenting time left with him. I want to help you make the best of it."

In this case, number 3 stimulated a lengthy review of how well Joe does in so many areas: He's friendly, kind, sensitive, bright, and never gives his parents big trouble. His mother summed up her feelings by saying, "We know so many kids who come from good homes. They're not exactly perfect, but you just know they're going to turn out all right. You know what I mean? Just that feeling that they're going to make it. I wish I had that feeling about Joe."

"It's very difficult to have that feeling right now," I said. "But if you listen to me and trust me as Joe does, I'll prove to you that Joe will make it. You see, I have that feeling."

I asked Joe to join us, and with all three disarmed of their guilt, fear, and worry, we spent considerable time talking about how Joe could shape up and how his parents could help. With a slightly different perspective, Joe's parents began to feel confident that they would be able to "arrest" Joe's deviance next time, instead of relying upon the police. Joe protested that he would never do it again. I replied, "Now, you know I don't believe you, Joe. You're still a kid, and you will mess up again. But I'll bet you'll be a helluva lot more careful next time!"

Although most parents hate to admit it, Joe's behavior was

not that different from that of other teenagers. The identities of most kids who spend an afternoon or evening raising hell and breaking the law remain unknown. Their path of destruction continues nonetheless, known only to their victims and, in some cases, to the insurance companies. To be sure, Joe was not alone in his deviant behavior.

Joe did stand in the minority on one count, alone on another. He got caught; that put him in a group that numbers 3 to 5 percent of law-violating teenagers. He received constructive help; that put him in a percentage too low to calculate.

I found out later that Kevin's parents had reacted violently. His mother screamed at him for days, and his father belted him around the family room, giving vent to his frustrations. After this scene, nothing further happened to Kevin. Amy's divorced mother lectured her daughter and finally, out of desperation, let the situation drop. She didn't even take Amy's car away. Joyce's parents grounded her for two months and demanded that she never see these three friends again.

These extreme reactions made matters worse. Kevin, faced with hysteria and physical abuse, stockpiled revenge that would probably be vented against another window or, worse, against people. Amy realized that her mother didn't care enough to be involved with her daughter's problems. Amy would eventually learn not to care, either. Joyce would circumvent the unrealistic punishment imposed by her parents. In all, these three kids belong to a majority who get caught in deviance but who will become repeat offenders, not giving a damn about what they do to other people.

Children of all shapes, sizes, and ages are in the grips of what appears to be a modern-day madness. With approximately 53 percent of all crime being committed by juveniles, one gets the idea that kids are trying to destroy the world they are supposed to inherit.

As I skimmed a recent volume of the FBI Uniform Crime Statistics (for 1979), two numbers caught my eye. On the surface, they seem to contradict my message of doom. In one column, it noted that 5817 kids were arrested for vandalism and

3329 for burglary in one year. Realizing that these were national statistics, I mistakenly concluded that at least two juvenile crime indexes were quite low. However, I took a second look at the page title and the column heading. The page read "Suburban Arrests by Age"; the column, "Age Ten and Under."

I quickly glanced at other numbers in the same column: prostitution, 19; car theft, 136; larceny theft, 7724; robbery, 68; murder, 3; rape, 13. I stuttered in shock, *"Rape—13!* You've got to be joking." I carefully reviewed the rest of the report, remembering that the FBI never jokes. I put together an interesting summary for a group of kids most representative of teenagers.

The FBI's crime statistics for 1979 report that 734,250 suburban youths aged thirteen through seventeen were arrested for crimes. Among the most frequent crimes were vandalism, larceny, burglary, and drug abuse. Violent crimes—murder, rape, robbery, and aggravated assault—accounted for 23,292 of these arrests.

If one believes what kids say about their own behavior,* this number of arrests represents many more actual crimes—about eighteen million, committed by 80 to 85 percent of this age group. Since projections from the 1980 census suggest that there are about two million kids aged thirteen through seventeen living in the suburbs, one can conclude that in every group of ten kids aged thirteen through seventeen, there are eight who break the law. On an average, *each* of these kids commits *eleven* illegal acts per year, or *one every thirty-three days.*

This conclusion staggers most parents. They find it hard to

From confidential interviews with 522 teenagers from a medium-size American city, it was learned that 89 percent of the kids admitted to some criminal act in the past twelve months. This included a wide range of illegal acts. However, 70 percent of these acts remained undetected by police or parents. (Martin Gold, Delinquent Behavior in an American City [Belmont, Calif.: Wadsworth Publishing, 1970].)

accept the fact that their well-adjusted, basically good kids could behave like criminals. Yet when I ask them to remember their own teenage years, they inevitably give me an embarrassed smile of understanding, quickly followed by a disclaimer: "But we weren't bad kids. Those were just youthful pranks. We didn't intend any harm."

Joe, Amy, Kevin, and Joyce weren't "bad kids." And they didn't intend any harm, either. At least, consciously, they didn't set out to hurt anyone. They just wanted to have fun. They had their own justification. Yet the motive behind their "pranks" didn't make any difference. The home owner, the farmer, and the taxpayers still feel like victims of a crime.

Calling illegal behavior "child's play" or labeling it a "prank" conceals the truth from authority figures. Looking at criminal behavior as harmless is an affront to law and order. Just because kids aren't inherently "bad" doesn't mean they can't act badly.

Parents often view such pranks as harmless, but the FBI summarizes them in hard, cold facts. I take another view. I think there is more to juvenile disruption than statistics or the broken windows and empty beer cans of childish pranks.

Kids are trying to tell us something. They're saying that they no longer believe in the authority expressed by the law. We adults have let them down. They express their disappointment by vandalizing, shoplifting, and making a shambles out of the educational process. Parents, teachers, principals, deans, judges, employers, and all other authority figures must take their disruption as a statement of need.

As I see it, kids want authority; if challenged, they will even admit to *needing* it. They feel secure when Mom, Dad, or the teacher says no, and makes it stick. They may complain or gripe, but they feel comforted by the realization that someone cares enough to put limits on their hell-raising. To take this one step further, I think the current epidemic of juvenile crime and violence is a message from our children. They are saying that they no longer want or need authority figures to be permissive.

Many parents and teachers rely on permissiveness because they are afraid that exercising power will harm the mental health of the child, stifle creativity, or bring the wrath of do-gooders down on their heads. They know that punitiveness backfires in revenge. They hang on to permissiveness, hoping that the child's natural inclination to be good will shine through. Yet there is little, if any, evidence that children receive morality as their birthright. If anything, they have genetic determinations to be insensitive to all needs save their own.

The time of look-the-other-way permissiveness must come to an end. We must stop trying to talk our children down from a precarious perch atop the ladder of deviance. We must put our well-intended words into action. Without action, kids learn that authority has no clout. Without clout, authority figures face continued deterioration of their power to control disruption, and disruption flourishes.

We must also give up our propensity for extremes. Give-all permissiveness and take-all punitiveness are equally undesirable. Too much talk without action and too much action without talk will erode authority. Using extremes without balance undermines our power, and our authority goes down the drain. Like it or not, authority figures have power; if we abuse it or fail to use it, then we'll lose it.

In a move away from permissiveness and toward stricter discipline and control, guidelines for appropriate, law-abiding, and responsible behavior must be carefully tightened. Understanding must be gently bridled. When faced with disruption, authority must give more guidance and less freedom. If guided well, freedom can be earned by responsible behavior, not given as some kind of gift from nature.

Recently, I heard of a seven-year-old who rebelled when told to quit screaming in a public building by the building's superintendent. As if prompted by a lawyer, this bright-eyed boy criticized the superintendent for depriving him of his constitutional right of free speech. He insisted that the Constitution and the Bill of Rights insured him the right to talk as he pleased, wherever he pleased. I had to chuckle at this boy's precocious understanding of his rights. However, I had concern whether or not this child was being taught that responsibilities accompany rights. He had the right of free speech, but he also had the responsibility to respect the rights of others.

Joe and his friends had the same blind spot as this child. They didn't recognize that responsibilities were part of their right to enjoy a party. Joe and his parents used the transgression to rediscover the balance of rights and responsibilities that comes with strict discipline. The other kids and parents did not.

There is a danger in advocating a shift toward strictness. Some parents may overreact and take my suggestion as a ticket to abuse, harass, and beat their children into submission. As stated earlier, going from permissiveness to punitiveness can be like jumping from the frying pan into the fire.

I favor strictness as an *alternative* to permissiveness and punitiveness. The definition of "strictness" differs from family to family, depending upon parental strengths, weaknesses, and morality. Whatever the definition, strictness contains a thoughtful balance of reason and power. Strict authority figures set rules and regulations that permit freedom to exercise rights and at the same time spell out responsibilities. The strict parent sets house rules that are justifiable but that also allow for a child to reason some things out for himself or herself. Also, strict parents have regulations that encourage trial and error while clearly spelling out the dos and don'ts. This balance permits the growth of a knowledge of right and wrong and the emergence of the cornerstone of morality: self-discipline.

Kids in the grip of a modern-day madness can not survive without self-discipline. The transgressions of Joe, Joyce, Kevin, and Amy testify to this need. If they had possessed self-discipline, they would have found ways to party without hurting anyone or anything, including themselves. It was only luck that prevented their deviance from becoming disaster.

I find that many parents take self-discipline for granted. "After all," they will say, "I learned how to control myself.

Why shouldn't my child do the same?" These parents think that self-discipline is imparted by some form of osmosis. In truth, they get so busy living, they forget how they learned self-discipline. It took the time and attention of strict parents.

I often hear parents say, "I want to give my children everything I didn't have." This is all well and good. But in giving children all the things you didn't have, don't forget to give them one thing you do have—the self-discipline necessary for law-abiding behavior. Just because we're moving into the twenty-first century doesn't mean we should throw away the survival strategies that helped us get this far.

In the push and shove to give our children material things, we make so much racket, we can't hear their plea. Listen more carefully and you'll hear kids say, "Show me how to survive in a world that wants to eat me alive. Teach, cajole, force, and even demand if you must. But help me make tomorrow better than today. Don't just fill my ears with words about how much you care or cram my room full of possessions. *Do more!* Love me enough to get tough!"

This cry for help is often difficult to hear. It emanates from somewhere between hair arranged in strange configurations and toes that rattle from soul-shaking music. It is often camouflaged by a fancy style and a cool rap. If you watch closely, you'll occasionally see how the heat from the inner fear melts their icy front. That's when you can hear their need. "Don't let me get away with this. Get tough. Stop me! I can't stop myself."

There are several crucial steps to follow for parents who want to get tough. The first is to get tough with yourself; otherwise, you can't get tough with your kids. Throw away guilt, ignore self-recriminations, and change worry into constructive concern. Don't be afraid of feeling disgust toward a hell-raising child. Accept it; it comes with love. Just make certain that disgust doesn't lead to prejudicial action against your child.

Second, be willing to admit your faults. Look at your own life, marriage, and social relationships. Discover where you are weak and how you should "get your head together." If you confuse yourself and others with lies and dishonesty, you can imagine how difficult it will be for you to help your child shape up.

Third, you must resolve to avoid the two extremes of permissiveness and punitiveness. You must be determined to find a moderately conservative manner of using strict discipline to teach your child how to live within realistic guidelines.

Fourth, you must look within yourself and find that part of your love that can be rough and tough. Every parent I know has a tough streak, which can surface when the child borders on trouble. Joe's parents thought that toughness meant they couldn't be warm and tender. When they realized that tough loving demanded sacrifice, they instinctively knew how to envelop their toughness in warmth and tenderness. In fact, once they put my "tough lessons" into practice, they discovered that they had more time to enjoy Joe and his friends.

The final two steps of getting tough involve setting and enforcing strict rules and regulations. This book, in fact, is dedicated to examining the art of putting toughness into action.

Mr. Decker found it difficult to implement these recommendations. His first inclination was to think that getting tough was going to take more work. He noted, "I have to be tough all day in my work. I don't want to be tough with Joe when I get home. I just want to enjoy him." It didn't take too long before he discovered that the quickest way for him to have time to enjoy his son was to make sure Joe lived with sensible guidelines. Consequently, the tougher Mr. Decker became, the more time he had to "play" with Joe, which in turn stimulated more respect and happiness, which required less toughness. In the final analysis, if you're willing to get tough and carry through with discipline, you will probably have to do it less often.

As you can tell, I advocate a return to conservative childrearing. Just when our children need us to be tougher than ever, we seem to be sticking our heads in the sand and hoping that the problems will go away. Despite the fancy clothes, fast cars, and occasional stories about teenage decency, I'm convinced our kids are becoming moral weaklings. And their timing is lousy. If ever there was a time when the courage of convictions and moral stability were needed, it is now.

The last time I saw Joe Decker, he chided me in a good-natured manner for taking the "good life" away from him. He told me that since I had worked with his family, he had a tighter curfew and less ability to confuse his parents with word games. He smiled as he complained about strict controls. He became excited as he talked about how he and his parents were talking more and arguing less. He expressed surprise that as his parents got tougher, he seemed to sense more love and understanding. He finished his remarks by saying, "I guess my parents really care about me."

I responded as I usually do: "Damn right your parents care about you. In fact, they love you enough to be tough. That's the greatest love of all."

3

How Tough Are You?

You don't have to be a parent or a teacher to be an author-ity figure. Anywhere you find a code of conduct and a person to enforce it, you find an authority figure. The swimming coach is an authority figure, as are the theater manager and the parking-garage attendant. We meet authority figures every day of our lives. So do our children.

Nor do you have to be a cop or a judge to be a *tough* author-ity figure. Toughness doesn't go hand in hand with carrying a gun or wielding power over life and death. Being tough requires two things: First, a belief that discipline means *to teach* and that teaching means *doing*, not saying; second, a practical knowledge of techniques of influencing children's behavior by tough action, avoiding brutality or rejection.

The following quiz gives you a chance to figure out how

tough you are. Put yourself into each of the twenty situations, examine the alternatives, and choose the action that you would take. I selected these situations because they are the ones in which parents often see their authority challenged by complaints, back talk, and defiance. If the action you would take is not listed, choose the one that comes closest to what you would do.

1. What is a good allowance for a 14-year-old (to be used for pleasure spending)?

   a. $6 per week
   b. $4 per week
   c. $2 per week
   d. none

2. What household chores should a 15-year-old do?

   a. keep his (her) room straightened
   b. a + help clean kitchen and take out garbage
   c. a + b + put dirty laundry in hamper and straighten drawers
   d. a + b + c +any special requests

3. What is a just curfew for a 16-year-old (not counting local curfews)?

   a. curfew should depend upon what he (she) is doing
   b. 11 P.M. on school nights; midnight on weekends
   c. 10 P.M. on school nights; midnight on weekends
   d. 9 P.M. on school nights; 11 P.M. on weekends

4. What is an acceptable age at which to let girls start unchaperoned dating?

   a. 13
   b. 14
   c. 15
   d. 16

5. What should you do if your 17-year-old drives home drunk?

    a. have a long talk with him (her)
    b. take away the car for 2 weeks
    c. ground him (her) for 2 weeks
    d. b + c + no phone calls, music, TV, or friends over for 2 weeks

6. Assuming your child has the potential to be a good student, what grade average should you expect in the core subjects (math, English grammar, reading, etc.)?

    a. C
    b. C+
    c. B−
    d. B

7. What is a good thing to do to a 14-year-old who gets kicked out of school for skipping the same class three times without an excuse?

    a. nothing; the school took care of it by kicking him (her) out
    b. take 1 hour off his (her) curfew for a week
    c. take 2 hours off his (her) curfew for a week
    d. ground him (her) completely for 1 week

8. What action, if any, should be taken if your 14-year-old had $100 of his or her own money to spend on school clothes and paid $75 for one pair of pants?

    a. nothing; it's his (her) money
    b. talk with him (her) about the value of a dollar
    c. make him (her) take the pants back
    d. c + make him (her) set up a budget

9. What should you do if you find out that your 10-year-old had three friends over while you were gone and they drank beer?

    a. forget it; it happens to the best of kids

    b. sit all four down and give them a good scolding

    c. b + don't let them come over for 2 weeks

    d. b + c + call the other parents and tell them what happened

10. If you decided to do something about your 16-year-old's smoking marijuana, which form of discipline would you use?

    a. a strong lecture about drug abuse

    b. make him (her) gather reliable information about marijuana covering *all sides* of the issue

    c. give him (her) a stiff penalty

    d. all of the above

11. To what extent should a college-bound student pay for educational expenses?

    a. not at all

    b. pay half of leisure-time expenses

    c. pay all of leisure-time expenses

    d. c + at least 10 percent of education-related expenses

12. If you let a 17-year-old have his (her) own car, how much should he (she) pay?

    a. nothing

    b. upkeep—gas, oil, repairs

    c. b + insurance

    d. b + c + half the original price

13. How old should your kid be before you expect him (her) to get a job?

    a. 17

    b. 16

    c. 15

    d. 14

14. What is the best action to take if you find out your 8-year-old took a dollar from your purse (wallet)?

    a. talk with him (her) about why stealing is wrong
    b. a + demand a formal apology
    c. a + b + make him (her) give the dollar back
    d. a + b + c + give him (her) no treats for a week

15. What should be done to teenagers who are caught vandalizing the local park?

    a. should be taken directly home by police
    b. should be taken to police station and parents made to pick them up
    c. b + give them a stiff fine
    d. b + c + make them work 3 weeks for the park department

16. If your 14-year-old runs away, how long should you wait before trying to find him (her)?

    a. overnight
    b. 6 hours
    c. 2 hours
    d. 15 minutes

17. What's the best thing to do if your teenager is unkempt in personal appearance and/or vulgar in speech around home?

    a. say to him (her) "Clean up your act!"
    b. yell or scream at him (her) "Shape up!"
    c. ground him (her) for a week each time the standard is violated
    d. don't feed him (her) until he (she) is clean and fine him (her) 50¢ for every vulgar word or expression

18. How many times should you explain to your 10-year-old why you want him (her) to do something?

a. as many times as it takes for him (her) to do it
b. 3
c. 2
d. 1

19. What should you do with your 10- and 12-year-olds who are constantly disturbing you with their bickering?

a. ignore them
b. keep them separated
c. figure out who started it and punish him
d. punish both of them no matter who started it

20. Assuming that you and/or your spouse smoke and you don't want your children to get the habit, what should your position be on your teenager's wanting to smoke?

a. let him (her) smoke
b. I don't approve but there's nothing I can do about it
c. he (she) can smoke only in his (her) bedroom
d. he (she) will not smoke in my home

As you may have guessed by now, the possible answers differ in degree of toughness. In each question, the first alternative is the softest solution, the last the toughest. Find your score by adding up the point value of the letters you circled using this scale:

a. 1 point
b. 2 points
c. 3 points
d. 4 points

Here's how I would categorize your total score:

65+   You're tough! There are very few of you around. On a scale of 1 to 10, with the marines a 10, you're a 7.

50–64   You're tougher than many parents. If you actually carry through on what you say you would do, you and I wouldn't disagree very much. You're a 5½.

35–49   You might disagree, but you're not so tough. You hesitate to take action, believing that talk will lead to disciplined behavior. It won't. On my scale, in which the angels are a 1, you're a 3.

20–34   You talk too much. You also worry too much about communicating with your children. Worry more about how he or she behaves, then concentrate on feelings. On my scale, you're just above a 1.

The explanations given below support my contention that "d" is the best answer to each question. If my sample group of 1000 parents is any indication, you may find my answers too tough. Less than 10 percent of the sample scored above 64. Approximately 15 percent scored in the 50–64 category. But more than half the parents (53 percent) were found in the 35–49 range, with the others (about 22 percent) scoring between 20 and 34.

Many of you will likely conclude that my disciplinary measures are unnecessarily harsh. But stick with me. I will give you ample opportunity to study each answer in more depth.

1. No allowance for a 14-year-old

By the time children reach the teenage years, they should be earning their own money to be used for pleasure. A program moving children toward financial independence should begin when they are quite young. Allowances are fine for younger children, but they are only a device for teaching the value of money and should self-destruct when children reach thirteen or fourteen years of age. Check chapter 14 for a careful look at this crucial subject.

2. A teenager should contribute substantially to order around the home

A teenager should be doing many chores around the house and should *not be paid for them*. Chores should be done as second nature and without reminders. The chores summarized in answer d are not excessive. Parents should always leave their options open for special requests, such as sweeping the patio or cleaning out the fireplace. Chapter 6 discusses this further.

3. A tight curfew for a 16-year-old

There was considerable disagreement on this question. The majority of dissenters pointed to their kids' complaints about unfairness as the reason they would establish later hours. However, coping with peer pressure ("Everybody else gets to stay out later; you're not being fair") is just one of the many things a 16-year-old needs to learn how to handle. They don't need to be subjected to the hell-raising that occurs after eleven o'clock at night. As you will note in chapter 6, curfew extensions can be opened to special negotiation if circumstances warrant it (proms, rock concerts, etc.).

4. Unchaperoned dating for girls should begin at 16

The disagreement encountered on this question related to the mothers who said that *they* started dating earlier than sixteen. When pushed to decide whether or not they should have waited, the majority agreed that they would have been more ready to deal with sexual pressures if they had waited until sixteen. Although chaperoned dating can be allowed, adolescents should be given time to experience various teenage traumas before confronting the "big one." Chapter 12, "Sex and the Single Kid," will cover exceptions to this rule.

5. Drinking and driving should result in a most severe punishment

The most severe punishment should be given to any kid (or adult for that matter) who treats his or her life and the lives of others with reckless abandon. More and more teenagers are violating this guideline, and more and more kids are dying because of it. This issue raises more toughness inside of me than any other. I've known too many beautiful kids who thought they were indestructible and who were proved dead wrong. See chapter 8.

6. Expect above-average grades in the basics

Children must be expected to take the study of math, grammar, reading, and other basic subjects very seriously. No child, no matter how smart or accomplished, can realistically say, "I don't have to study English; I know it." Once a child gets above-average grades in core subjects, then he or she may pursue self-directed interests. In case you're wondering, I do *not* believe that all learning must be fun to be effective. Chapter 7 has more on this.

7. Parents should retain the option of disciplining a child for violations of conduct in school

A family must have a code of educational conduct that says to children, "Your major job is to learn as best you can in school." If a child has skipped the same class three times, there are three things parents must consider. First, the penalty for such blatant violation should be strong. Second, this penalty is in addition to the school's punishment, acting as an "insult penalty," so to speak. Third, the child is saying something about that particular class, and parents should investigate the reason for the child's skipping it. However, the investigation does not excuse the child from the penalty, no matter what the reason might be. Chapter 7 discusses this further.

8. Parents should exercise financial control if the child does not

Even if a child makes his or her own money, parents have the responsibility to see that it is spent wisely. Parents should not turn their backs on poor judgment with the excuse "Let him (her) learn the hard way." That may work sometimes, but not in this case.

Children should be given ever-increasing freedom to spend the money they earn as they see fit. But when a child violates a sense of balance and budget, parents should step in, make the child return the purchase, and teach the child a lesson in budgeting. Using three fourths of clothing money on one item is unreasonable, calling for parental intervention. The time for parents to stay out of their children's financial affairs is *after* the son or daughter has left home and become self-supporting. See also chapter 14.

9. Use strong measures to fight peer pressure

Three or four kids who get together in your home, and behind your back, to experiment with right and wrong should be shown that they are wrong. Though you might have a private chuckle or laugh with the kids later on, you have to take a tough stance at the time it occurs. The difficult task of involving other parents must be taken. It's an effective weapon against peer pressure. Let your child know that child's play is one thing, law violations are yet another. Chapter 9 gives you further advice on peer pressure.

10. Use a combination of measures to discipline kids caught smoking marijuana

Marijuana-smoking is widespread among teenagers. That doesn't make it right; it's still illegal. Using the three methods of discipline mentioned in question 10 enables you to drive home a serious point. Make the child do some homework on marijuana. His learning the pro *and* the con affords a better chance to learn self-control. Whether you like it or not, you can't *make* your child quit smoking dope. But you can give him or her strong encouragement to be careful. More in chapter 8.

11. *Kids go to college to learn, not to party*

Most parents I know have let the educational funding for their children get out of hand. Efforts to save money so that a son or daughter may have time to study are backfiring. Parents usually deny themselves things in order to gather money for their kids' education, and some kids show their lack of appreciation by partying instead of studying. When kids have to pay before they play, they take their education more seriously. Chapter 14 has more to say about this.

12. *The good life is expensive*

A teenager who owns a car is enjoying the good life prematurely. I'm against a kid's owning a car. However, if you decide to approve, make the kid pay his or her own way. If he has been exceptionally responsible, you may choose to help out with part of the purchase price. Otherwise, he foots the bills. The more he has to pay, the more he'll protect himself as well as his investment. I was tempted to give a fifth alternative, calling for a complete pay-as-you-go program. See chapter 14.

13. *Give the work ethic an early foothold*

Working is usually not fun, at least not for children. However, promoting the work ethic provides an outlet for energy, a source of satisfaction, and the necessary means for survival. The earlier a child experiences the benefits of work, the better his or her chances of cashing in on the rewards of the real world. Children must go through the frustration of learning that life is not all fun and games. Chapter 14 suggests ways in which you can teach this lesson.

14. Take all possible steps to teach that stealing is wrong

Children who steal should be taught several lessons. Talking about what theft does to others conveys the strength of the golden rule. Giving the dollar back teaches the invaluable lesson of retribution. The formal apology (without guilt) exposes the child to the victim and drives home the points made during the talk. Finally, a tough penalty—no treats for a week—gives the child the fear he needs to avoid stealing again.

We often fail to realize that talking is only part of the solution to theft. I know many kids who realize that stealing is wrong, but they still do it. Why? Because it is fun to rip off, and talk does not teach avoidance. Chapter 11 has more on this.

15. If vandals are frightened, they'll spread the word

The most difficult thing about the epidemic of vandalism is that very few of the bandits are caught. When evidence is conclusive or the kid is caught red-handed, a lesson that carries heavy clout is in order. Making the parents come to the station and imposing a fine that the kids must pay off with work will take much of the excitement out of destroying another's property. These kids will spread the word to their friends: "If you're going to rip off, be careful; you're in deep trouble if you get caught."

The only drawback to this program is that parents, out of a sense of embarrassment, may belittle the kids rather than teach them an important lesson. Worst of all, they might dismiss the vandalism as child's play. More in chapter 11.

16. Runaways should be dealt with immediately

Kids who run away are sending out a distress signal. The message may be as simple as "I don't like being grounded" or as complicated as "You and Dad would be better off without me."

Whatever the message, parents can't deal with the trouble unless the child is *in* the home. Therefore, I advise the pursuit of a runaway within a short period of time. Fifteen minutes gives the child an opportunity to blow off steam and still return without a hassle. I do not agree with the libertarians who demand that runaways should be permitted the "space" to find themselves. If parents don't resolve the underlying problem, runaways will "find" themselves in more danger than they ever imagined. See chapter 13.

17. Improper dress and/or language should not be tolerated

Unkempt appearance and vulgarity can come and go as unpredictably as a breath of foul air. It's a waste of time to figure out why it happens. It's important that rules enforcing proper dress and appropriate language be enforced, no matter what the argument.

"Wash up before you eat at this table" and "That nasty word will cost you a quarter" are no-nonsense ways to convey right and wrong. Be prepared to listen to a lot of complaining about how other kids can do what they want to. You can listen, but you don't have to take action on what you hear. See chapter 6.

18. One explanation is enough

Parents erode their authority by talking too much. If you have explained a situation once, and your child has heard you, repeating yourself is a waste of time. After ten years of exposure to your morality, your child knows why you want him to get home by dark or clean up his room. His demand for explanations is a stalling technique. Don't give yourself a case of nerves by worrying about a child's accepting your explanation. Your child won't fully understand your reasons for discipline; that's why you're a parent and he's a child. See chapter 4 for help in avoiding complaints.

19. *Peace and quiet* first, *then investigation*

You deserve peace and quiet. It's up to you to make certain your children know *and* respect that wish. Constant uproar from bickering children calls for a quick lesson in silence. When you hear "That's unfair; I didn't start it," say "Sure it's unfair. You two find a way to make peace or you'll get another lesson that life is unfair."

If there is an underlying problem between the children, this approach will bring it out in the open. Then, you can investigate, handle the problem, and save yourself a headache. See chapter 10.

20. *Rank has its privileges*

Whether you like to admit it or not, age and experience give a person rank, and rank has its privileges. If this offends you, take a look around and find examples in your own life. Then help your children learn how to deal with this reality.

Pulling rank on the smoking issue is appropriate. If you or your spouse is hooked on nicotine, that does not automatically mean that you can't do everything in your power to discourage your child from making the same error. It's still your house, and you can exempt yourself from rules given to your children.

Sure, it would be best for you to quit smoking. It would be healthier, and it would make it easier to enforce a no-smoking rule. But as an adult and as authority in your home, you have the privilege of being foolish. Just be honest about it. "I'm pulling rank on this one. When you have your own home and family, then *you* can pull rank. Until then, you'll have to live with unfairness. Sorry."

An important warning: The more often you pull rank, the greater the likelihood that your children will rebel at your directives and reject your guidance. Don't do it very often.

After studying these twenty problems and my get-tough answers, you may still be up in the air on the question "*How* tough is tough?" It was Joe Decker who helped me understand the complicated meaning of this question. He also aided me in seeing that the question must be answered within the confines of your conscience.

Toward the end of our time together, he reflected on the changes that had occurred after his parents tightened control. He spoke of Amy, Kevin, and Joyce and how they still pushed him to continue his old ways of recklessness. He noted that it was hard to resist their overtures. He described a little voice inside him that kept repeating, "It's not worth it, Joe. It's not worth it."

He spoke with conviction when he said, "I can get outside myself now and look beyond today. I see a lot of things in my future that scare me. But I can handle it, you know. I'm tough now—tough enough to survive—and I know it.

"You know, my parents made this happen. I mean, they started it to happen; I *made* it happen. They were just as scared as me. But once they got tough, they gave me a reason to want to be responsible. That's pretty important for a kid. I only hope I can be tough enough to love my kids the same way."

Mr. and Mrs. Decker had obviously found the answer to the question "How tough is tough?" They loved Joe enough to overcome their own fears and to give him the toughness to survive.

But one question remains: "How much love is enough?" My answer: more than yesterday, but not as much as tomorrow.

4

His Word Was Law

Once the Decker family regained a healthy balance of dis-
cipline and understanding, there was time for quiet reflection.
Mr. Decker felt a strong twinge of nostalgia. He recounted his
days of growing up, comparing his father's method of child-
rearing with his own.

There was both compassion and insight in Mr. Decker's
eyes. "Gosh, it's amazing how I could get so far off track and
not realize it. I was letting Joe get away with murder. I turned
my back, expecting him to quit his hell-raising simply because
I told him to. I of all people should have known better. Why,
when I was young, I wouldn't have dared to do to my father
what Joe was doing to me. I knew better. My father's word
was law."

Mr. Decker was fortunate. He had had a father who prac-
ticed the time-honored method of maintaining clout. You

could tell from Mr. Decker's stories that Grandpa Decker had talked softly and carried a big stick. Mr. Decker had responded with a fear of reprisals from the head man. This fear of unpleasant consequences is what makes the word become law to a child. And, in moderation, there isn't anything wrong with this type of fear.

Our speaking softly and carrying a big stick gives our children security. They feel good when we refuse to be baffled by their words of complaints and stubbornness. Even though many of you probably tend to agree with me, most parents are hesitant about taking tough action. Rather than act, we listen until our ears get sore. We struggle to understand, labor to gain rapport, and endure back talk en route to what we hope will be meaningful communication. In short, we overdo a good thing.

Meanwhile, our children use words to forestall compliance and confuse us. They hope to find the right combination of phrases to cover their insecurity and camouflage their wish to be spoiled rotten: "Give me a break. . . . Give me space. . . . I need room to do my thing. . . ."

With a loving hug and a nod of understanding, we should reply, "I'll give you room to do your thing, as long as your thing is in line with *my* thing."

In many homes, talk is cheap. It's been devalued by parental inactivity and, subsequently, by the child's belief that nothing is going to happen to him if he ignores his parents. What's worse, children get away with it. No wonder that the parental word has become impotent.

Kids don't believe your word because they don't believe you will put any bite behind your bark. They think that your free will, control, and sense of moral balance can be easily destroyed by the right words. When this happens, words of warning are treated as just so much chaff among the grain, blown away by a strong wind of protest.

If you do put bite behind your bark, don't expect your children to roll over and play dead. A certain degree of defiance is a sign of healthy self-confidence. I worry a great deal about any kid who is always compliant and never challenges authority. He could be a whipped puppy, lacking any backbone. In the long run, this type of child may suffer more than any other.

When you set a restrictive guideline, children will be unhappy about it. Even those who clearly know it's for their own good will experience a moment or two of frustration. It's natural. When your guidelines clash with a child's will, a major threat to the power of your word arises, in the form of *complaints*. Your word can be law to the extent that you effectively deal with complaints.

Here's how this threat might sound: "You didn't give me a chance"; or "Why do I have to do it now? That's not fair"; or "You never let me have what I want." When you define limits to a child's growth space and he or she wants more space, such complaints are inevitable. In many ways, complaints are a pivotal point in parent-child relations, especially as they affect children's doing as they are told.

In most homes, complaints begin and end with a mad mixture of do-nothing words. These words muddy the waters of action and sharpen negative feelings. Parents get sidetracked from action when they respond to complaints, and they react with anger, guilt, or some other useless emotion. As a result, complaints make matters worse.

Kids don't help the situation. Many of their messages are wrapped in hidden meanings, half truths, and exaggerations. When these interact with parental uncertainties, complaints make a difficult situation intolerable.

However, complaints don't have to erode authority. They can serve constructive purposes. They can clear the air, indicate emotional involvement, give you a chance to discuss problems, and, best of all, stimulate constructive action. Complaints, if well managed, can be the first step toward implementing a get-tough approach and making the word mean something. You don't have to bury your head in the sand just because your kid is challenging your authority.

I will present twenty frequent complaints of children. Review these one-line clout-destroyers and I think you'll find yourself nodding: "Yeah, that's happened to me." I will then explain how or why these one-liners befuddle your authority. These complaints represent games. The child is saying one thing and meaning another. In my language, the kid is trying to con you.

I will also give you a possible response to the complaint. Then you can use my recommendation to find your own way of surviving the attack.

In each instance, the kid is engaging in a con job for the purpose of stealing your clout. Study these complaints, recognize the trap, and consider my suggestions. The more you can avoid the con, the more likely you'll retain your clout and your word will become law.

"You're not being fair."

Mom replies, "Well, Kathy, you have twenty dollars to spend on clothes."

Kathy wails, "Ah, Mom, c'mon. All I can buy with that is a half a dress. You're not being fair."

Mom protests. "I am, too, being fair. If you had to live with my budget, then you'd know I'm being more than fair."

Arguments about fairness are destined to go nowhere fast. When you have to make a judgment about financial matters, you must keep your eye on justice, not fairness (or equality). Children want to be treated as special. Use your unconditional love, not your checkbook, to give them a message about being special.

Mom might have said, *"I'm not trying to be fair. I'm making a financial decision. If you want to understand my reasoning, I'll be glad to show you our budget when you're finished complaining."*

"You just don't understand me."

Dad says, "Joe, you go out with your friends or else you stay home. You don't need to be with your girl friend again this week."

Obviously hurt, Joe replies, "No use explaining; you just don't understand me."

Dad retaliates. "I understand you more than you think. You don't understand what it's like to be a parent."

This exchange could continue all night. Dad might get so upset as to give up in frustration and give in to Joe's request. Dad could have saved himself some grief by not sticking his nose into whom Joe sees when he leaves home. However, once he does, he must admit that nobody, including Joe, understands Joe.

Dad could have replied, *"You're right. I don't understand you. Explain what you see in this girl and maybe I can worry less about your seeing her so often."*

"You never help me."

After a discussion, Mom says, "No, you can't go to that party tomorrow night."

Jim grimaces and retorts, "I'm just trying to make friends. But you never try to help me."

Mom is offended. "I help you more than you'll ever know."

A kid will often play victim in order to get you to play rescuer. When a child uses the word "help," be prepared to count to ten before responding. The general rule is to dump the responsibility for help back in the kid's lap.

Thus, Mom might have said, *"I'll be glad to help you, but my help has nothing to do with the fact that you are not going to that party tomorrow night."*

"You like to see me suffer."

Amy leaves the car a mess, and Dad punishes her. "You can't use the car for three days."

Amy, with tears in her eyes, says, "You're only doing this to see me upset. You like to see me suffer."

Touched by her emotion, Dad consoles her. "You're wrong, Honey; it hurts me to see you suffer."

"Oh, poor me" has many faces, all of which are destructive. Playing the martyr complete with a long face and tears is a favorite way for kids to erode parental punishments. The message of life's hard knocks can be given compassionately, but should be given nonetheless.

Tough-minded Dad could have said, *"I'm sorry you're hurt. It's not the first time and certainly won't be the last. Next time, maybe you'll remember to take better care of the car."*

"Why can't you treat me like an adult?"

Betty, the nineteen-year-old college student home for the summer, gets this message from Mom: "You will have a one-A.M. curfew during the summer."

Outraged, Betty complains. "Why can't you treat me like an adult?" Mom gets defensive, "I do, Honey. I just think you should be home so I don't worry."

Mom is going to lose this battle. Betty will give all sorts of reasons why she is mature, not the least of which is her ability to handle herself when she is away at college. If Mom is going to avoid the trap, she must stick closely to the facts of life.

Mom could have said, *"Betty, as long as you live under this roof, even for a couple of months, you will follow some rules. Curfew is one of those rules."*

"All my friends get to do it."

Dad looks out the window and states, "It's going to storm. You can't go to the park today."

Billy, quite distraught, replies, "But, Dad, all my friends will get to go. They'll all be there."

"No they won't, Billy," replies Dad. "Their parents will keep them home, too."

The use of peer pressure to counteract authority is the most frequent con job kids pull, no matter what their age. If you attempt to argue about the legitimacy of what other kids will or will not do, your clout will go down the tubes. Treat the child as an individual and he or she will learn how to respond in kind.

Dad should have said, *"I don't care what other kids get to do. You will not go outside when it looks like it's going to storm."*

"You think you're always right."

Mom penalizes Chris for leaving his bike in the rain. "You lose your bike for a week."

Nastily, Chris says, "Just because you're my mom, you think you're always right."

"Mom's not always right, Chris. Just wait until you're a parent; you'll see how tough it is."

Chris made a direct attack on Mom's authority. Mom, worried about whether or not she was being too tough, got defensive. She introduced a needless comment about Chris's maturity, which Chris, if he's devilish at all, will use to escalate the argument.

Mom should have stuck to her guns and said, *"My being right all the time has nothing to do with your penalty."*

"If it weren't for your harping, I'd have no problems."

Mom confronts her son. "You left the kitchen a mess last night. If it happens again, you'll be grounded for two nights."

David takes a very aggressive stance by answering, "If it weren't for your harping, I'd have no problems cleaning up."

Mom retaliates. "No. If it weren't for your messiness, I wouldn't have to get so upset."

Mom was close to a good answer for this complaint. However, she used the same words that David used: "If it weren't for. . ." These four words are regularly used by kids to abdicate responsibility. Parents are well advised to avoid the idea that they cause their children's emotional reactions.

Mom could have changed the emphasis of her statement by replying, *"If you want me to stop harping, keep the kitchen clean. You started it; I didn't."*

"You're just afraid of what your friends will think."

Mom seriously questions Diane's low-cut blouse. "You shouldn't wear that to church. Change into something else."

Diane is offended. "I don't have to. Anyway, you're just afraid of what your friends will think."

Mom counters. "I am not. I just don't want my daughter looking like some kind of tramp."

Diane may have a good point. Many parents are influenced by peer pressure and don't recognize it. Your job is to figure out whether it's your morality or your need for approval that's operating when you make a statement like that of Diane's mother.

A restatement of the point might sound like this: "*Sure, I like approval from my friends. But that blouse is inappropriate according to my standards, not theirs.*"

"*I know what you're going to say, so spare me the lecture.*"

Dad, concerned about his son's partying, warns, "Be careful tonight, Todd. I know there's going to be drinking at that party."

Todd protests. "No you don't, Dad. And I know what you're going to say, so spare me the lecture."

Frustrated, Dad answers, "I'll lecture to you as long as I wish, and you will listen to me."

With this complaint, Todd demonstrated that his father had become predictable. Dad would talk a lot but he wouldn't take any action. This is an all-too-familiar situation, resulting in children's feeling safe in ignoring parental warnings.

Dad might have said, "*Spare me your back talk or you won't go to the party at all.*"

"*You just don't know what it's like to be young.*"

Watching his son pull a comb through shoulder-length hair, Dad says, "Why don't you cut that hair? It really looks crummy."

Fourteen-year-old Ben replies, "Get off my case, will ya, Dad? You just don't know what it's like to be young."

"What are you saying, Ben?" Dad is angry. "I was young much longer than you have been."

Dad lost a big chunk of his clout engaging in a petty argument with Ben. Ben took a cheap shot, and Dad responded in kind. Dad could have got his point across much better by sticking to the issue of long hair, refusing to be sidetracked by comments about age.

Dad might have said, *"Get serious, will ya, Ben? I want your hairstyle changed a little bit. Knock off the cheap shots and let's talk about the length of your hair."*

"You don't care about my feelings."

Mom says to her daughter, "That guy's not right for you, Fran. I don't think you should date him."

In a bit of a tizzy, Fran responds, "Oh, Mother, really! You wouldn't say that if you knew him as I do. Obviously you don't care about my feelings."

Put on the defensive, Mom replies, "Honey, I *do* care about your feelings. I care so much I just want to make sure you don't get hurt."

This interaction is another example of how a terrific fight between parent and child gets started. Mom should not invoke her care and love for her daughter. It makes it sound as though she's trying to convince herself that she does care. You can bet that Fran will pick up on that defensiveness and escalate the argument. The whole scene could be redirected quite simply.

Mom should have said, *"I'm not talking about your feelings right now. I want to give you my viewpoint about your boy friend."*

"You treat my sister (brother) as your favorite."

Mom tells her eight-year-old, "Tammy, clean up the bathroom. You left it a mess."

Tammy complains. "Oh, Mom, Sissy is just as messy as I am. Why don't you tell her to clean up the bathroom? You treat her as your favorite."

Mom quickly answers, "I do not! Your sister gets just as much punishment as you do."

Many parents are very sensitive to any complaints about

their showing favoritism. They've been led to believe that any difference in discipline is "playing favorites" and that this is automatically damaging to the children. If you keep your eye on action, you can justify playing favorites.

Mom could have said, *"I play favorites when it comes to a messy bathroom because your sister doesn't leave it a mess. If you would clean up after yourself, I'd favor you too."*

"You're always yelling."

After ten minutes of begging and cajoling her daughter to eat properly, Mother loses her cool. "Mary, you shut up and eat right now or else I'll spank your bottom until it's red."

Mary hangs her head and whines, "You're mean, Mommy. You're always yelling at me."

Mom's voice gets even louder. "I am not always yelling. And as for you, you're really going to get it!"

If you lose your temper too often (say, more than two or three times a week), your clout tends to diminish. There are times when a yell, a growl, or a temper outburst can get a child's attention. Just make certain you follow up with constructive action instead of more temper. This mother got hooked by Mary's complaint. She should have gone to the stove, put the pan in the sink, cooled off, and made more constructive use of her anger.

After returning to the table, Mom might have said, *"If you don't want me to take your food away, you'd better straighten up right now."*

"I never get what I want."

Dad says to eleven-year-old Kevin, "You'll have to wait until next year to get a new baseball mitt."

Kevin complains. "Aw, Dad, I never get what I want."

Dad replies, "You do, too. In fact, you get more than most eleven-year-olds I know."

This short exchange will certainly build into a confrontation. When Dad told his son he'd have to wait, he should have expected some type of complaint. Kevin wants a new mitt *now*. Dad should have stuck to his guns instead of slipping into a reference to other kids, thereby inviting peer pressure to be used against him.

Dad should have replied, *"Many times you don't; that is true. For instance, you will have to wait until next year to get a new mitt. Sorry."*

"You wouldn't say that if Dad (Mom) was home."

Mom looks at her son's messy room and penalizes him. "Marty, your room is a mess. You will not get your allowance this Friday."

Marty doesn't take that lying down. "I don't believe you. You wouldn't say that if Dad was home."

Mom appears flustered. "Oh, yes, I would. Your father will agree with me after he sees your room."

Trying to play one parent against the other is a key strategy for any kid who wants to get out of a punishment. You can expect it. This mother took Marty's bait and sounded unsure of her husband's support. If indeed Marty was correct in what he said, Mom and Dad need to clean up their act before they can expect their son to clean up his.

Mom could have said, *"Dad isn't here right now, and the punishment will stick. If Dad doesn't agree, then he can use his own punishment, next time."*

"You won't be bothered with me much longer."

Dad turns to his gregarious eighteen-year-old daughter and say, "Karen, you've being going out too much. Starting tomorrow, I want you home at least two nights a week."

Karen acts more offended than she really is. "Fine, Dad. Have it your way. Just remember, you won't be bothered with me much longer."

Dad is taken off guard. "What do you mean 'bothered'? You're not a bother to us. We love you."

If Karen is on the ball, she will follow up on Dad's comment by saying, "Well, if you love me, then you'll let me go out as often as I like." Dad will find himself in a trap, caught between his original directive and Karen's statement about how love is expressed. The best way to avoid such traps is to react to the implied threat in the complaint rather than to the complaint itself.

Dad could have responded, *"I don't like being threatened. It only makes me want to keep you home three nights a week."*

"You always take somebody else's side."

After talking to the teacher, Nancy's dad says, "Nancy, your teacher says you're starting to goof off in class. Stop it." Nancy is snotty in her reply. "Oh, Dad, the teacher doesn't know what she's talking about. But I should have expected your position. You always take somebody else's side against me."

Dad is defensive. "That's not true, Nancy. Just last week, I stood up for you when your mother was complaining about your attitude."

Dad really blew this one. He allowed Nancy to take him away from a pertinent subject into an area of confusion. You can imagine how Nancy will want to argue about what Mom said last week. Dad should have stuck to the topic of the teacher's complaining about Nancy's performance. Even if the teacher was wrong, Nancy would have to learn how to deal with her.

Dad should have said, *"This is not a popularity contest, Nancy. Your teacher had some examples of your goofing off. We'd better talk about it before your grades slip."*

"You don't have enough proof."

Mom confronts her fifteen-year-old son the morning after he comes home late. "Randy, you acted funny last night. You were either smoking or drinking something you shouldn't have been."

Randy protects himself. "Mom, you're wrong. Anyway, what do you have to back up your story? You don't have enough proof."

Mom replies, "I don't have enough proof? Well, I have your staggering and singing funny songs. That's proof."

Once again, this is an example of a parent's losing sight of the original purpose of the confrontation by responding to a half-baked complaint. If you confront your child about shady behavior, you are well advised to stay away from playing cops and robbers. Don't argue about degrees of guilt or get bogged down in rules of evidence. Even if you are a lawyer by training, your child will beat you with emotional arguments. Stick with the facts. If you think you have strong evidence, prosecute; if you don't, wait and watch.

Mom could have said, *"Maybe I don't have enough evidence this time, but I'll be watching. You'd better keep yourself on a tight string, Randy, or I'll play judge and jury."*

"You don't trust me."

Dad tells his sixteen-year-old daughter, "Sherry, your mother and I will be gone this weekend and your aunt will be staying with you."

Sherry replies, "Why my aunt? I can stay here by myself. The problem is that you just don't trust me."

Dad answers, "That's not it at all. Of course we trust you. We just want to make sure you don't get hurt."

"You don't trust me" may be the most frequent of all complaints coming from kids. And it is the one complaint that parents usually lie about when they hear it. I know of very few sixteen-year-olds who could be trusted to have the house all to themselves for an entire weekend. It's a lie to say you trust your kid when you don't. Trust is not an either-or matter. You trust kids with some responsibilities but not with others. Let your kids know the truth; then they can improve.

Dad should have said, *"You're right, I don't trust you, not at your age. Show me responsibility and I'll improve my trust."*

Analyzing these complaints one by one is somewhat misleading. Rarely do they occur so simply. More often than not, a conniving kid will put two or three complaints together, thereby multiplying their effectiveness.

Joe Decker was a pro at stringing complaints together. One time, when told he must earn his own spending money, Joe replied, "You don't understand; it's not fair. All my friends get an allowance. If you trusted me, for once in my life I would get what I wanted. Obviously, you don't care about my feelings. You just like to see me suffer."

The Deckers had plenty of opportunity to practice the skills of listening to such complaints, avoiding the traps of a con job, and putting their words into action. Joe was quite adept at using many of these complaints to confuse his parents and to get them off his back. We worked at them one at a time, and with practice the Deckers spent less time being defensive and more time making their words lead to constructive action.

Mrs. Decker summed up her and her husband's frustration when she said, "Why does Joe delight in confusing us? Doesn't he know that we're just trying to help him grow up? He acts like he doesn't want to become an adult."

I explained to the Deckers something that is often overlooked by most parents. For the most part, kids don't want to grow up. They like the irresponsibilities of being kids.

When she expressed surprise, I explained further. "Have you read the papers or watched the news lately? The grown-up world is full of war, inflation, crime, taxes, and ruthless competition. If you had to leave fast cars and hot music and face a world that demands more than you can give, would you want to grow up?"

Mr. and Mrs. Decker smiled as they acknowledged my message. They had greater insight into Joe's attempts to thwart their efforts. Mrs. Decker noted, "I guess I can't blame him. I'm glad I don't have to be a teenager just starting out. I wouldn't like it, either."

Thoughtful and reflective, Mr. Decker finally concluded, "I wanted to grow up. You know why? I wasn't afraid of the world. We had problems then, just like we do now. But I knew how to survive. My dad taught me how to be tough. I need to give Joe that same sense of security that my father gave me. I have to make my words more than a bunch of sounds. If I don't, then I just add more noise to Joe's world. And, God knows, he has enough of that now!"

5

Principles of Prevention

When I tell kids they'd better shape up, or parents that they must get tough, I often use the phrase "taking care of business." Applied to children, it means acting responsibly; to parents, it calls for disciplining children when they act irresponsibly.

When kids are taking care of business, parents can relax, have fun, and enjoy the fulfillment of raising well-behaved children. When kids fail to act responsibly, parents must take care of business by pulling the control rope, getting them back in line.

To define "taking care of business," I shall list my principles of prevention. I rarely give absolute directives, but in this case, I make an exception.

These principles also give my view of the foundation upon which effective child-rearing should be built. I've divided the principles into general and specific categories, adding some explanations and corollaries to the principles when necessary.

The five general principles apply to all age groups and will help you become a better disciplinarian, even if you don't implement any other actions. The fifteen specific principles expand upon the five general principles and cover the key problem areas of child-rearing. They will be examined in detail throughout the rest of the book. If you study these twenty principles and take care of business, you'll have fulfilled the requirements for getting tough.

GENERAL PRINCIPLES

1. Move your body, not your mouth

More than any other, this statement tells parents what they and their children should do in disciplinary situations. Too much talk and too little action will destroy the law and order of a family faster than anything. Parental clout has been seriously eroded by too much worry about effective communication and not enough active follow-through.

I'm all for good communication of emotions between parent and child, *but not when children need discipline*. Discipline is infinitely more important than heart-to-heart communication. When children fail to act responsibly, it's no time for understanding and dealing with feelings; it's time for action.

Don't yell or scream (at least not more than twice a week) or waste time explaining why the act was wrong. Don't search for reasons why the child did what he or she did. Take action. Make the child sit down if that's what you asked. Gently but firmly pull the child indoors if that's what you requested. If your child is late getting home, forget the reminders and make him pay a penalty: for instance, extra work, one night's grounding, or a fifty-cent fine.

We all learn to do what we do, not what we say. Matters of discipline follow the same law. If you only talk, that's what your child will learn to do. If you act, so will your child. When it comes to learning right from wrong, talk is not only cheap; it gets in the way. We have thousands of children who know how to mouth the words of morality, but they don't translate those words into action. Why? Because their parents don't back up words of warning with constructive follow-through.

I suggest you develop an early-warning system to alert your children to the importance of doing what you asked the *first* time you ask. The key elements of this system are changes in tone of voice and in posture, speed of speaking, facial expression, or any other nonverbal action you can think of to stimulate your child into doing what he or she is supposed to do. A snap of the finger, a pointed nod, and a growl are three good ones. My favorite is some version of the evil-eye technique. Some parents have perfected this warning system so that they can stare a hole in the back of a wild child from across the room.

No matter what technique you use to implement this principle, keep your talking to a minimum. For example, don't use more than ten words in making the child do as he or she was told.

2. Keep responsibility where it belongs

Just as you make mistakes and must shoulder the burden of responsibility, so must your children. If you try to take responsibility for children's errors, you're being irresponsible and none of you will be able to shape up. That's why I remind you to keep responsibility where it belongs.

If a kid makes a mistake, he needs somebody to point out the when, where, what, and how of his error. You must look at his behavior and show him what parts were right and what were wrong.

If a seven-year-old won't eat his veggies because they're "yucky" or the "wrong kind," you shouldn't condemn yourself for fixing peas and rush to the kitchen to fix corn. If you made a well-planned meal, then you should expect your family to eat it. You are being very responsible. It's the boy who's being irresponsible. He must learn that it is *right* to eat the foods that you prepared and wrong to expect you to conform to his whims.

If you feel like being irresponsible and the child acts irresponsibly, who's going to teach him or her to be responsible? Obviously, nobody.

You need to enforce the position "Eat your peas or you won't eat at all." If you take and hold this position, you're simply following through on your responsibility to prepare nutritional meals and make sure the children eat them. There's certainly nothing irresponsible about that.

This principle permits you to avoid the bottomless pit of guilt that so many parents fall into. Guilt is a destructive emotion, leading only to depression and repetition of the same old mistakes. Throw away blame, shame, and any other form of self-recrimination. Keep your eye on responsibility. Take-charge parents don't bear the burden of responsibility if they didn't do anything wrong.

3. Keep a list

You can reduce some of the hassles of discipline by maintaining an up-to-date list of the dos and don'ts that affect each of the children. The list should include the rewards and punishments you intend to use in disciplinary situations.

In making the list, treat each child individually. Write down the five most important rules for the child, making the statement simple and to the point. The rules should take into account the child's age, stage of development, strengths, and weaknesses. They also should be ranked in importance.

Make the rewards and punishments on an individual basis. List two rewards for every punishment. This will remind you that rewards are twice as powerful as punishments.

For your seven-year-old, you may say that cleanliness around the home, putting his things away, playing nicely with his sister, controlling his temper, and eating properly are the five most important realms of behavior. Furthermore, you may elect special treats and money as rewards and no TV as a punishment.

For your fifteen-year-old, you may accentuate honesty, good grades, proper dress, curfew, and use of money as the five top expectancies. Good rewards for a teenager might be extra clothes and time added to curfew, whereas grounding or restricted use of the phone would constitute an excellent punishment.

If you feel adventuresome and have the time, make the kid come up with his or her own list *before* you sit down to work one out together. Explain your reasons for the rules *once*; then, don't succumb to the "Why?" Your children know what you stand for by the time they are five or six years of age. They will recognize your reasoning; they may not like it, but that's okay. Nobody ever said that parents were supposed to win a popularity contest.

Concentrate your disciplinary efforts on these five areas of behavior. Let your children know that there will be times when you will choose to overlook certain disruptions that aren't included in the list. If the child is warned, he or she will not push his or her luck. There's no reason that you can't add another behavior area to the list. In the interest of conserving your mental energy, don't try to be all things to your children all the time. The list of the top five rules will help you remember to save plenty of time for yourself.

A footnote to this principle: You may elect to keep a written statement of nonnegotiable rules and regulations attached to the bulletin board or refrigerator. Nonnegotiable rules apply to all children and represent regulations that are absolutely unbending. You will not discuss exceptions. For example, three nonnegotiable rules might be "no illegal activity in this home," "no kids in the house when parents are gone," and "no coming and going as you please."

Violations of the nonnegotiables result in most severe punishments; repeated violations indicate deeper problems and may result in family counseling.

Keep nonnegotiables to a minimum. The more you can negotiate with your children *before* errant behavior occurs, the better your chances for instilling self-control and accommodating the individual traits of the "little people."

4. Rank has its privileges

You work hard to be parents. You struggle with bills and other harsh realities, trying to protect your children until they are old enough to protect themselves. You're in charge of the home. "In charge" means power, and power means rank, and rank has privileges.

You have a set of rules and regulations that your children must live by. These are not necessarily the same guidelines that you use in running your own life. Rules concerning curfew and sex, for example, do not apply equally to you and your children. With a soft but firm hand you can help your children accept this fact of life.

When you act as a parent—directing, organizing, warning, punishing, rewarding—you are exercising your rank. You are engaging in a supervisor/subordinate relationship. Just as you wouldn't expect to tell your boss how you will earn your paycheck, you shouldn't expect your children to tell you how to discipline them.

When you teach children right from wrong, you must assume the role of benevolent dictator. You are in charge. *There is absolutely no question about that!* You can not be fair (as in "equal"). You cannot be a democrat (as in "one person, one vote"). When you parent, you're a dictator. If you dictate well, you shouldn't have to do it often, and you should have plenty of time to enact other roles.

As I noted in chapter 1, there should be no question that you are disciplining your children out of love. Love is unconditional; you love your children no matter what they do. But control procedures are conditional: They depend upon what the child does and does not do. When you discipline, you pull rank on your children, and this makes you a dictator. When you discipline out of love, this makes you a benevolent dictator.

As I pointed out in the quiz, the more often you violate a rule—for example, speeding or littering—the more you chip away at your clout. The more you exercise the privileges accorded to you as authority, the more you invite rebellion. Thus, though rank has its privileges, it also has its price.

5. *Avoid the extremes; find the happy medium*

Part of being human is having a propensity to go to extremes. We tend to see things in black and white. Thirty years of stressing communication of feelings has resulted in the extreme of permissiveness. As I view parenting history, this permissiveness followed a period of strict punitiveness. As I advocate a return to strict discipline, many may interpret my suggestions as abandonment of understanding and empathy, picking up where punitiveness left off. This is not so. My get-tough recommendations are intended to avoid the extremes of do-nothing permissiveness and harsh punitiveness. I encourage you to find a happy medium between the extremes represented by such statements as "My kids will mind me without exception; what I say goes; I don't care what they think; I alone determine what is good for them"; and "I want my children to have all the space they need to choose their own life; authority should only guide, never direct; I should never interfere with my child's growth space."

The first set of statements reflects abuse of power that will backfire sooner or later in rebellion and revenge. The second group gives children little or no idea of limits. Without limits, children have inadequate exposure to self-control.

When finding your happy medium, I advise leaning slightly to the conservative side. Imposing controls on children permits leeway for them to experiment with being wrong and at the same time lets them know what is right.

SPECIFIC PRINCIPLES

Following are fifteen principles and appropriate corollaries that will guide you in approaching difficult situations.

1. *Children will have house rules and regulations*

All children will have a curfew.

Television-watching will be controlled and balanced by active learning.

All children will practice respectful language.
Children will help with household chores.
There will be no illegal activity in the home.
Dinnertime and bedtime will be orderly.

2. Children will maintain high standards of cleanliness, neatness, and propriety in meeting adult expectations

Back talk and disrespect will be treated as two separate issues.

Provocative clothing, inappropriate dress, or other excesses in the name of fads or fashion will constitute violations of reasonable standards of neatness.

Children will keep themselves clean and their surroundings neat.

Vulgarities will be dealt with according to the standards of the given situation.

3. Children will demonstrate achievement in fundamental academic skills before pursuing self-directed studies

Creativity will be encouraged after competency in basic academics has been demonstrated.

The performance of children having trouble in the basics will be monitored more often than the official grading period.

School grading system will be accepted as the best possible indicator of performance.

Children will be expected to have a job; their main job is to obtain the best possible education.

4. Students will hold a primary responsibility for discipline; they will be guided, assisted, and directed by a hierarchy of authority figures

Teachers, deans, and principals will discipline students only when students can't or won't do it themselves.

Student discipline will not involve any more authority figures than absolutely necessary.

5. All drug abuse, including that of alcohol, will result in some type of disciplinary action

Children should understand that abusing drugs is flirting with death.

Whether good or bad, the law is the law, and it will be honored.

Parents will use a process modeled after the judicial system in dealing with drug abuse.

When disciplining drug abuse, punishment will be used to promote rehabilitation.

6. Children will express their desires in terms of individual preference, not of the pressure to conform

"All my friends get to" and "Everybody is" do *not* represent a reason for granting privileges.

Children will be encouraged to compete against their last performance, not against another person.

Children's opportunities for individual expression will be maximized.

Communication between parents concerning children's activities will occur regularly.

7. Children who display temper fits will be expected to "cool off" and use their rational senses

Control of aggression is best achieved through development of the choice process.

8. Children who lie, cheat, steal, vandalize, or commit any other act of deception will be taught a lesson in developing and protecting a reputation

Reputation depends upon performance. A bad reputation develops quickly; a good reputation takes longer.

Work is an excellent preventer of deception.

Deception often brings out the investigator in parents.

Deception should result in two actions: restitution and punishment.

9. When dealing with sexuality, parents should focus attention on the circumstances surrounding sexual conduct rather than the conduct itself

Sexuality begins when kids talk to, not touch, each other.

Since sexuality is complicated and emotional, parents should separate hang-ups from morality.

The development of trust is crucial to healthy sexuality.

10. When it is time for them to leave home, children will do so in a responsible manner

Runaways will be found and the problem solved.

When disruption persists, kids may be asked to shape up or ship out.

Children will be encouraged to leave home after their eighteenth birthday.

11. Children will learn the work ethic early in life

The foundations of pride and self-confidence grow from development of work abilities.

Work has more positive influence on children than any other factor.

12. Children will begin a program of financial independence as soon as possible

Money should be tied immediately to work.

Allowance is an artificial means of teaching the work ethic.

Earning what they spend and allowing for savings are expected of teenagers.

13. Children will be permitted to enjoy possessions as long as they use them appropriately; this is especially true of the car

Use of a car is the strongest incentive for his or her spending money carefully.

Parents will institute a program of "snoopervision" when children are first driving.

14. Exceptional circumstances or crises will not excuse children from responsibility

Divorce, disease, death, or other calamity should stimulate the attitude "When the going gets tough, the tough get going."

Teenage pregnancy, arrest, violence, and similar crises require parents and other authority figures to sort out responsibilities and work for constructive change.

15. Parents will remain alert to the blind spots of loving, which can diminish their effectiveness

Myths, half truths, misdirections, and falsehoods are often masked as common sense.

These fifteen principles and corollaries act as an outline for the rest of the book. You can choose the manner in which you continue your review of my get-tough policies, since the remaining chapters can be treated sequentially or independently.

I've relied heavily on a question-and-answer format in those areas that are largely dependent upon specific circumstances. The collage of information gained from questions and answers establishes ground rules by which you can develop your own brand of toughness.

I encourage you to pay close attention to chapter 14. In reviewing work, money and possessions, I found that what was called for was a new definition of the "facts of life." In my view, these matters represent the main course of living.

6

Law and Order Begin at Home

Principle #1. Children will have house rules and regulations

Principle #2. Children will maintain high standards of cleanliness, neatness, and propriety in meeting adult expectations

Every home has a personality. Whether it be a two-room apartment or a twenty-room mansion, there is something very special created when people express their individuality in whatever space they can afford. When children are present in this space, the home's personality becomes infinitely more complicated.

Homes also have "atmosphere." This is impossible to define, but you feel it the moment you walk through the door. It sets the tone for the home, accounting for how you feel and whether or not you want to stay. Some homes have an atmosphere that makes you want to kick off your shoes and relax; in others, you feel like you shouldn't even sit down.

When I walk into a home (I still make house calls), the atmosphere hits me immediately. I have a sense of the home's personality. I may know nothing about the people who live there, but I can sense the day-to-day events that compose their lives.

The home's personality or atmosphere is best reflected in how the children behave. When I sit down at the kitchen table or plop down in the family room, the children quickly gather around to check out the strange visitor. Inevitably, they show off a bit. It's when Mom or Dad attempts to discipline them that I discover the major ingredient of the home's personality.

When Sissy jumps up and down on the sofa, Dad snaps his fingers, and she sits down, I feel comfortable and secure. When Billy screams and Dad's threats are ignored, I get tense and feel uneasy.

If I feel this way as a one-time visitor, imagine what the children feel like. There's every reason to believe that children feel secure when disciplined and uneasy when permitted to be wild. That's why I say that when law and order dominate the home's personality, the children will have a feeling of security. After all, they must live there every day.

There's no simple way to review the two major principles of prevention and the corollaries that define them. There is just enough difference in each home and family member to make any hard-and-fast disciplinary procedures obsolete before they're implemented.

I decided an interesting way to organize my recommendations concerning law and order around the home was to do it according to the floor plan of a given house. Thus, I will discuss in-home discipline by reviewing one room or area at a time, examining the disruption that might occur in that area as well as suggesting what you can do about it. Here's an outline of my floor plan with accompanying areas of behavior:

Entrance Hall: Curfew
Kitchen: Household Chores
Dining Room: Dinnertime Disruption

Family Room: Television Use
Living Room: Misuse of Mouth; Back Talk; Vulgarity
Bathroom: Personal Cleanliness
Bedroom: Messiness; Bedtime Disruption
Basement: Illegal Activity
Backyard: Dangerous Play

ENTRANCE HALL: CURFEW

Rule: All kids will have a curfew
Disciplinary measure: Some restriction of freedom
   depending upon degree of violation

The entrance hall is where kids should be met if they're coming home late. Coming and going under parental supervision should begin when the five-year-old first goes next door to play with a new friend and end when the kid is completely independent. Curfew is the cornerstone of all other household rules and regulations. It is so important that I've developed an unwavering policy toward it, as follows:

All children who do not maintain a home of their own will be subject to curfew regulations. This curfew may range from seven P.M. for a twelve-year-old to one A.M. for a college junior spending the summer at home. At no time should the curfew be later than one A.M.

All exceptions to this curfew must be negotiated ahead of time. It is possible that you will permit extra time out provided that the child has demonstrated reliable behavior in the past and is willing to pay for the extra privilege. For example, you might say, "I'll give you an extra hour this Saturday if you give me a B on the German test this week."

Violations of curfew should result in the loss of future curfew privileges. Being one hour late means coming in one hour earlier the next weekend night. A second offense leads to progressively stronger restrictions. (See Appendix.)

All curfew agreements must be based on the family's moral code and take into account local and state ordinances affecting curfew.

Parents don't pay enough attention to the curfew issue. Based on my experiences, the later kids stay out, the greater the chances that the ghosts of irresponsibility and wanton recklessness will rear their destructive heads.

If kids are going to enjoy the pleasures and comforts of living at home, they should realize that with these rights come responsibilities, one of which is to come and go under some regulation of curfew. If parents don't take this stance, they are contributing to the child's notion, "Life owes me a living."

Parents should not be afraid of compromise when dealing with curfew. If you're bombarded with complaints and are unsure of your position, try an approach such as this: "I worry about your being out at night. Show me something that will help me see your maturity and I will have fewer problems with your staying out late."

KITCHEN: HOUSEHOLD CHORES

Rule: Children will help with household chores
Disciplinary measures: Restriction of freedom; fines;
    *ostracism**

I chose the kitchen as the focal point for discussing household chores because it seems to be the center of work in the home. You must admit that children need to learn how to work and that you deserve help with daily chores, be it in the kitchen, bathroom, garage, or wherever.

I hesitate to say that doing the dishes or emptying the garbage is good for a child's moral fiber. I prefer to think that it is part of being a child. A parent might say, "I had to take out the garbage when I was a kid, and now it's your turn. Someday, you can make your kid do the jobs you don't want to do."

This and other facts of life are important for a child to learn as soon as he or she is old enough to help you set the table. Here's a list of household chores you might elect to assign to

Must not be used without professional consultation.

your children, depending on their age and their stage of development:

Set/clear table	Help with laundry
Take out garbage	Help with shopping
Sweep floors	Dust
Vacuum rugs	Mow grass, shovel snow, rake
Clean out tub, basin	leaves
Do dishes	Help with meals
Pick up living/family room	Make beds

Keep the door open for other jobs by reminding the child that you expect him or her to run errands and help with special projects as they arise.

There are many things you can do when the children fail to do their chores. Three preferred recommendations are restriction of freedom, fines, and ostracism. Check the appendix for these and other measures. Pay close attention to the precautions concerning ostracism.

DINING ROOM: DINNERTIME DISRUPTION

Rule: Dinnertime will be orderly
Disciplinary measures: Removal of food; fines; loss of treat

"Eat your corn," Mom says.

"I hate corn," the four-year-old replies.

"I don't care. *Eat your corn!*" Mom sounds tough.

"You can't make me," the boy says defiantly.

This is the first battle of a war that rages nightly in many homes. Following this exchange will be more demands, louder denials, screaming, yelling, and possibly a spanking. Compared to other problems of child-rearing, dinnertime disruption is often viewed as a "little thing." However, little things have a way of piling up on parents to the point of angry outbursts and remorse about things that shouldn't have been done.

The dinnertime battle is a frustration stand-off. When it happens, you are surrounded by a child's refusal to eat, temper tantrums, your need for peace and quiet during dinner, and your expectation that children learn to eat properly.

The short-term outcome of this encounter is painful to all; the long-term effect is even worse. The boy will enjoy the hassle and learn how to gain attention by being disruptive. He will also learn to defy authority and will lose respect for rules and regulations. I daresay that in most cases, the boy will *not* eat his corn.

The disciplinary measures suggested are to be used after only *one* warning, which may follow *one* request or directive.

Removal of food is carried out as indicated in the appendix, as are the fine and evil eye. The loss of a treat: "For not eating your corn, you lose one piece of your candy [or cake or other dessert]. If you don't eat your corn now, you will lose another piece in a minute. If you eat your corn, you may keep the rest of your dessert."

Refrain from yelling or spanking, even though your four-year-old sticks his sister's teddy bear in the gravy. Take tough-minded action before it gets this far. If all else fails, don't be afraid of leaving the table and eating later.

FAMILY ROOM: TELEVISION USE

Rule: Television-watching will be controlled and balanced by active learning
Disciplinary measure: Loss of privilege

Television is a cheap and convenient babysitter. Though you must supervise program selection, the TV can occupy a child's time and provide marvelous entertainment. There are two things that bother me about television-watching: scheduling, and control over passive learning.

To schedule television-watching, sit down with your children and a TV listing. Ask them to circle the programs they intend to watch over the coming week. The oldest child gets first pick if there is a conflict in scheduling. I suggest you set TV-watching hours in much the same way that you would curfew hours and that you let your children pick within those hours. Exceptions are always negotiable as long as they're done ahead of time.

Control over passive learning is best accomplished by demanding that active-learning situations take place as well. My rule for this is based on an equal-time-compensation plan. That is, for every hour of TV-watching, children must participate in some type of active learning. For a two-year-old, it might be educational games; for a ten-year-old, active learning might be studying or scouting; for a teenager, it might be reading or a project or hobby.

If children fight over the TV, violate agreements, or don't follow through with their active-learning commitments, take the privilege away. Adapt my recommendations to the particulars of your home (number of TV sets, number and age of children). Once again, if things become too complicated for you, take tough action and turn the darn thing off for two or three days.

LIVING ROOM: MISUSE OF MOUTH

This section covers a multitude of problems, all of which I've grouped under "misusing the mouth." Because of the violent nature of temper tantrums, I've elected to cover the topic in a separate section.

> *Rules: Back talk and disrespect will be treated as two*
> *separate problems; vulgarity will be dealt with*
> *depending upon circumstances*
> *Disciplinary measures: Ignoring; time-out; startling;*
> *fines; loss of privilege; restriction of freedom*

Back talk and disrespect

Although these two terms are used interchangeably, I view them as separate problems. Back talk expresses rejection of a directive or warning. An example of back talk would be a child's saying, after he has been told to pick up his toys, "I don't have to" or "You can't make me" or "No, I won't."

Disrespect indicates a rejection of the person giving the directive. An example of disrespect: "You're a mean mommy" or "You stink" or "I hate you."

I advise treating back talk differently from disrespect.

For back talk, I suggest ignoring, active ignoring, and then loss of privileges. Parents must remind themselves they want compliance, not complaints. The cardinal rule in dealing with back talk is "Never talk back to a child's back talk."

Disrespect calls for two parental actions. First, some type of disciplinary measure to confront the disrespect; for example, you could use time-out or a fine as a punishment. The long-term goal in dealing with disrespect is to teach the child to use the three magic phrases "Please," "Thank you," and "Excuse me." These few words can teach children that what they think of another person's actions doesn't preclude common decency.

Vulgarity

There's no such thing as a "dirty word." There are, however, situations in which a person's reputation or desires will be damaged or frustrated if certain words labeled as "vulgar" are used.

Children should learn that many people don't like certain words. Grandma will be upset if you say "damn." Out of respect for her, you should learn to control your words. The boss doesn't like the word "shit." You are well advised for your own benefit not to use it. When policemen give you a ticket, it's probably not a good idea to curse at them. On and on the examples go. Vulgarity depends on the nature of the situation, not the intrinsic worth of a given word.

Children must learn to discriminate between appropriate and inappropriate words in given situations. Bring home the importance of such discrimination by using fines as a method of control. As you can see in the appendix, fining doesn't have to be a horrible situation. Parents might even choose to discipline their own mouths by imposing fines on themselves. No matter what your position on "bad words," controlling vulgarity is, at the very least, good public relations.

BATHROOM: PERSONAL CLEANLINESS

Rule: Children will maintain high standards of
   cleanliness and propriety of dress at all times
Disciplinary measures: Restriction of freedom; loss of
   privileges; ostracism

Nothing pleases me more than to see children play hard and get dirty from head to toe. Likewise, nothing disgusts me more than to see a child stay that way after he or she should have been cleaned up. The way some kids look these days, you'd think they forgot about the availability of soap and water.

A frustrating problem for any parent is the matter of personal presentation. It's not a serious matter; therefore, many parents don't elect to include it on a list of five major concerns. However, other parents want their children to be clean and neat. If they aren't, the tranquillity of the home can be upset.

As kids experiment with their individuality, they inevitably try out new types of appearance. They check out their appearance in the mirror and imagine what other people will think. Parents have to be the front-line censor when children's experimentation gets out of hand.

Censoring a child's appearance is a risky business. If you do it too often, you invite arguments, rebellion, and revenge. If you look the other way, you give your children no guidance in propriety. For parents who are concerned about their children's personal appearance, I advise the following: Expect your children to meet *your* standards of cleanliness and neatness. You define what is proper and what isn't. Explanations may fall on deaf ears, and review of morality and values will probably lead to heated debates. Back up your expectations with restriction of freedom, loss of privileges, or ostracism when children violate the standards. One precaution: The older a child becomes, the less your demands will work and the greater the risk of rebellion. So if you make a big deal of personal appearance, do it early in the child's life.

BEDROOM: MESSINESS; BEDTIME DISRUPTION

Rules: Children will keep their surroundings neat;
  bedtime will be orderly
Disciplinary measures: Restriction of freedom; incentives;
  ostracism; "Premack principle" (suspension of
  privileges until compliance); natural consequences

Messiness

Nobody can mess up a house better than a kid: three pairs of slacks, two pairs of shoes, and assorted underpants, socks, and shirts strewn about the bedroom; a wet towel in the hallway; three dirty glasses and a half-empty cereal bowl in the family room; crumbs, open jars, dirty dishes following a late night snack. No one would guess that Mom cleaned the house that morning.

More often than not, Mom stays up late or gets up early to reclean the house. She doesn't complain openly, but once in a while she expresses a wish that the family would help out more. In turn, they shrug their shoulders, mutter some poorly contrived promises, and return to what they were doing.

Most kids take cleanliness for granted. They don't know what it's like to peel mud off their shoes after an hour of outside chores in the mud and sleet. They have no way of remembering when bathroom duties had to be done without the convenience of an indoor john. And their jaws surely would drop if they had to clean their jeans with lye soap and a hard-bristled brush.

I'm not saying that kids should suffer in order to appreciate cleanliness. There are other things just as important. However, I think it's totally inappropriate that they grow up believing someone else is supposed to clean up after them. Though I usually help families face bigger problems than messy rooms, I still believe every child should know how to clean up after himself or herself.

If you are faced with a litterbug, check out the appendix and review the "Premack principle," lecturing, natural consequences, and loss of privileges.

I'm not saying that cleanliness is next to godliness. However, I do think we should help our kids maintain a moderate degree of "spit and polish" in their daily lives. Then, when they encounter chaos and turmoil, they'll know how to make things better on the outside. This can often be the first step to making things better on the inside.

Bedtime disruption

I've seen parents get exasperated trying to make their children go to bed and *stay* there. "I want a drink," "Let me watch just one more show," and "I'm scared of the dark" are common ploys of delay. When these fail, the child simply walks out of his or her bedroom and goes to the room where the parents are.

Typical parental reactions are yelling, spanking, and constantly returning the child to bed. If parents can muster the tolerance for two or three nights, a program of ostracism usually works.

BASEMENT: ILLEGAL ACTIVITY

Rule: Parents will not permit illegal activity in the home
Disciplinary measures: Fines; suspension of privileges;
  "snoopervision"

I had a mother in my office recently who had given up arguing with her teenage son about smoking marijuana in her home. He had hassled her so much with "Everybody's doing it" and pressured her with complaints that she finally gave in and looked the other way whenever she saw the glassy haze in her son's eyes or sensed the bittersweet odor of "grass" coming from his bedroom. I think she was absolutely wrong.

You must not permit illegal activity to take place in your home. Many parents elect to take exception to this rule when it comes to sitting with a son, drinking a beer, and watching a game, or when sharing wine during the holidays and special occasions. In certain cases, I can support this exception, *provided* that parental supervision is maintained.

If you find your kid breaking the law, I strongly advise a hard-nosed approach. The disciplinary measures listed above should be used successively. Whatever you do, don't look the other way. You may overlook illegal activity, but the judge won't.

Backyard: Dangerous Play

Rule: Parents will take immediate action when children
are in dangerous situations
Disciplinary measures: Spanking; family counseling;
outside reinforcement; restriction of freedom

Many parents believe that natural consequences are the best of all teachers. "Let the child crack his head" and "It'll teach the kid a lesson to be arrested" represent extreme examples of this viewpoint. I believe this can be taken too far. There are times when parents can see the child heading for danger. When this happens, strong-arm preventive measures are called for.

When a four-year-old is about to fall off a swing set or a two-year-old is playing in the streets, parents must take action. These are times when I think spanking is very necessary.

When a fifteen-year-old is flunking most of his courses or is keeping constant company with older kids with bad reputations, parents must also take no-nonsense action. Permitting the natural consequences to take their toll is inadvisable. At least you can give it the good old college try.

Spanking a child loses its effectiveness at about the age of five. After that, severe restriction of freedom is called for when children are clearly heading for danger. For older teenagers, the "Shape up or ship out" program may have to be initiated. Some unfortunate parents must resort to calling in the police or a social agency to aid them with a wild child. If at all possible, my favorite recommendation for outside help is family counseling.

QUESTIONS AND ANSWERS

Here is a sampling of typical questions and answers that follow my presentation of law and order around the home.

My kid's hair is too long. I want it cut, but he says "Never." What do I do now?

Step back and reconsider. Keep your eye on clean, neat, and styled hair, not the "short and sassy" look. Do what you must, but admit to yourself that there are many more important issues than hair length. Reevaluate your list of behavior priority and question whether hair length is in the top five before taking action.

I hate to admit it, but my teenager stinks. I always notice it at dinnertime. Do I make a big deal out of it?

I think you should. There are some who argue that people should smell like people. Since you obviously share my view that people should smell like clean people, tell the kid, "If you stink, you don't eat."

I've got the opposite problem. My daughter is so clean she won't get her hands dirty scrubbing floors or washing dishes. Now what?

Make her a deal she can't refuse. Using the "Premack principle"—or, calling time-out—say to her, "You will do nothing you want to do until you help me clean up the kitchen."

My tall, handsome son has the worst posture. He just won't stand up straight, no matter what I tell him. What do I do?

Tell him that you won't bug him about his posture if he will remind himself to stand up straight. Advise him that you will snap your fingers twice every time you see him slouch. If he corrects it, you won't say anything. If he doesn't, you will remind him orally. Let him know that you will do it all the time, even when his friends are around. This action should be taken only after physical problems have been ruled out.

Aren't you using peer pressure? You've said it was wrong.

Yes, I am suggesting that it be used. Peer pressure is a negative influence, but sometimes you can use it to stimulate individual choice, which in turn outweighs the pressure coming from peers.

My daughter refuses to wear a bra, and I refuse to let her out of the house unless she does. Where do we go from here?

The more you fight her on this issue, the less chance you have for compromise and tranquillity. Maybe you could consider letting her go certain places without a bra in exchange for wearing one at other times.

Okay. But isn't that giving in to her demands?

Not really. You are compromising with her, something I don't believe you've done yet. And as long as you compromise on your terms—that is, retaining parental control—it'll work out okay.

My daughter calls me a "bitch" whenever she gets mad at me. I just don't think I should stand it anymore.

Neither do I. Tell her you want her to stop it immediately. Warn her that the next time she does it, she will have no phone privileges for three days. After all, if she can't use her mouth appropriately, then she shouldn't use it at all on her favorite toy.

My kid wouldn't stand for that. She would yell and cry, accusing me of taking her rights away. How do I answer that?

Tell her that she has responsibilities as well as rights. When she uses a vulgar, disrespectful mouth with you, she is being irresponsible, and you will teach her to live by rules of respect.

I caught my son smoking cigarettes in his room. He's been told not to smoke in the house. What can I do?

Put clout into your warning by giving him a lesson in respecting the privacy you've afforded him. Take the door off his room for four days. Each time he wants to close his door to gain privacy, he will be reminded that in order to enjoy privacy, he must learn how to protect it.

My eight-year-old doesn't want to go to bed, because he has terrible nightmares. How can I cope with that?

Children's nightmares often reflect a traumatic day or unresolved fears. For example, children experiencing their parents' unfriendly divorce may be victimized by insecurity expressed in nightmares. If this condition persists, outside help should be sought.

I swear my ten- and twelve-year-old bring their friends over just to make so much racket they'll drive me nuts. I hate to dampen their fun, but I can't stand it much longer.

Noise pollution threatens the health of our ears. Superjets, rock music, and the urban crunch aren't the only culprits. The wild play of children may be worse than all the others put together. Check out my recommendation in the appendix on the use of startling. Use some noise of your own to stop your soul from shattering.

My eleven-year-old drinks more than his share of pop. I decided not to buy it all the time. But then everyone else suffers because of him. Any suggestions?

You can try two different angles, depending on how tough you want to be. You could fine him for excessive soda-drinking or you could buy everyone except him a special dessert. Let him see what his indulgence is costing him.

You said that the oldest should go first in selecting TV programs. I've always thought the youngest should have first pick.

I've heard the same thing repeatedly. However, giving the youngest first pick teaches everyone that weakness gains special recognition. I prefer to think that the oldest, provided he or she is responsible, gets the recognition. By the way, the oldest must also have more responsibilities, which pay for this privilege.

But that's not fair.

You're right, it isn't. Children must learn sooner or later that life isn't fair. However, I think you should try to exercise justice. By the way, I think parents should have first choice on television programs if there is only one set. Remember, you pay the bills.

I tried your suggestion, but my oldest traded his TV time for the youngest's dessert—one whole week of desserts for one half hour of programming. What do I do about that?

First of all, don't overprotect the youngest. Help him learn from his mistake; that is, how to barter and not get cheated. It's almost traditional that older siblings rip off younger ones. My brother took my favorite knife in exchange for a special secret. The "secret" turned out to be that the dirt road at the corner led to New York. That road is still a dirt road, and it still heads west. Yet every time I drive past, I have a warm spot in my heart for a time that is gone forever.

I think grounding is more trouble than it's worth. How about that?

Grounding, if used correctly, is a very powerful punishment. What makes grounding troublesome is when kids don't care about going outside. If kids like to play alone, grounding probably won't work. Likewise, the power of grounding is often usurped by overdoing a good thing. Any grounding that lasts longer than two weeks will lose its effectiveness.

What do you think of mothers who punish their kids in public or when friends are around?

I think they are the salt of the earth. Recently, I was shopping for fruit at my local supermarket when a mother nearby disciplined her four-year-old with ultimate efficiency. The little warrior was trying to climb a shelf of canned goods, getting ready to play superman. Without hesitating, the mother pulled the child off the shelf, popped him once on the rear, pulled a heavy cord of yarn out of her purse, tied it to the straps on his playsuit, and turned him loose. He was on a short rope, and he knew it.

While three mothers gawked at the lady, I stood proudly and applauded her. She smiled, embarrassed, and walked away, pulling her wild child behind her.

As for what to do when Uncle Charlie and Aunt Minnie come to visit? Discipline the kids just as you would if you had no company.

You've said that parents can punish kids when they disturb their peace. Isn't that a bit dictatorial?

Yes.

What can I do about a child who never takes a chance?

There could be many things that cause such a situation. The child may be naturally backward and will grow out of it. He may be withdrawing from challenging situations because he fears being rejected if he fails. Or you may be too tough on him. If you participate with him and he still backs away, you may want to seek outside consultation.

It never seems to fail that when my kid is late coming in, he always argues that his watch says that he's on time. How do I get out of that one?

It's not *your* problem. Designate an official clock—say, the one in the hallway or on the stove—and make all judgments about curfew violations based on that clock. Do *not* argue. If the official clock says he is late, he is late. Period!

When my child leaves the bathroom a mess and goes off to school, do I leave the mess or go ahead and clean it up?

That depends on whether or not you can tolerate having the bathroom a mess. My first reaction is to leave it until the kid cleans it up. But that could be punishing yourself, especially if you're having some friends drop by. If you decide to clean it up, you may add an insult penalty to the restriction of freedom or loss of privileges. A good insult penalty would be washing out all the toilet bowls. Use the Premack principle, to enforce the penalties.

What if the child would simply refuse to do the penalties?

Parents in this situation face a significant loss of clout. Some parents have successfully used a mild form of ostracism in getting the kid's attention. I caution you to seek outside consultation if this situation persists. You may be unintentionally contributing to such obstinacy and need some objective help.

How does a parent know how much responsibility to give to kids—say, to a four-year-old?

My working rule is this: If a child can mess it up, he can clean it up.

What's your position on TV violence?

Personally and professionally, I don't like violence. The violence on television is not only offensive but unreal. It's unreal because the viewer never gets a solid taste of the painful results of violence. The hero is worshiped and the victim is forgotten. If violence is to be portrayed in the media, then it should be played honestly. That means the viewer or listener encounters the depression, horror, and destructiveness of violence.

What do you think about the argument that TV violence causes children to be more violent?

I have some problems with pointing the finger of fault at the television when kids *choose* to be physically violent. Television doesn't *cause* violence; people who are violent do. However, there is every reason to think that parents and authority figures must monitor children's exposure to violence; and, incidentally, not just violence in the media.

I can't agree with your "ostracism" as a punishment. Keeping children outside the family completely is too harsh, and you've said punishment should never be harsh.

Ostracism is very powerful. If not carefully implemented, it can become harsh and therefore unacceptable. That's why I suggest it as a last resort.

My husband and I both work and can't control our children's TV-watching. Now what do we do?

Forget about it. Don't try to control something you can't. Focus on another reward/punishment system. Remember, you can't be all things to your children all the time.

What's your position on the working mother?

I think Mom or Dad should stay very close to an infant. Once the child starts exploring the world, Mom or Dad can feel better about reentering the work force. I think the worry about the working mother's not paying enough attention to the children is much ado about nothing. Fifty or sixty years ago, mothers worked from sunup to sundown and didn't have much time to pay attention to the children. The children had to work, play, and take care of themselves. Most of these kids turned out just fine.

Yes, but Mom was at least there.

I've talked with many older people who said that their mom was so busy just keeping the house running that they didn't see her except at dinnertime and a few precious minutes at bedtime. I'm a great believer in the quality of time spent with children, not the quantity. There have been many mothers I've advised to return to work and quit "smothering" their children. Both they and their children benefit in the long run.

What's a good curfew for a twelve-year-old?

I advise this position: "You will report home when the streetlights go on (when the sun goes down). Then we'll talk about where you go from there."

What do you think of the situation in which Mom says, "Just wait until your father gets home. Then you'll get it"?

I don't like it. This mother is copping out on her role as disciplinarian. I have to wonder how many other times her lack of self-confidence gets in the way. If it happens very often, then this mother needs personal counseling, not advice on discipline.

It seems to me that your get-tough action without communication would create rebellion in older kids. I want to avoid the war that most of my friends seem to have on their hands.

I daresay that your friends have a war on their hands because they talk too much. My experience tells me that arguing, constant explanations, name-calling, and rebellious back talk do not represent communication.

You can reduce the polarization and the resultant "war" by stating your rules, explaining them once, and enforcing them with a minimum of talk. Kids who are faced with *unshakable*, just rules won't waste their time making a war they can't win. They will get on with the business of having fun *and* they will be more apt to seek you out as a trusted adviser. *Then* you can have communication.

Being tough often means taking action that is difficult. Yet you must keep your eye on reality and help your children learn to live with it. Don't let your love smother your kids to the point where they don't learn the valuable lessons that the school of hard knocks can teach them.

Bring reality to bear on your children by imposing law and order around the home. The simplest reality to begin and end with is borrowed from educational psychology; that is, we learn to do by *doing*.

School Daze

Principle #3. Children will demonstrate achievement in fundamental academic skills before pursuing self-directed studies

Principle #4. Students will hold a primary responsibility for discipline; they will be guided, assisted, and directed by a hierarchy of authority figures

When children walk in the door for their first day of school, they enter a mental maze. They leave the familiar haunts of their home and grope their way down the hallways of formal education. They must learn new procedures and faces. They must become adapted to the pressure from peers as they struggle with structured learning and new authority figures. Like it or not, when kids enter academia, they also enroll in the school of hard knocks.

The first few months are hectic. Feeling anxious, many children go to one extreme or another to find security. With practice and time, patterns begin to unfold. Kids experiment with new ways of behaving while exercising some self-discipline. They come to grips with the three R's while participating in extracurricular activities. They develop friendships and group identity while trying to remember who they are as individuals. They react to teachers and principals, working to understand how these people compare and contrast with their parents. In short, when faced with the maze of the educational setting, kids eventually find their own middle ground. Unfortunately, it's not always a happy one.

It's easier to be shy or sassy to a teacher than to learn respect and compliance. It's simpler to be either a loner or one of the herd than to be a group member with an individual identity. It's more convenient to study only what feels good, or not at all, than to budget time, giving equal emphasis to difficult and delightful subject matter. There are other challenges that stimulate movement to the extremes: drugs, rough language, hallway violence, skipping school, endless pranks. No wonder students, big and small, appear to be suffering from "school daze."

Even parents who have refined my get-tough policies experience the uproar of school daze. They tend to go to one extreme or another to protect their children from the turmoil inherent in finding the happy medium. Some parents interfere, solving the child's problem; others ignore the situation altogether, believing that it will all "work out." These parental reactions hinder rather than help children's search for their own happy medium.

In reviewing school daze, I've limited my discussion to the two issues most relevant to my get-tough policy: achievement and discipline.

ACHIEVEMENT

It's never too early for a child to learn that living demands working. Mom has her job, Dad has his and children should have theirs. The child's first and foremost job is to learn as best as possible from the formal and extracurricular activities associated with school. Education must be seen as the key to freedom, personal as well as social. Without knowledge, independence—social as well as individual—cannot be maintained.

Beginning with kindergarten, kids must learn that knowledge opens the door to enjoyable activities. If children learn and produce *evidence* of that learning, they should have freedom. If they don't, their freedom should be curtailed commensurately with their failure to achieve.

Because of this philosophy, I place great emphasis on grades. If a child's grades coincide with his or her abilities and aptitude, then the parent need not implement any disciplinary procedures. If and when a problem develops, I recommend regular review of grades. I will outline this procedure, giving you a note or two on how I implemented the program with Joe Decker.

First, determine the grade average you expect your child to maintain. Expectations for achievement must be based on measured aptitude, taking into account any special learning disabilities. Given the sophistication of achievement and aptitude tests and the availability of communication between parents and teachers, most parents know what to expect from their children. If there is doubt, psychological or educational testing should be sought.

(Joe Decker had a B+ potential and a C− average. He was an underachiever. He was a sophomore at the time we implemented this program. He had plenty of time to pull himself together.)

Second, discuss your expectations with your child in language he or she can understand. Take time to ensure that the child realizes that learning is reflected in grade performance. It may not be the best system ever devised, but grades are here to stay for a while.

If the child is quite young, lighten the burden of "getting good grades" by discussing your expectations in terms of a game. For example, take a trip to the zoo and say, "If you can name two animals we saw today, you get a C in remembering; three animals gets you a B, and four will be an A." With a somewhat older child, you might say, "You get an A in dishwashing because you do a good job without being reminded.

However, you get an F in brushing your teeth because you never do it without being reminded."

For a kid Joe's age, you simply have to say, "You will improve your performance in terms of grades or you will lose some privileges." Joe knew he was doing poorly and needed only to hear "Shape up!"

Third, decide how often grades should be reviewed. The frequency of review depends upon the age of the child and how well he or she is doing in school. If the child is in the first few grades, some type of daily review of papers is advised to prevent serious problems from developing. If you see that your child is doing well, keep your review informal and completely positive; that is, praise the good work and ignore or counsel the bad.

Children who have developed achievement problems need an organized program of review. This program must include clearly defined increments of achievement and a list of rewards, penalties, and precautions.

The fourth step in the procedure begins the formal program of review. The child must go to the teachers and seek their help. With parental guidance and prompting, the child should say something like this to his or her core teacher or teachers: "I've been doing poorly lately. I want to do better, but I need your help. I would like you to give me my grades every week [or every two weeks]. If you want, I'll save my papers and tell you the grade I think I deserve. On Friday, I would like you to write my grade and your name on a piece of paper that I can show my parents. If you have any questions, you can call my dad or mom."

This is a critical step in the program. If the student doesn't ask for help with a positive spirit, the teachers involved may tend to think it's more trouble than it's worth. Teacher cooperation can be ensured by the student's being very serious and willing to do almost anything to get weekly feedback on grades. In cases in which a student is very serious about improvement, I've yet to meet a teacher who wouldn't help.

You should minimize your contact with the teacher. If the teacher wants to talk with you about the program, explain it briefly but remind him or her that you want your child to do most of the work. Getting the teacher's signature or initials discourages cheating. Teachers who think weekly reports are too much bother must be confronted by the parent.

Joe tried to tell me and his parents that his teachers wouldn't like the whole idea. I replied, "Then you'd better find a way to make them like it." Joe was so slick with words that he had no trouble enlisting teacher cooperation. In fact, I found out later that the very fact of Joe's asking for help was worth half a grade point.

Once the teacher expresses a willingness to help, you take the fifth step in the program by setting a standard for summarizing grades. Since life usually operates on an average—some days are better than others—the grade summary will average the weekly grades.

Only subjects usually designated as "core" should be included in the summary. Activities such as band, shop, chorus, art, and gym should be excluded unless deemed of special significance to a particular child. A tough-minded parent is interested in the basics, which include, but are not limited to, English, arithmetic, language studies, social and physical sciences, health, consumer education, and specialized vocational-training courses.

The Decker family and I agreed on these numerical equivalents of letter grades. Joe wrote down these numbers in front of his parents so that there would be no arguments later on.

A+	= 4.33	C+	= 2.33
A	= 4.00	C	= 2.00
A−	= 3.66	C−	= 1.66
B+	= 3.33	D+	= 1.33
B	= 3.00	D	= 1.00
B−	= 2.66	D−	= .66

An F, of course, equals zero, giving no credit toward the average.

Several precautions should be noted at this time. Do not be misled by arguments that a "+" is halfway toward the next grade. There is *no* grade that equals 2.5 or 3.5. If a school system assigns numbers different from mine—for example, grades based on a five-point system—convert the letter grades to my system or convert my system to yours. But remember: no credit for an F.

The sixth step in this program is an extension of the numerical equivalents worked out in the fifth step. You and your child should work out a reward-and-penalty chart to be used in deciding how to convert the grade average into positive and negative consequences.

Several more precautions are in order. Do not expect the child to emerge from a bad grade average in a matter of weeks. Set your sights on improvement, no matter how small. When you agree on rewards and punishments, make certain the actions you take are seen clearly as rewards and punishments *by the child*. If they aren't, the program won't work.

Here's how the reward-and-penalty chart looked when applied to Joe Decker's grade average and his likes and dislikes. We agreed that in the first eight weeks, Joe would be expected to raise his grade average from C− to B−.

3.40 and above	=	all privileges + $5 toward special purchase
3.1 to 3.39	=	all privileges + $3 toward special purchase
2.9 to 3.09	=	all privileges + $2 toward special purchase
2.7 to 2.89	=	all privileges + $1 toward special purchase
2.66	=	all normal privileges
2.4 to 2.59	=	loss of 1 hour off curfew each night
2.1 to 2.39	=	loss of 2 hours each night + no phone after 8 P.M.
1.9 to 2.09	=	loss of 3 hours each night + no phone after 7 P.M.
Below 1.9	=	total grounding and no phone

The increments gave Joe a chance to earn or lose privileges and money in degrees. The lesson became clear: "The more you improve, the more goodies you receive." Joe wanted to purchase a stereo. The more he moved toward a B+, the more money he received. The following stipulations were made as to the accumulation and expenditure of the special money:

- the money was put in a savings account with Joe's and one parent's name on it;

- the money was to be used only for that special purchase;

- the purchase was to be made only *after* the achievement program was over—that is, when Joe reached his overall B+ average and maintained it for one grading period;

- the parents had the right to approve of the amount of the purchase;

- if Joe failed to maintain gradual movement toward the goal, part of the money would be taken out of the fund and spent to take everyone out to the Hamburger Palace.

The implementation of the procedure is the seventh step in the program. The kid collects the grades on the appointed day. All slips of paper should be gathered and the grade average computed. The average should be rounded off to the second decimal figure, or hundredths.

Joe's average the first week was 2.60. He was on the borderline. In this case, Joe was showing good faith, so his parents elected to allow him to retain all normal privileges. However, Joe was warned that the reward-and-penalty chart would be strictly enforced the following week.

The program hit a snag during the second week. Joe "forgot" his math grade and demanded that three instead of four grades be used to find the average. If Joe had been doing well the previous week, I would have approved of giving him the benefit of the doubt. But since he had missed the cutoff, the forgotten grade was counted as an F.

Usually, barely missing the cutoff or forgetting to collect a grade can be overlooked—that is, the first time it happens. But you must not tolerate continual "just misses" or habitual forgetting. If the child has a bad week in one class and does not compensate by bringing up the other classes, he will never learn to exceed the cutoff. If a kid forgets to collect a grade, he may be pulling a con job. If this is allowed to continue, the entire program will fail.

Since Joe was already on thin ice from missing the cutoff, he was penalized for forgetting one grade. It's possible that he truly forgot, no con intended. But, tough luck! His average the second week was 2.30, and he lost privileges until the following Friday evening. He never forgot a grade again.

Following this, Joe had five good weeks in a row. One week the teacher said she could not give Joe a grade. In that case, we agreed that one slip of paper should read "no grade" and be signed. Joe earned ten dollars toward the purchase of a stereo. Then he goofed off and another snag developed.

During the eighth week, Joe got two B's, one C, and an F. But he changed the F—made it look like a B—and computed a 2.75 average. He enjoyed his privileges until Thursday of the next week. That afternoon, a teacher called and said he was glad that Joe had brought his F of the previous week up to a B.

Joe's lie resulted in eight days of total grounding and regular checking between his parents and his teachers for two weeks. Joe learned his lesson about cheating more from his parents' constant checking than from the grounding. He didn't like being treated like a first-grader. Consequently, he quit acting like one.

After Joe maintained his B— average for six weeks, the average was increased to a flat B. He had no trouble maintaining that, so six weeks later, the expected average was raised to a B+. Joe maintained A's and B's in all core classes for the rest of the year. His parents were so pleased that they kicked in an extra hundred dollars, and Joe got his stereo slightly ahead of schedule. He had improved so dramatically that I heartily approved.

As I always do, I recommended that the weekly review program be suspended once Joe reached and maintained his expected grade average. If he had not been so consistent so quickly, I would have suggested that they monitor his grades every two weeks for a longer period of time. But it didn't take long for him to realize that he had to shape up. So he shut his mouth and put his brain into gear—something every under-achiever must learn to do.

DISCIPLINE

Discipline in the home is tough to handle. When children raise hell at school, the difficulty multiplies. The introduction of new authority figures complicates matters, as do children's drive for independence, parental concern about how others will view their children, and the kids' realization that Mom and Dad don't know it all.

Pushing, shoving, shouting, screaming, hitting, punching, talking out of turn, name-calling, are a few of the symptoms of children's testing the limits of a new situation. Classrooms, hallways, locker rooms, playgrounds, and the school bus become battlefields upon which the experimentation takes place. This disruption in all corners of the school world causes teachers and principals to age faster than God intended them to.

In my view, student discipline is more than a problem for parents, teachers, and principals; it's a community concern. Citizens must demand that children behave themselves while on school property. Furthermore, they should back up their demands with action. I'm not saying that you should break up a fight in the alley behind the school. That could prove unhealthy. But you can report disruption to the proper offi-cials, threaten to call the police (anonymously), write letters to the school board and the newspaper, and lodge complaints during school-board meetings if nothing is done about your complaints. You can agree to be a witness in a prosecution. Most important, you can support your school board when the members come under fire for trying to stop tyranny on school grounds or when the star basketball player is expelled for sell-ing drugs.

Whereas you have a right to expect the school to operate an

efficient and effective educational program, you also have a responsibility to help them do it. Simply to pay taxes and then expect teachers and principals to handle a monstrous problem is irresponsible. If you can't be responsible and help the school do its job, then you get the same advice I give to kids: Rights and responsibilities go hand in hand; you can't have one without the other.

Teacher-training programs don't help matters. Every manual I've read in the past few years contains the same message: Teachers are responsible for student discipline. The trainers urge teachers to find the right reinforcer, reward positive behavior, and ignore disruption. They are admonished to avoid punishment while maintaining the pressure for outstanding achievement. They are cautioned to keep troublemakers separated from one another without allowing the "good kids" to be slighted. What do they think teachers are—God's assistants?

Most training programs in disciplining students are unrealistic. Though I agree that rewards are strong incentives for good behavior, I've been around long enough to realize that many kids just don't care about praise from authority figures. Kids who will work hard for special recognition are probably doing well already. Thus, though I support the use of rewards, I recognize that a system of punishments must be made available to school personnel.

Teachers add to their own problems. In concert with administration, they believe what the training manuals tell them. They try to shoulder the burden of being responsible for all student discipline and then wonder why their backs are bent. It's getting so ridiculous that when students do well, it's the parents who receive the praise. When they do poorly, it's the teachers who must shoulder the blame.

Meanwhile, students spend their time figuring out which teacher will let them get away with what disruption. Kids have repeatedly confided in me that one of the first things they do when confronted with a new school or teacher is to find out from other kids which rules they can break and which teachers enforce the rules.

Those of you interested in an effective student-discipline system must remember one important fact: Student disruption is caused by kids, not by adults, and the kids should be held accountable for it.

Parents find this hard to accept, in their belief that children are too young to know how to cope with the problem.

My reply would be "If they're old enough to start a problem, then they're old enough to help solve it."

My attitude toward student discipline seems to have some contradictions. On the one hand, I advocate that authority figures lean slightly to the conservative side in imposing controls on children. Yet I espouse children's being held accountable for their own actions. This apparent conflict is resolved by the notion that whereas authorities must retain control of disciplinary situations, children can be given room to discipline themselves whenever possible. If they are successful, authority can back off and give them more room; if not, authority must step in, but only after children have demonstrated that they can't handle the responsibility. Thus, I suggest that children be given more responsibility to solve their own problems, or at least be made constantly aware that disruption is *not* the fault of the teacher, principal, and other authority figures.

My recommendation for dealing with student discipline is contained in a hierarchy of procedures, starting with children and ending with the most powerful agency in the community: the courts. Each stage in the hierarchy involves more intervention by authority figures. As you will see, each step of authoritative intervention is taken after the kid fails to handle the disruption or when the problem becomes too large or time-consuming for the kid to deal with.

(I've borrowed from several school systems in building this hierarchy, and from my experience in administering such a system as supervisor of a residential program for disruptive youths.)

The stages in the hierarchy are:
    Student Control
    Advice from Counselors
    Teacher-Parent Teamwork

Principal/Dean Review
Police Liaison
Citizens' Advisory
School-Board Intervention
Court Disposition

Student control

In my experience, nobody can control kids better than other kids. Though I basically don't like the "herding" that often results from the pressure for conformity, peer pressure is a reality and sometimes can be harnessed to achieve effective student discipline. Taking into account the peculiarities of the school (size, location, composition, student values), I recommend that the idea of a student council be expanded to include a committee on student discipline.

With the help of parents, teachers, administrators, and interested citizens, the student discipline committee should draw up a written policy that will guide the actions of the committee. This policy should include the types of problems to be referred to the committee, with the understanding that problems could be added or deleted as experience demanded. The policy should also cover how referrals are filed, what due process all participants are ensured, and how the hearing will be conducted. Under administrative restrictions, the committee will compose a list of rewards and penalties to be used in disposing of a referral. Any level of authority should be able to refer a case to the committee, and referrals for special recognition of positive behavior are encouraged. If informed volunteers (for example, lawyers) help the students write and execute a judicious policy, administration would not have to use the veto power it must retain.

When I implemented this procedure, I helped the student council form a committee on discipline. They were guided in developing simple rules for due process. They routinely disposed of problems involving vulgarity, messiness, disrespect, intimidation, and class disruption, and often helped the poorly motivated student. One time the students worked effectively to help several classmates who were chronic underachievers.

The group also made provisions for recognizing special achievements. Limited cash awards were given to the student of the week, and special privileges (all within the school code) were given to anyone who showed significant improvement or otherwise distinguished himself. We found that public praise as well as criticism from the teachers and administrators made a strong impression on the kids.

The kids took their responsibility very seriously. However, we found that sometimes they got in over their heads and had to be bailed out. For example, we learned not to refer drug-abuse cases to the committee, since 90 percent of the committee had at least flirted with drugs at one time. They were unable to review the merits of the individual cases objectively.

Even though violence was a problem to be handled immediately by authority figures in the school, we found that when referred to the committee, the students often discovered the cause of the fight and took it upon themselves to negotiate a lasting peace.

Theft was another problem that the committee handled, even though the principal had already been involved. We found that the more we administrators stayed out of theft cases, the sooner the items were returned to the rightful owner, the more equitable was the restitution, and the more forthcoming were the apologies.

I used the Premack principle (see the appendix) to promote efficiency and discourage pointless arguments. Free-time activity was delayed until all cases scheduled for that day had been disposed of according to due process. This particular application of the principle also tended to reduce the number of referrals made by students as well as to encourage cooperation and avoidance of disruption.

Advice from counselors

Counselors should be assigned to advise the student discipline committee as well as to monitor its activities. Kids may want to have closed hearings at which no authority figure is present. Since this student government cannot be allowed to run without adult guidance, counselors, with the freedom to keep nondangerous information confidential, should sit in on all meetings.

The students must realize from the outset that they will never have free reign. In the language of chapter 2, the student disciplinary committee must be tethered to some control rope. They will have as much slack as they demonstrate they can handle.

Counselors are present to insure that the students remain a body governed by laws, not by prejudices or negative peer pressure. This provides a safeguard that the system won't self-destruct before it gets off the ground. This also gives counselors the opportunity to single out certain students who may need individual attention.

The counselors I used were respected by the students. After the ground rules were established, I allowed the students to pick their own counselors. The counselors' main job was to help the students learn to carry the burden of self-discipline. As long as the committee worked toward a constructive resolution of the problem at hand, the counselor remained a monitor or adviser. If the students failed to act responsibly or otherwise violated the ground rules, the counselor disbanded the meeting and explained to higher authorities what had happened. Since the students didn't want me to know they had failed (and thereby give me permission to take charge of their lives), they worked harder to achieve self-control.

Teacher-parent teamwork

Teachers are the front-line authority figures in the school. They have the responsibility of letting the children know that someone is in charge. Teachers must run their classrooms. If they don't, an atmosphere conducive to learning cannot exist. However, this does not mean that teachers must discipline *every* rule infraction. Nor does it mean that they must clear every disciplinary measure with the principal.

There are times when immediate action is needed, and there are also times when discipline could be referred to the students. When my teachers encountered such problems as vulgarity, disrespect, intimidation, and the class clown, they used the student-control element to alleviate a student-teacher confrontation.

The teacher would say, "The rest of you had better talk with Tom about his mouth, or else I'll have to do something about it." This vague reference to imminent punishment served as a warning to Tom as well as a request for the students to control Tom. The more the students were accustomed to handling disciplinary referrals, the quicker they told Tom to "cool it."

An effective student-control program gives the teacher more clout. If the teacher is able to hold the students accountable for classroom propriety as well as for other self-control problems, the students will work to protect their own interests.

It is crucial that other levels of authority support this system of accountability. I've included parents at this level of the hierarchy because they must support the teacher's authority. Parent-teacher conferences are the established mechanism whereby this mutual support can be developed. I would also like to see more active parental involvement in such matters as monitoring hallways, investigating truancy, and supervising in-school suspension programs.

Administration must, of course, support the teacher's authority, not supplant it. As "Keeper of the Clout," the principal could simply whisk into a disruptive class, take the reins from the teacher, make warnings of dire consequences, and then disappear. However effective for the moment, this action does little to establish that the teacher has clout of his or her own.

Principal/dean review

The principal or dean represents the highest degree of authority in the building. Consider the following, which is taken from a summary of a congressional report on violence and safety in schools: "In case studies, the single most important difference between safe schools and violent schools was found to be a strong, dedicated principal who served as a role model for both students and teachers and who instituted a firm, fair and consistent system of discipline."*

In my hierarchy of authority intervention, the principal is pulled into the problem only after the student committee, counselors, parents, and teachers have failed to dispose of the case. There are instances in which offenses necessitate the direct intervention of the principal. Even when this occurs, I recommend that the principal point out to the students that he or she is taking action because the students failed to "take care of business."

Following is a list of disciplinary measures available to the principal.† I've arranged the entries according to students' rating of their effectiveness, starting with the most effective.

> Individual counseling
> Serving suspension time on Saturday
> Withdrawal of extracurricular privileges
> Parent conferences with teachers or principal
> Referral to court authorities or police
> Student conferences with teacher or principal
> Expulsion
> Restrictions on participation in activities
> Out-of-school suspension
> After-school detention
> Strict supervised study
> Referral to social worker
> Special class for social adjustment
> Referral to school psychologist
> Giving student pamphlets on school rules
> Referral to community social-service agencies
> Giving student demerits
> Transfer to another school
> Oral reprimand
> Corporal punishment (paddling)

---

*The Safe School Study Report to the Congress, *Vol. I, U.S. Government Printing Office (January 1978).*
†*"Survey of Student Discipline," compiled by the Illinois Educational Association, completed by students in District 186, 1978.*

This sample of students' judgments supports my contention that, within limits, kids can discipline themselves. These students selected individual help and the hard penalty of losing precious weekend time as the most effective one-two punch for dealing with disruption. Their thoughts about the effectiveness of talk (oral reprimands) and hitting were equally revealing.

All authority figures, especially principals, would do well to take a similar survey in their respective schools. It could be a natural first step in implementing student control.

Police liaison

Many schools have working agreements with local police departments in which an officer is assigned to the school. In my experience, these officers keep a low profile except at times of crisis. They usually wear street clothes and view themselves as the students' friend. They try to avoid confrontations if at all possible. I'm not convinced that police liaison has been effective and I view its use as optional.

If police are to be assigned to a school building, I think it should be after the students have requested it. I would like to think that the students, counselors, parents, teachers, and administrators could form a team to solve student discipline without outside intervention. I do accept the fact that some schools suffer from such a degree of disruption that police must be on duty. However, when this step is necessary, I think the police should be clearly identified as peace officers, complete with uniform and weapon. If the kids find this offensive, then I would suggest that the principal say to them "We will get rid of the cop when you get rid of the violence."

Citizens' advisory

Another optional agency of intervention is the citizens' advisory committee. The committee would be composed of citizens from all walks of life. As a group, they would be asked to give advice to the student discipline committee, organize and monitor any parent involvement in school discipline, and act as public-information brokers.

Our program had a citizens' advisory committee that was instrumental in giving procedural recommendations concerning discipline as well as suggestions for community activities that would benefit the students. One committee member volunteered to help kids learn how to use the community's banks; another gave students excellent lessons in buying clothing; still another took the students to several car dealers, where they learned the facts of life about purchasing "wheels."

The best reason for the existence of a citizens' advisory group is to signal to all concerned that the average citizen has a responsibility to aid the school in its overwhelming task.

School-board intervention

School-board members have a rough job. They are blamed for high taxes and low achievement. They are criticized when students fail and ignored when reading scores go up. School boards take a lot of heat. I think they should.

The more heat board members take, the more they'll be motivated to do something about the deterioration of discipline in our schools. As the central policymaking organization, the school board cannot pass the buck, saying that some psychosocial bogeyman causes all the trouble. I should add that I consider central administration—superintendent, director of departments—to be on the same level of intervention as the school board. Too often these people are permitted to hide in their offices and write memos about what should happen when they should be stepping into the kitchen and taking the heat with the rest of the policymakers.

Board members and central administration could help their own cause by supporting a system of student control. If all other levels of intervention knew that the board would back them in demanding student discipline, we could have safer schools, higher achievement, and school-board members who wouldn't have to wear a disguise when they appeared in public.

Court disposition

My recommendation for involving students at all levels of disciplinary intervention falls to pieces without the willingness of the courts to support strict discipline in the schools. There will always be at least one student who will test the limits of the system. If this student gets a strong dose of justice in the courtroom, he or she will spread the word that the school means business when it says to behave.

Crowded court calendars are a major drawback to this recommendation. But I will argue that if the courts *made* time to handle unruly and incorrigible cases, the school would have fewer referrals to the justice system. When a kid can sell dope in the hallway and six months later still be doing business after being "disciplined," the principal's or teacher's statement that there will be law and order at school becomes just a bad joke.

My recommendation for implementing a program of student discipline raises more questions than answers. I will attempt to answer some of the more frequent questions that arise when I discuss discipline and achievement.

These two programs sound complicated and time-consuming. Is all this really necessary?

It's necessary only if the child demonstrates an inability to handle problems by himself or herself. Monitoring achievement on a regular basis and encouraging kids to participate in their own discipline is an investment that can eventually save time and money. More pressure should be taken off teachers, principals, and school boards and placed where it belongs—on the kids.

Isn't underachievement really a result of a child's being spoiled?

I think it is, at least in part. A child who thinks that the world will conform to his or her every whim won't have any reason to study reading, grammar, math, and so on. Underachievement can also be a sign that the student is experiencing problems in daily life. The more these issues are brought into the open, the better the chances of helping the students improve their grades.

When do I start this program of formal review?

In general, whenever you think underachievement is taking place. My program has been most successful with children from seventh to twelfth grade.

In your case with Joe, you made him wait almost a year before he got his stereo. Isn't that awfully tough?

Absolutely. He had to learn sooner or later to work hard for things he wanted.

My son is a freshman in high school, and when he gets in trouble at school, I give him a paddling. It works every time.

If it works every time, why do you have to keep doing it? Restriction of freedom works better.

My daughter is fourteen. I just got two failing slips in the mail. I thought she was doing fine. What do I do now?

I'm concerned that you didn't know she was failing two courses. You need to review her work on a regular basis for at least half of a semester. The program outlined above should work. You should also consider imposing a study period, possibly two hours at first.

I wanted to give my son a study period, but he said that there is nothing to study. When I checked, I found out that the teacher doesn't give homework. Is there anything I can do?

If the boy is getting good grades and he scores well on achievement tests, then you need not worry. Keep your eye on the outcome, not the way the boy reaches the outcome.

That doesn't sound very good. It sounds as if you would approve of lying or cheating—anything to get good grades.

I do not condone such underhanded activity. However, you can't do much about cheating. You can only explain your morality and hope that the school policing activities will spark enough fear that the child will decide to follow your values.

The principal called me the other day and said my son was caught cheating. He's an excellent student; he doesn't need to cheat. What should I do?

First see how much pressure to achieve the boy feels. You may be putting too much pressure on him; he may think he can never meet your expectations. Then let him know that you are angry about his cheating. Reemphasize the importance of honesty. Then give him an insult penalty; for example, extra work around the house or two hours off his curfew for a week.

My daughter cheated on a test and I grounded her for the rest of the semester. It's been rough, but she learned her lesson.

Don't be too sure. She may have learned to be more careful, but at what expense? Grounding for that long punishes you more than your daughter, and she will become immune to grounding, so that next time it will be less effective. If you want to punish her, make it shorter and harder.

My son said I shouldn't punish him for skipping class, because the school already did. He accused me of "double jeopardy."

Well, at least he learned what a legal term meant. Explain to him that when he skipped class, he violated two laws—the school's and yours.

You seem to put a lot of faith in our grading system. Don't you realize that it is mostly unfair?

I'm not convinced that it's *mostly* unfair. However, it probably isn't as fair as it could be. But you should know that I'm not impressed by arguments about fairness. Grades are real, whether fair or unfair; so are the opportunities for advancement that are tied to grades. Grades are here to stay, at least for a while. Until that reality changes, kids must learn how to work within the confines of the reality they must face every day.

Do you believe in the pass-fail grading system?

Not when it comes to core subjects. I've seen kids in English and math use the pass-fail system to goof off and not learn what they should. They lack the background that comes with daily studying and rigorous application of what they have learned. The real world is graded, not based on pass or fail.

You sound as if you wouldn't approve of the Montessori method.

Rather than comment on a system I don't totally understand, let me say this: I don't think that learning is always fun. Nor should we try to make it something it isn't. It's not fun to make mistakes, yet making mistakes can be the first step to a lifelong lesson.

My kid complains about unfair teachers. In one case, I agree with him. What can I do?

The world is filled with unfair people. Help your kid learn how to cope with that reality. Engaging in name-calling or revenge tactics is unfruitful. Let your kid gripe, and if you agree, let him know it. Then discuss strategies for change or other methods of coping with the situation. Talk with him about the power of public relations, or "apple-polishing," if you like. Formal complaints by you could be lodged if classroom justice becomes a mockery.

How can teachers discipline children in the classroom when parents don't do it at home?

As I mentioned, it's tougher, but it still can be done. If children receive no discipline at home, a teacher has the opportunity, with help from other levels of intervention, to teach the child that there is another way to live.

What's your opinion about dress codes?

I think standards of neatness and cleanliness are important. Dress codes should be made by students after being given some ground rules by authority figures. The length of a kid's hair is not nearly as important as what he or she does with the brain underneath.

What if a teacher won't give weekly feedback when requested to do so by the student?

Then it is time for a parent-teacher conference. I would be very interested in a teacher's response to a parent who says, "Is it true that you don't want to help my child work his way out of the hole he got himself into?"

In the quiz, you said kids should average B in the basics, but you supported Joe Decker in his maintaining a B— average. What gives?

Joe was working himself out of a hole. It's defeating the larger purpose to expect him to do it in a matter of weeks. We took several steps to get the desired result. Also, I expect a B average in the basics from students who have the potential to do it. Not all students have this potential.

What's your position on drug abuse in the schools?

Unfortunately, many parents, teachers, administrators, and citizens view it as "inevitable." I think this is a disastrous, defeatist viewpoint. It also becomes a self-fulfilling prophecy. If we accept drug abuse as part of the "modern scene," then we are being more irresponsible than our kids. As you will see in chapter 8, I take a hard-nosed, legalistic approach to drug abuse. I encourage you strongly to do the same.

But how can you expect children not to smoke dope?

By expecting them *not to do it* and backing up your expectations with hard-nosed action. Too many authority figures, including many law-enforcement agencies, are shaken by the flimsy argument that it's no big deal, because everybody is doing it. If we aren't going to enforce a law, then the law is useless and serves only to erode our clout.

But what if the family supports dope-smoking?

Arrest the whole darn family.

C'mon, Dr. Dan. Aren't you being a little hard on kids? Don't you remember what it's like to raise hell?

A long time ago my parents taught me the difference between having fun and flirting with danger. For those of you who've never heard how an old-fashioned parent would explain the difference, it goes like this: If you're going to have fun, you "raise hell." If you let fun get out of hand, you "raise hell and put a brick under it."

You've said nothing about racial prejudice in schools. Isn't it the biggest cause of violence?

Violence is "caused" by a combination of personality traits; among these are the absence of self-discipline, low frustration tolerance, poor impulse control, and low self-esteem. The provocation that results in violent actions could be many things, including the complicated issue of racial prejudice. But focusing on prejudice takes us away from the cause and, consequently, from the cure.

By the way, the 1978 report to Congress on violence in schools notes, "In a majority of cases, victims and offenders are of the same race."

What's your position on disruption on the school bus?

The school bus is an extension of the classroom, and the bus driver is an authority figure. Kids who do not mind the bus driver should be referred for disciplinary action. Likewise, bus drivers should be trained in managing the behavior of children.

Questions relating to achievement and discipline could go on forever. Some answers are absolute, many are relative, and others are no more than logical speculation on what could or should be done. To be sure, there are many more questions than answers.

When I encounter the confusion of school daze, I long for the one-room schoolhouse where students worked, played, laughed, and cried together in a spirit of brotherly and sisterly love. The school was an extension of the home and the teacher a part of the family. Learning was as natural as kissing Mom good night.

Those days are gone. So is the simplicity of achievement and discipline. But we can still bring the beauty, peace, and harmony of those times to our children. To do so, our words and actions must convey a no-nonsense message: "Your main job is to learn as well as you possibly can in school. That includes how to behave yourself on the school grounds and in the classroom. The teacher will help you learn and you will do your best. If you goof off, you will answer first to the teacher and then to me."

8

Coping with Drug Abuse

Principle #5. All drug abuse, including that of alcohol, will result in some type of disciplinary action

Taking drugs for what ails us has become a national pastime. As drug use has increased, so has drug abuse. Although drug abuse respects no age limits, the young seem most often victimized by its evil. Since it is assumed that our children have less maturity and self-control than do adults (which is not necessarily so), and that adults should be old enough to know what they're doing to their bodies, concern about drug abuse usually focuses on our children. I support this emphasis.

In providing guidance for authority figures in coping with drug abuse, I often find myself embroiled in controversy and confused by subjectivity. Parents drink martinis and then tell their children that alcohol is bad. Adults take pills to "solve" their problems but tell children that they are wrong when they take dope to cope. Kids argue and parents get defensive. Teenagers vacillate between becoming alcoholics and overdosing with every imaginable piece of garbage while authority figures struggle to understand. The lack of constructive activity in the face of death is enough to drive me to drink.

Stirring up controversy regarding drug abuse is easy. Solving the problems is not. I have worked for years in search of a way to approach the drug-abuse issue so that solutions are workable for all children. I've reviewed all types of drug-abuse programs, looking for a common thread. However, the only thing they have in common is that all their clients are kids who have already fallen into the trap of taking drugs as a way of life.

I have been dismayed at the lack of agreement among people who make the study of drug abuse their life's work. As a layman friend of mine says, "The expert's answer to drug abuse depends upon what drugs the expert is taking."

I used to hope that the scientific community could give us an infallible system for dealing with drug abuse. Yet contradictory evidence in professional journals and poorly controlled research still dominate the scene. The problem is magnified when one realizes that even the strongest narcotic might be a godsend to a person suffering from terminal cancer.

Religion can be counted on to provide guidance in difficult issues, but drug abuse is not one of them. Moral platitudes, quotes from Scripture, and clerical admonitions give help only to those who want it in the first place. Religion is a deeply personal and subjective experience and cannot provide acceptable solutions for everyone.

The philosophies of ethics, logic, and psychology are too esoteric to confront the harsh realities of drug abuse. Common-sense beliefs are too subjective to give stability. They also tend to give explanations, not answers. In the case of drug abuse, common sense might dismiss the problem by saying "If nature didn't put the drug in your body in the first place, then you have no business putting it there yourself." However easy this is to understand, it doesn't give us a foundation upon which to build answers.

The standard I've come to rely upon is an expression of the need for objectivity in human affairs. In dealing with drug abuse, I see no other viable alternative except the legal system. The law provides us with a time-honored mechanism for making sense out of the senseless. The justice system provides us with a standard, grounded in common sense and representing the best that philosophy, religion, and science have to offer.

Despite the arguments about "bad" laws, I believe we must *make* the law work for us in coping with drug abuse. Without the discipline inherent in the law, we will continually face the deadly effects of drug abuse and remain helplessly confused. The law gives us answers in black and white while permitting a discussion of the type of rewards and punishments that will promote rehabilitation. Best of all, it gives us a logical foundation upon which to build workable solutions to fit all segments of society.

I ask you to join me as I apply the legal system to solving drug-abuse problems. I intend to take the logic of the courtroom and bring it into the living room. If you will, don the robes of justice, place yourself in a high-backed chair, and consider cases of drug abuse brought before you.

I will present four types of cases, all of which can and do occur where you live (there may be slight differences depending on state statutes). The *people*, representing the interests of society, will bring charges against children or parents for drug abuse, neglect, or delinquency. To give you a refreshing view of the latter two, I shall call neglect "malparenting" and delinquency "malpractice of childhood."

If you're willing to put yourself on the "hot seat" of justice, then come into our "moot court of drug-abuse justice" and be prepared to reside.

First case ...

PEOPLE V. WILSON

CHARGE: Fifteen-year-old Joe Wilson is accused of the malpractice of childhood because of his persistent smoking of cigarettes and showing no regard for his mother's directive that he quit.

EVIDENCE: Joe smokes one and a half packs of cigarettes a day. He contends that he has a right to smoke, that all his friends do, and that his mother is just hassling him for no good reason. Joe points out that any teenager can buy cigarettes just about anywhere. He believes that the law prohibiting minors from smoking is "dumb."

FINDING: Guilty.

MITIGATING/ AGGRAVATING CIRCUMSTANCES: Joe's mother and father are divorced, and Joe doesn't see his dad very often. Joe is insecure in his male role and easily influenced by peer pressure. His friends smoke, and Joe needs to assert his independence from Mom. His anger and resentment run deeper than smoking.

COURT'S OPINION: Joe will undoubtedly continue smoking. The Court is distressed with Joe's defiance and hostile indifference. Attempts to enforce the ruling will result only in more sneaky behavior. However, some remediation is still in order.

DISPOSITION: Mrs. Wilson will enforce the following:

a. Joe will sign up for an exercise class at the YMCA, where he will learn about physical fitness and interact with adult males.

b. Joe will be grounded whenever there is indication that he is smoking.

c. Joe will donate two dollars per week from his paper route to the local Cancer Society.

"Next case . . ."

People v. Thornton

CHARGE:
Paul Thornton is charged with possession of a controlled substance.

EVIDENCE:
Sixteen-year-old Paul was apprehended by the dean at the high school as Paul was attempting to sell barbiturate tablets to another student. Paul has taken the pills from his mother's prescription without her awareness.

FINDING:
Guilty.

M/A
CIRCUMSTANCES:
Paul is an average student, helps around home, and is generally well-behaved. His mother has a history of "bad nerves." Paul's father is a traveling salesman with little time to spend with his son. Mother doesn't have the strength to supervise her teenage son, so often avoids confrontation.

COURT'S
OPINION:
Paul must receive a stiff punishment. He is playing with fire and needs to get burned. The mother, father, prescribing physician, and pharmacist bear some responsibility in contributing to Paul's actions.

DISPOSITION:
The pharmacist and physician will be alerted to the problem. The school will carry out its suspension as planned. As for the family, the following is recommended: the family enter counseling; the pills be put under lock and key. Paul receives this penalty: no driving privileges for two weeks; no outgoing phone calls for two weeks; curfew cut back to eight P.M. weeknights and ten-thirty on weekends for one month. Paul will be placed under Court supervision for six months and the case will be reviewed at that time. If the recom-

mendations have not been carried out, the parents will be charged with malparenting.

"Next case ..."

PEOPLE V. WHITE

CHARGE:

Mr. and Mrs. White are accused of malparenting in that they knowingly contribute to the delinquency of their two children, ages fourteen and sixteen.

EVIDENCE:

The children's paternal grandparents have observed that Mr. and Mrs. White have condoned the consumption of alcohol by both teenagers during family gatherings in the parents' home. It is determined that this typically happens during family gatherings.

FINDING:

Innocent.

M/A
CIRCUMSTANCES:

The parents supervise the consumption of wine during family gatherings and, as such, are acting in accordance with the law. Both parents believe they are teaching their children sensible and proper use of alcohol.

COURT'S
OPINION:

It is well within the parents' rights to conduct themselves as noted. The Court believes that they are not engaging in illegal behavior and that as long as they can demonstrate responsible supervision, the Court sees no reason to interfere with their parental rights.

DISPOSITION:

The Court would like evidence from Mr. and Mrs. White that they have had conferences with the grandparents so that the children will not suffer in any way from the disagreement that led to this charge.

"Next case...."

PEOPLE V. SCHOTZ

CHARGE: Eighteen-year-old Stanley Schotz is charged with possession of alcohol and marijuana, disturbing the peace, and contributing to the delinquency of a minor.

EVIDENCE: Stanley was arrested by the sheriff at his home in the exclusive suburb of Lakefront Lagoon at three A.M. There were approximately fifty youths present, many of whom were minors. Several cases of beer, two ounces of marijuana, and assorted hard liquor were confiscated. When confronted by the sheriff's deputies, Stanley became abusive, unruly, and attempted to strike one of the officers. Stanley's parents were out of town at the time.

FINDING: Guilty.

M/A CIRCUMSTANCES: Stanley's parents often leave him alone during their overnight absences. They say he is an adult and should be expected to act like one. Stanley had been arrested twice before, once for speeding and once for possession of marijuana at school.

COURT'S OPINION: Stanley is considered an adult in this matter, but the Court seriously questions the parents' judgment that Stanley could be expected to behave like an adult just because the law considers him one. His behavior was and has been immature. Severe action must be taken against Stanley so that he will have adequate warning as to the eventual end of the reckless path of behavior he is pursuing.

DISPOSITION: a. $100 fine to be paid by Stanley, not his parents.

b. Stanley and his parents must visit each of the parents of the other children at the party and explain what occurred.

c. Stanley is to visit the nearest penitentiary to see where his next contact with the legal system will take him.

d. One year's probation.

"The Court is recessed ..."

To add realism to your role as judge, follow me into my chambers and take a look at what I think is the human side of such a court.

"Today was tough. That Wilson kid and his attitude really burned me! When he started smarting off about the 'stupid rules' against a minor's smoking, I wanted to take him over my knee and teach him some respect.

"What am I saying? Good heavens, judges aren't supposed to have such feelings. But I'm human; I can't help it. I am swayed by my own emotions. I care. I didn't count on this human involvement when I put that black robe on. When I see childish immaturity, disrespect and disregard for the law, my blood boils. What ever happened to 'justice is blind'?

"I'd better relax. I'll drink a couple of martinis. Tomorrow will be interesting. There is a test case on marijuana. It'll help me regain my objectivity."

"Next case ..."

PEOPLE V. FULLERTON

CHARGE: Mr. and Mrs. Fullerton are accused of malparenting.

EVIDENCE: At a meeting of the PTA, Mr. and Mrs. Fullerton said that the marijuana laws were wrong and they would not contribute to the double standards of drinking alcohol in front of their children while not permitting them to smoke marijuana. They quoted several studies that suggest that the effects of marijuana are no more harmful than those of alcohol. They also mentioned the folly of prohibition and that it was only a matter of time before marijuana would be decriminalized.

The children noted that they had smoked marijuana in plain view of their parents and the parents took no punitive action.

FINDING: Guilty.

M/A   The parents are moral individuals who have
CIRCUMSTANCES: a belief in what they are saying and have the
                    courage of their convictions. The children
                    are generally well behaved, but their grades
                    could be improved.

COURT'S   The Court does not question the stability of
OPINION: the parents; nor are the children to be held
                    as delinquent. However, there are no specific
                    or general circumstances that permit *any*
                    exception to the laws concerning marijuana.
                    The legislation is clear.

                    The Court is aware of conflicting research
                    and sympathetic to the parents' concern
                    about double standards. But the Court can
                    find no evidence of double standards when
                    viewing the case from the legal perspective.
                    It is legal for the parents to drink; it is illegal
                    for the kids, or for any other person, to
                    smoke marijuana.

                    The Court reprimands the parents for con-
                    doning illegal behavior. The Court is not
                    pleased with the conspicuous absence of reli-

able information concerning the effects of marijuana.

DISPOSITION: The parents will immediately institute a system of penalties for possession and/or use of marijuana by the children. If evidence is brought to light that the parents have not followed this course of disciplinary action, they will be held in contempt of court. A hearing shall then be held to determine their fitness as parents. The case shall be reviewed by this Court in six months.

"Next case . . ."

PEOPLE V. JOHNSON

CHARGE: Through the state, eighteen-year-old Kathy Johnson accuses her parents of malparenting.

EVIDENCE: Kathy's petition to the Court reads, "My parents drink every evening before and after dinner. When they drink, they don't listen to me and are mean for no reason. Now I'm drinking. I know it's not right, but I feel better. Two weeks ago, I got drunk and my boy friend broke up with me, calling me an alcoholic. It's my parents' fault."

The parents respond that Kathy has been disruptive for several years. She won't do what they tell her to. They don't deny that they drink every evening, but they disagree that they treat Kathy any differently.

FINDING: Innocent.

M/A
CIRCUMSTANCES: The parents refuse to seek family counseling and deny any problems with alcohol. Kathy is doing poorly in school and is in danger of

not graduating. In general, the parents feel this is a family matter and resent court intervention.

COURT'S
OPINION: The parents and Kathy appear blinded to their real problems. The child's charge has some substance, yet the Court does not agree with her contention that her parents "cause" her drinking. Kathy is old enough to resist temptation, no matter what her parents choose to do.

Kathy does not present any emotional, intellectual, or physical defects and must be held accountable for her own actions.

The Court further recognizes that Kathy is legally an adult, and though there may be cause supporting malparenting, it cannot be applied to this situation, because Kathy is no longer a minor.

DISPOSITION: The Court has no authority to enforce the following directive, as it finds no guilt. However, the parties are strongly encouraged to comply.

a. All parties attend at least five meetings of Alcoholics Anonymous.

b. Family counseling be added to recommendation #1.

c. Kathy be admonished that her drinking is still illegal.

"Next case . . ."

PEOPLE V. HENRY

CHARGE: Fifteen-year-old Dan Henry is charged with illegal consumption of alcohol.

EVIDENCE: Dan was taken by his teacher to the dean's office because of "wild classroom behavior." The dean states that Dan smelled of alcohol and was easily identifiable as being "falling-down drunk." Further investigation yielded the information that Dan regularly bragged to friends about how much he could drink— morning, noon, and night. While still drunk, Dan admitted to having consumed five beers and a half pint of vodka before school. His girl friend states that his drinking has been getting worse for months.

FINDING: Guilty.

M/A CIRCUMSTANCES: Mr. and Mrs. Henry are conscientious, hard-working parents. They attend church regularly and have raised Dan's four older brothers to be productive members of society. They admit to spoiling Dan by giving him much more freedom than they ever gave their other children. They sensed that Dan was getting out of control but felt so much guilt and so little control that they simply looked the other way. They are willing to take a tighter stand with Dan if they can receive help.

COURT'S OPINION: Dan Henry must be considered a teenage alcoholic—not a very pleasant conclusion. Though Dan is being singled out in this case, the Court wishes to admonish all parents that alcoholism is not confined to adults. It often gets started when junior-high students look to liquor as a substitute for marijuana, both of which they use to avoid responsibility. The lesson of responsibility and self-control must be the cure for the disease noted in this case.

DISPOSITION: The following order is entered:

a. Dan is to attend ten meetings of AA.

b. Dan will have a highly restricted curfew for six months.

c. Dan must actively seek a part-time job.

d. Dan's parents are to keep close tabs on his whereabouts, to the point of implementing a program of "snoopervision," during which they check up on his coming and going.

e. The Court will review this case in six months.

"Next case . . ."

PEOPLE V. BLACK

CHARGE: Seventeen-year-old Ron Black is charged with malpractice of childhood for use of marijuana.

EVIDENCE: Mr. and Mrs. Black sought the Court's help because of Ron's strange behavior, which they judge to be evidence of his smoking marijuana. In the past six months, Ron has been more irritable, hostile, and argumentative. His father says, "We've lost our old Ron."

A junior-high basketball star, Ron has become overreactive to every little frustration. In addition, his once-excellent level of responsibility has all but disappeared. He has admitted smoking marijuana and on many occasions has come home with a glassy stare and smelling of bittersweet smoke.

His mother enters this statement: "The other night, he (Ron) came home late and stood in the kitchen staring at the dishwasher. Then he babbled something about how wonderful the dishwasher looked. Without batting an eye, he began sweating and pacing, saying that somebody was hiding in the closet, ready to pounce on him. I was scared."

When confronted, Ron denied all allegations.

FINDING: Guilty.

M/A
CIRCUMSTANCES: A drug counselor noted that Ron's strange reaction was most likely a negative side effect to marijuana, what LSD users would call a "bad trip." Further, it was learned that kids with heightened sensitivities and substantial insecurities can become "shaky and unstable" after smoking marijuana.

It was also learned that Ron has been quite worried about leaving home and making it through college. He also feels tremendously insecure with girls. He gets good grades, and this is the first time he's been in any trouble.

COURT'S
OPINION: Ron appears to be at a stage in life where he cannot handle the psychological factors associated with the use of marijuana. The parents are correct in seeking help with a situation that Ron has lost control over. Though the drug use is clearly illegal, the Court recognizes the importance of rehabilitation in this case. Ron's past record suggests that he be given the opportunity to learn from this experience without undue punishments. Obviously, if he refuses to do so, the Court

will take that fact into account should Ron ever appear in court again.

DISPOSITION: a. The parents are to help Ron find a counselor with whom he can talk about his problems.

b. Ron is to tour a facility housing young people who've become physically or emotionally damaged due to drug abuse. A lecture on drug abuse is also in order.

c. Ron should return to sports and to budgeting time for improving his studies. He is hereby admonished that any future contact with this Court will result in strict punitive action against him.

"Next case . . ."

PEOPLE V. SHAW

CHARGE: Sixteen-year-old Joe Shaw is charged with disorderly conduct and possession of drugs.

EVIDENCE: Joe became uncontrollable after returning home from a late-night party. He was very agitated. He became angry when he bumped his elbow on his bedroom door, and he smashed the door to bits with a steel chair. He took his father's hunting knife and ripped his bed to shreds and then crushed his lamp into pieces. Finally, he threw a chair through the family-room window.

His parents, fearing for his and their safety, took Joe to the emergency room of the hospital. Police on duty investigated and found a substance in Joe's possession that later turned out to be PCP, or "angel dust."

Joe says he does not remember any of these events.

FINDING: Guilty.

M/A   Joe's grades have been going steadily down-
CIRCUMSTANCES: hill for several years. He is disrespectful
             toward all adults and indifferent to penalties.
             Joe wouldn't tell the police where he got the
             drug, and was abrasive and uncooperative
             when asked.

             Mrs. Shaw appears to be a well-inten-
             tioned mother. However, she seems more
             interested in reading the Bible than in apply-
             ing its teachings. She makes excuses for Joe's
             disruption and denies any responsibility. Mr.
             Shaw states that he wants to discipline Joe
             but feels that Joe is beyond his control and
             that the forceful measures he'd like to take
             do not meet with Mrs. Shaw's approval.

COURT'S   The "bad trip" experience that Joe had with
OPINION: PCP is only a symptom of a bigger problem.
             It appears that Joe is very low in self-esteem
             and even lower in self-confidence. He seems
             to be basically a good kid with a warped
             sense of allegiance and responsibility. He
             seems to be looking for the security of some-
             one strong enough to control him.

             Obviously, this Court would like Joe's par-
             ents to provide that control and security.
             However, they need outside reinforcement,
             at least for a period of time. Whereas the
             Court will punish Joe severely, it does so with
             the hope that he will pull himself together
             before he sinks any deeper.

DISPOSITION: Joe is sentenced to weekends (Friday eve-
             ning until Sunday afternoon) in the juvenile-

detention center for three months. This sentence is reduced to one month provided that:

a. Joe sees a counselor of his choice for three months.

b. Joe also participates in family counseling.

c. Joe's curfew be limited to no later than nine P.M. on all nights for three months.

If compliance is not forthcoming, the Court's investigators will so inform me and the reduction of sentence shall be reversed.

"Next case ..."

PEOPLE V. LITTLE

CHARGE: Sixteen-year-old Jean Little accuses her mother, through the state, of malparenting in that she used unreasonable search and seizure in reacting to Jean's use of marijuana.

EVIDENCE: Jean's mother searched her daughter's room after getting suspicious about possible drug use. Jean was coming home later than curfew with red eyes, a strange, hazy look on her face, and was acting very silly. The mother also reports smelling a bittersweet odor in Jean's clothes when washing them. She read a couple of articles on marijuana and decided to search Jean's room. She found several crudely rolled marijuana cigarettes and two letters with references to "pot parties."

Jean argues that her mother had no right to invade the privacy of her room and search her things. The daughter also points out that she has an excellent school record, attends church regularly, and is helpful around the house. Jean was most upset about the punishment that her mother gave her after finding the marijuana: grounded for two months and told that she could not see her boy friend during the grounding.

When asked if she smoked marijuana, Jean politely refused to answer.

FINDING: Mrs. Little is innocent of the charges.

M/A CIRCUMSTANCES: All evidence points to the fact that Jean is above average in responsibility. She is sociable, popular, has not been in any trouble, and is given strong recommendations by the school counselor and her minister.

Jean's mother is doing an excellent job of caring for her two daughters as a single parent. The use of marijuana seems to be the only negative behavior on an otherwise spotless record.

COURT'S OPINION: Though the Court has no proof that Jean smoked marijuana and recognizes her admirable record, she is reminded of two very important facts:

First, the possession and/or consumption of marijuana is illegal. The popular use of this illegal drug is *not* a basis for any supportive argument. The use of an illegal drug by the majority of any age group does not change the law concerning the abuse and the enforcement thereof.

Second, the plaintiff is in error when she raises her complaint by saying her mother "Had no right to invade the privacy of *her* room and search *her* things." In fact, the mother had not only a right to do what she did but a responsibility to do it. Any parent who suspects a child of illegal or immoral action can and must search and seize any contraband.

The Court warns all parents that search and seizure can have harmful consequences and should be carried out only under clearly dangerous circumstances.

The Court also appreciates the mother's judgment to punish. However, it should be modified.

DISPOSITION: The Court recommends a punishment for Jean that is short but tough; for example, grounding for one week, with either no visitors, no shopping, no snacks, no TV, no car, no stereo, or no phone privileges after six P.M.

The Court reminds the mother to discontinue the "snoopervision" when Jean proves she can handle the responsibility of self-control.

The Court also reminds the mother and daughter that "snoopervision" is playing the role of policeperson. This role is inappropriate in many instances, but it is approved of in cases where parents have reason to suspect that their child is engaged in illegal behavior.

"Next case . . ."

PEOPLE v. CASSIDY

CHARGE: Mrs. Cassidy accuses her fifteen-year-old son, Mark, of malpractice of childhood.

EVIDENCE: Mrs. Cassidy states that Mark, the oldest of three children, is "addicted" to marijuana. She notes the following observations: Mark's grades have been moving steadily downward for four months; he exhibits sudden, unpredictable changes in personality from morning (when he is "his old self") to evening (when he is "jumpy, irritable, and acts very strange"); he leaves the house after being told that he is grounded; he has become fast friends with older boys, known to have drug arrests, and he usually comes home twenty to thirty minutes after curfew with red eyes and a hazy look on his face.

Much to the Court's surprise, the divorced father of Mark doesn't support his ex-wife's making a "big deal" out of smoking marijuana. He wants Mark's mother to handle it or else give custody to him.

The Court also heard Mark say that he smoked marijuana, but he was quite hostile and disgusted that his mother said he was "addicted." He concluded his curt statement by saying that marijuana has been proved *not* to be physically addictive and therefore his mother was wrong.

FINDING: Guilty.

M/A CIRCUMSTANCES: Mark has been permitted to assume an indifferent attitude toward illegal behavior. His father and mother are pulling in opposite directions.

COURT'S OPINION: The Court has several important observations to make in this case.

First, the word "addiction" is appropriate when speaking of physical addiction, but it is also applicable when referring to emotional "addiction." Mark's deteriorating behavior is reflective of an addictive personality, and therefore he must be considered "hooked."

Second, the Court wishes to make clear that the psychological dependency indicated in this case can lead Mark to deeper involvement in the drug culture. Hence, it is imperative that all possible steps be taken to help Mark out of his "habit."

Third, the Court is displeased with Mark's indifference and denial. His attitude is a strong indicator of psychological dependence.

Finally, the Court is distressed that the father does not see the need for outside help. Possibly he needs to spend more time really understanding and getting to know his son.

DISPOSITION: Mark is to be referred to a drug-abuse program. If he does not attend voluntarily, then he shall serve a six-month sentence in juvenile detention.

The family is advised to seek counseling for themselves in order to prevent a repeat of this pattern with the two younger children.

If the parents display any aggressive actions in which the children are targets of revenge, the Court will entertain a motion to charge either or both of them with malparenting.

The Court will review this case in six months.

"Next case . . ."

PEOPLE v. JACKSON

CHARGE: Larry Jackson is accused of trespassing on school grounds.

EVIDENCE: Seventeen-year-old Larry was found wandering in the school hallway Saturday morning by a janitor. He was incoherent, babbling about homework and looking for the leader of a nationally prominent rock group. The janitor called the police.

Larry was arrested for trespassing but was obviously "out of his head." He was hallucinating about sights and sounds that were unrelated to any events occurring at that time. He was taken to the hospital where he admitted to an emergency-room nurse that he had taken a potent form of LSD. He was admitted for observation and released to his parents the next day.

He now denies the implication that he abused a drug and laughs at the trespassing charge, saying that he was told to come to the school to play basketball with some buddies. His parents are upset with the police and the hospital personnel, saying that they badgered Larry into admitting the use of LSD. Larry says that he was just pretending to be "spaced" in order to make fun of the janitor and police.

The physician cannot absolutely validate the use of LSD.

FINDING: Guilty.

M/A   The parents appear to be blind to the possi-
CIRCUMSTANCES: bility of serious deviance in their son. If this is true, then it is impossible for them to help him learn from mistakes. Larry's morality appears to be suffering from malnutrition. Since medical evidence leaves room for a reasonable doubt, the possible use of LSD must be taken into consideration during the disposition.

COURT'S
OPINION:
The Court is very concerned about the use of such a dangerous substance as LSD. The involvement of this drug dwarfs the trespass charge. The Court believes the observations of the janitor, police, and hospital personnel.

Hence, the Court sees fit to levy a strong punishment for the trespassing, believing that a much more serious charge could have been brought against Larry.

DISPOSITION:
Larry must earn and pay a fine of $500. The Court will accept a payment of $25 a week. When this case is reviewed in six months, the Court will expect evidence of remediation of the parents' insensitivity to Larry's lack of discipline. Larry is reminded that because of his age, he will be sent to the adult penitentiary if he gets in any more serious trouble.

"Court adjourned."

There you have it: two days in "drug-abuse court" with yours truly as the chief judge. If you placed yourself in the high-backed chair alongside of me, you should have a fairly clear idea of how I suggest we deal with drug abuse in our society.

The major lessons to be learned in using the legal system to help us solve drug-abuse problems are these:

• The court must collect all relevant information concerning the situation, including the child's school performance, the family's history and present functioning, and the known information about the drug involved.

• The legal system demands an answer to the charge. The gray area involves mitigating or aggravating circumstances that increase or decrease the severity of the act, thereby suggesting the nature of the discipline needed for remediation.

- Dispositions must involve pragmatic solutions that go beyond guilt or innocence.

- Parents can be held accountable for helping a child with a problem but are not to be held accountable for the illegal act itself.

- The court must enforce needed recommendations.

- Punishment should always contain an element of teaching. Rehabilitation must always be the final goal of any punitive action.

Following are a few of the questions most often asked about drug abuse.

Why do kids take drugs in the first place?

There are all sorts of answers. If you ask the kids, they'll say, "Hey, wow, I take them to get high and feel happy," or "I take them to forget my worries," or "All my friends are doing it, so what's the big deal?"

In grown-up terms, kids take drugs to escape reality. But that's no big news. With crime and inflation trying to outdo each other, I'm not sure I want to stay around, either.

The important thing is not what kids want to escape from but where they want to go after their escape. Kids, like all of us, want to achieve happiness. However, they think they can get to happiness just as they can hop a plane and go to Chicago. Obviously, happiness doesn't work that way.

Kids take drugs to find a special meaning that brings happiness. Yet happiness that comes with drugs lasts as long as the drug holds kids hostage. Then they're released, to wander around until they throw some more "happy drugs" into their bodies.

Kids should be helped to use love, not drugs, to find meaning and happiness. It may be old-fashioned, but I still think kids can "cop a buzz" from the loving warmth of true friendship much more easily than from alcohol or those funny-looking cigarettes.

Where do kids get drugs?

My first inclination is to say "Where *don't* kids get drugs?" To which I would answer, "At home and at church." But there's dope passing in the pews and there are thousands of tranquilizers in the cupboard.

Kids who want drugs can get them just about anywhere. Street corners and alleys are thought to be the dope pusher's paradise. However, respected recreational facilities such as the Boys' Club and the YMCA are also places to find dope. Unfortunately, most schools have become smorgasbords of drugs.

Kids usually don't have to pay for moderate amounts of marijuana. Passing around a joint is a big part of being "friendly." It's a very effective way to show off. "Hey, there's our buddy—the guy with the joint. Boy, is he cool!" Kids who buy dope do so by spending their allowance, lunch money, or some of their paycheck.

For concerned parents, the question of where kids get drugs is not as important as the challenge of what to do about the *fact* that kids get drugs.

What do you think of this so-called "research" I hear about all the time?

Not very much, I'm afraid. The problem, as I see it, is that most of the subjects of the studies are either scared little rats running around a cage or burned-out addicts who are institutionalized or too strung out ever to be called "typical." I sincerely wish we all could support better research so that science could tell us the long-term effects of the drugs we often throw carelessly into our bodies.

Isn't the dramatic increase in teenage alcoholism and drug abuse a result of the increased stress in the world today?

Though I'm not sure there is a "dramatic" increase, I will grant you that there is an overall percentage increase in drug abuse by teenagers. However, I don't think this is caused by an increase in stress. We all had stressful times growing up. There wasn't much more stress imaginable than that of the Depression days. The point is not how much stress is present but how the kids are taught to cope with it. If anything is causing the increase in drug abuse, it is the fact that our children are too soft, both physically and mentally. They are not responsible enough to cope with stress without running into a blind haze caused by drugs.

To say that increased stress causes drug abuse is to take attention away from the real culprit—rampant irresponsibility.

But, then, are you saying that parents are causing drug abuse?

Absolutely not. I believe that kids are responsible for their own actions. *Kids* cause teenage drug abuse.

I know you say that "everybody is doing it" doesn't make any difference. But what am I to do about the fact that just about everybody is smoking marijuana, even many adults, and my child wants to know why I'm so against it?

Continue to do what it sounds like you have been doing: letting your child know that it doesn't make any difference what the "herd" is doing, that he or she is going to be an individual. Your morality must not melt when faced with the hysterical pursuit of conformity. If you are surrounded by people who point their finger at you and say, "Ninety-nine percent of people think you're wrong," you can still have the courage to say, "Well, I'm the *one* percent!"

My husband and I tried a different approach when we found out our daughter was smoking pot. We confiscated some, rolled it up, and smoked it in front of her and her friends. She almost had a nervous breakdown. She ran out of the room and didn't talk to us for a week. Did we do wrong?

Absolutely! It sounds as if your daughter has more respect for the reliability of your moral code than you do. Remember, *never* throw away your morality for the sake of "teaching a lesson." The best lesson can be in *not* bending your morality. It sounds like your daughter was testing the strength of the limits you were placing on her. You flunked.

Okay, if I do the same thing, is there any way to make it up?

Yes. Admit you were wrong, point out how you are going to mend your ways, and then say, "I'm sorry." Apologies can work miracles.

I want my kid to admit that she is "straight" to all her friends. That way, they won't tempt her to take drugs. What do you think?

I think you are setting your child up for needless hassles and possible rejection. Kids don't want to hear that a friend is straight. It scares them. It also makes them think that they don't have the courage to do likewise. They typically take out their frustration by making fun of the straight kid or spreading rumors that hurt popularity. Teach your daughter how to say no to offers of booze or other drugs without sounding like she's a goody-goody. If kids say "Maybe later" or "Not right now" or "Gotta keep my head clear for a while," I've never seen other kids make fun of them. Once again, with a little tact, honesty triumphs!

I hear that marijuana leads people to commit crime. Is that true?

Not exactly. My experience suggests that people high on marijuana want to make love, not war. However, using marijuana as an alternative to coping with stress can become addictive. And a person addicted to taking the easy way out can commit a crime.

My son says that marijuana helps him relax and do better in school. I must admit he does better. Should I let him smoke dope and forget about the legal problems?

No. It's not the drug that causes him to get better grades; it's paying attention and coping with boredom that does it. I'd hate to think he has to have a drug to do that.

We know our daughter is going to smoke dope and would rather she do it under our supervision. Is that okay with you?

No.

Even though my kid assures me that he doesn't smoke marijuana, all his friends do. How can I be sure he's telling me the truth?

If you don't trust him, evaluate his behavior in school, around home, and in the community, looking for signs of irresponsibility. If you find evidence that he is undependable, tell him that you don't trust him and institute a program of "snoopervision."

My daughter thinks it's "cute" to give beer to my grandson. Could this make him an alcoholic?

That is a medical question, and I'm not qualified to give you a professional answer. However, as an informed layman, I say yes, it's possible.

No matter what your question or how it was answered, if at all, you must admit that coping with drug abuse is difficult.

When faced with fear, confusion and half truths, I take great comfort in the solution offered by the law.

Whenever we put drugs into our bodies that weren't put there by nature or aren't intended for medical treatment, we are guilty of drug abuse. In this light, all drug abuse must be seen as body abuse. And it's certainly no surprise that all of us abuse our bodies in one way or another.

The best way to cope with drug abuse is to face the facts, gather all possible and pertinent information, and use the legal process to figure out an answer that will solve the problem. It isn't just our children who indulge in drug and body abuse. Many adults are just as guilty as they are. So let's quit pointing the finger of blame at the other guy or gal, and get down to the business of solving a very nasty problem. I assure you that if you don't find an answer, your local judge definitely will.

9

"Everybody": The Ghost of Peer Pressure

Principle #6. Children will express their desires in terms of individual preference, not of the pressure to conform

I had three teenagers in my office recently participating in a group counseling session. They were victims of peer pressure. This is how one bit of the conversation sounded:

"Hey, Doc, everybody gets to stay out till they want to." Bill was getting redder by the minute. "I'm sixteen and got my license. I shouldn't have to come home at midnight."

Stan supported his buddy. "No lie! I'm gonna be seventeen pretty soon—a 'man,' so says my father—and all my friends set their own curfew."

"Yeah," Vic squeaked. "I don't think it's fair. Everybody I know don't have parents that are so strict."

And so it went. Two hours of moaning, groaning, and complaining by three boys convinced that they were being ripped off by unreasonable parents. This type of argumentation is a

165

pain in the neck to any of us who want our children to be individualists. The verbal gymnastics of "Everybody is doing it" embodies peer pressure, possibly the most challenging aspect of parenting. Parents feel that "everybody" is somehow a pointless concept, but they don't know how to cope with it. They usually throw up their hands, give the kid what he or she wants, and say, "I just can't win."

If you want to win in the battle with peer pressure, you must understand how it works. Then you can implement procedures that will enable your children to make decisions based on choice, not on the pressure to conform.

The popular view of peer pressure as a self-contained energy field that surrounds teenagers and drives them into the reckless pursuit of sameness is erroneous. As a teenage social phenomenon with its own intrinsic power, peer pressure simply does not exist. In truth, "everybody" is a ghost that stalks about, feeding off self-doubt and fear of rejection. Like a parasite, it consumes psychic weakness as it destroys individual freedom. It exists whenever people throw away their free will in favor of seeking approval from others. Although the ghost is most active during the teenage years, it is potentially present in all of us.

Peer pressure does not start on the outside and work inward. It operates in reverse. As kids lose self-confidence, they are weakened on the inside and vulnerable to outside attack. Knowing they have more questions than answers, kids hide their ignorance by pretending to be "cool." As coolness becomes contagious, self-doubt replaces self-confidence. As kids dump their self-doubt on one another, peer pressure continually undermines individuality. As a result, a psychological vacuum develops within the child. This vacuum is filled with ghostlike forces that scream for stability: "But everybody is doing it!"

The pressure created by this ghost exists for millions of teenagers. It pushes them toward conformity because they falsely believe that in order to gain recognition and friendship, they *must* behave as the group behaves.

Proof of the ghostlike quality of peer pressure is found in the precious few kids who retain their free will as well as group identity. Peer pressure doesn't swipe these kids' free will, because what they think of themselves is more important than what other people think. They may think about what the group wants or demands, but they don't let the group run their lives.

I've talked to a few of these kids who refuse to lose their individuality. They are the strong ones who've learned to say no to the pressures to drink, smoke, shoplift, engage in promiscuous sex, and experiment with dangerous "thrills." Yet these kids still have many friends. What's their secret? Let me tell you about one of them, a good-looking sixteen-year-old named Cindy.

By most standards, Cindy ran with a "fast crowd." Her friends smoked pot, drank beer, and had sexual relations with their boy friends. Since they did these things in moderation, Cindy did not view their behavior as immoral. She simply chose *not* to follow their example.

Contrary to the rumor mill, Cindy was "straight as an arrow." She didn't smoke anything, rarely drank any alcohol, and was still a virgin. She was happy with her choices and was considered part of the group. She had plenty of friends *plus* her individual freedom. She had the best of both worlds. She even provided an example of straightness to her friends.

Her secret was simple. She knew how to say no without offending or belittling her friends. She avoided put-downs when saying no. She never said "No, I won't smoke pot, because it's bad for you," or "If you drink beer, you can't be my friend." She never took responsibility for what her friends did. As she noted, "Hey, I can have them as friends without doing everything they like to do."

When she was at a party and the marijuana was passed around, she would say, "Not now, maybe later." But "later" never came. When a beer was shoved into her hands, she'd say, "Can't take any more right now." In fact, she hadn't taken any. When a boy friend wanted to have sexual intercourse, she'd thank him for the compliment and say, "I'm not into that right now; check me next time." Next time, she'd say the same thing.

Cindy never let self-doubt and the pressure for conformity rule her conscience. To her, peer pressure did not exist, because she never opened herself to the ghost. She didn't have to be cool, forcing her thoughts on others or succumbing to fear of losing friends. She respected her choices, and so did her friends. I have had other kids tell me the same thing. They say, "If you don't make a big deal out of not smoking or drinking, you won't lose any friends. They will respect your choice."

Unfortunately, the majority of kids are not like Cindy. They are more like Bill, Stan, and Vic. They have lost respect for their choices, feel empty inside, and the ghost of peer pressure has taken over their consciences. They exhibit the signs of the ghostly presence: lousy school performance, use of drugs, curfew violations, and general disrespect for household rules and regulations.

Bill, Stan, and Vic were deeply within the grasp of the ghost of peer pressure. Being best friends and constantly using the "everybody" argument, it was difficult for them to see that "everybody" existed only in their minds, not in reality. They didn't realize that their ability to exercise free will had been replaced by a badly worn but still functional recorded message.

The "everybody" ghost even blinded them to their own contradictions. They sat not an arm's length away from one another, yet each protested that he stood *alone* in being ripped off by his parents.

A brief analysis of the parents' positions will give you further insight into the workings of peer pressure.

Bill's parents were convinced that Stan and Vic were a bad influence on Bill. According to Stan's parents, Bill and Vic were leading their son down the path of delinquency. And, without hesitation, Vic's mom made it very clear that Bill and Stan were poisoning her son's personality.

Yet if Bill and Stan represented a poison to Vic's personality, and Stan and Vic were a bad influence on Bill, then it couldn't be true that Bill and Vic were leading Stan down the path of delinquency. Are you confused yet? Well, similar propositions accusing any combination of two with pressuring a third into deviance would be just as circular and meaningless.

Listening to these parents and watching how Bill, Stan, and Vic were chasing their own tails reminded me that the ghost of peer pressure is fed by confusion. It was well nourished in these three families.

These parents were losing a battle with a ghost that was living in the emptiness vacated by their children's self-confidence. The more the parents fought the ghost, the stronger it became, flourishing amid self-doubt and "bad vibes." If the parents ignored the situation, the kids' self-doubt would spur on their disruption, and they would feel justified, since "Everybody is doing it." They were in a dilemma: "Damned if I do, damned if I don't." They needed a third alternative.

If you face the ghost of peer pressure, I recommend a three-step solution: Confront the peer pressure in your own life; rediscover a healthy sense of competition; and implement some dos and don'ts that are aimed directly at the ghost.

Peer pressure in your life

Kids aren't alone in battling the ghost of peer pressure. You, too, may subject your free will to the pressure toward conformity.

Review your values, asking the simple question "What do I believe is right and wrong?" Examine the issues of sex, money, freedom, car, alcohol, and respect for law and order. The answer to the fundamental question of right and wrong gives you the basic values necessary for confronting the ghost.

The greater the agreement of two parents over these values, the better their chances of diffusing the power of peer pressure. A single parent must search his or her soul several times, gaining two or three times the courage of conviction enjoyed by two-parent families.

In searching your values, you may need a refresher course. You may turn to reputable sources such as ministers, philosophers, teachers, and counselors. You may review your own upbringing, seeing what your parents did correctly and incorrectly, learning from both. The more information you use to form your viewpoint, the stronger your self-confidence will be. Confidence in your values is an indispensable tool when confronting the "Everybody is doing it" frenzy.

Be honest about the effects of peer pressure in your daily life. Ask yourself, "Do I buy the newest, most improved product simply because of advertising?" "Am I disappointed when not invited to the 'best' parties?" "Do I feel ashamed (instead of compassion) when my son dribbles the ball out of bounds or my daughter forgets her lines in the Christmas play?" "Do I have a tendency to judge my work performance through the eyes of my coworkers?" The more of these questions you answer yes, the more peer pressure influences your life. Here's how parental peer pressure existed in three parents.

Bill's mom judged her son through the eyes of others. She noted, "We want Bill to look his best. Our friends really gloat when they see him standing so tall and handsome. He makes us so proud."

Stan's dad was not aware of how the peer pressure from other parents shaped his viewpoint. He was extremely fearful that his son might be arrested, and he didn't know how he was going to explain "his failure" to his coworkers.

Vic's mom explained that she allowed Vic special privileges whenever he hung around "middle-class" kids. His being "college-bound" was more important to her than Vic's following rules about curfew, appropriate use of the phone, and household chores.

If these three parents had been more aware of the enemy within, they would have seen that they were passing along the ghostly influence of peer pressure like a family curse.

If Bill's parents judge their son in their eyes of how their friends see him, it will be natural for Bill to look to others to make decisions about his own life. If Stan realizes that his father is frightened of what his coworkers might think, it is not surprising that Stan seeks to please others in order to avoid rejection. If the "middle class" is Vic's mother's rationale for what rules Vic is to follow, it is understandable that Vic would believe that the concept of "everybody" has clout.

Your children may be learning to give in to peer pressure by watching you. If your morality and self-confidence are stampeded by the thundering herd of sameness, then the power of "Like father (mother), like son (daughter)" could work against you.

Competition rediscovered

In the past twenty or thirty years, we've lost sight of a healthy sense of competition. With the push for money and recognition growing by leaps and bounds, we've gradually slipped into the belief that the key to fame and fortune is beating another guy or gal at some activity. As a result, we evaluate our performance as it compares to that of someone we judge to be a pacesetter. We look outside ourselves for a standard of reference. This is a mistake. It opens the door for the pressure of conformity to take controlling interest in our free will.

The second step in winning the battle against peer pressure is a recommendation adults must implement. It involves a practical rediscovery of the value of rugged individualism. That is, *competition is an* intra*personal event. Never compete with another person.*

The key here is the word "intrapersonal." It means that competition should occur *inside* your head, not between you and another person. Thus, I suggest that you compete with what you accomplished yesterday in setting out what you want to achieve tomorrow. In this way, each day you improve your own performance, not the performance of somebody else. You set your own pace.

If you put this value into practice, you free yourself from worrying about what the other guy will think of your performance. You are able to concentrate on *your* goals, *your* morality, *your* limitations, and *your* wishes. You willingly accept criticism, since anything that can improve your performance is valuable, no matter who says it or how it is said. Best of all, you have a precious gift to pass on to your children.

One other quality is needed before you can put this value into active use. It's the old-fashioned virtue of humility. If you accept that you will never be perfect, never be totally acceptable to everyone in your life, and never be the greatest human being that ever existed, you can use this humility to say to yourself, "I may never be the greatest thing on two legs, but there's no reason I can't do better than I did yesterday."

Dos and Don'ts

If your children are still in the crib or crawling around the family room, you may think you don't need to battle peer pressure. You're wrong. The sooner you start, the better. You can always work on the value outlined above. As many parents will testify, waiting until your son or daughter is firmly in the clutches of the ghost of peer pressure can be too late.

Following are a few dos and don'ts that apply to the battle against peer pressure. You may see some of these recommendations elsewhere in this book, but the ones I outline below are directly applicable to the issue of peer pressure. They will help you send the ghost to the graveyard, where it belongs.

Don't be baffled by words. Upsetting you with wisecracks is a child's tool to get your sense of right and wrong off balance. It can ultimately become the kid's test of your values. Kids are looking for something to believe in. If a word or two can destroy your sense of right and wrong, the kid has little reason to believe in something that is so easily shaken. You can do many things with a child's wisecracks; just don't let them take you off the track of moral behavior. Your stability will enable the child to find individuality when he or she is confronted by words from friends.

Do follow through on directives. Nothing can teach a kid the strength of morality as parental follow-through can. "No" must mean "No." There can be no exceptions. If you don't mean "No," and intend to follow through, keep your mouth shut in the first place. As I learned in my quiz, many parents know how to talk or think a good game, but playing one with their children becomes a whole different matter.

Ignoring wisecracks or laughing them off while concentrating on following through with action is an effective way to handle a child who doesn't want to take no for an answer. This firm stance gives kids courage to say no to their friends without sounding self-righteous. Furthermore, once your child says no to a bad influence, he or she will be able to follow through with action. Following a parental directive is a perfect preparation for following society's laws.

Don't set too many absolutes. Parents who set too many absolute rules in their home tread on dangerous territory. Too many absolute nos, which I would call punitive, add fuel to the fires of rebellion and give kids more reason to follow the ghost of peer pressure into death-defying actions. If you prohibit trial and error by saying no too often, you force your children to turn to peers to discover the "real truth."

Do compromise. Give and take can be an important strategy in winning the battle against peer pressure. However, it should occur *after* the child has demonstrated that he or she can live within the guidelines of the home. Thus, a compromise over staying out until two A.M. on a Saturday night could be allowed only after the seventeen-year-old proves that he or she can get home regularly by one A.M.

Without such a "Show me" attitude, it is very easy for kids to get the notion that they are running the show. When this happens, kids don't protect their freedom. They believe that if it didn't cost them anything, it has no value. They are more likely to follow the first guy or gal who comes along with a wild, impulsive notion. However, if kids have to earn their freedom, they will be more disposed to protect it from the irresponsibility of "Everybody is doing it."

Don't attack choice of friends. You cannot directly control your child's choice of friends. If you try, you'll suffer continual frustration and eventual rebellion from your son or daughter. If you make fun of or unduly criticize your children's friends, you will drive them away from confidence and trust in you and your family. Keep in mind that the friends who hang around your kids reflect how your children feel about themselves. If you make fun of children's friends, you're making fun of the children themselves.

Do promote individuating activities. Kids need to learn how to be different. They can't do that if they're always hanging with a crowd, doing what everybody else is doing. Give your children chances to be successful in hobbies, games, and other activities that will highlight their individual talents or interests.

I personally am very impressed with all variety of sporting activities, especially the ones calling for individual achievement (swimming, bowling, track and field, archery). Also, look into activities at the YM-YWCA, Boys' Club, 4-H, Junior Achievement, and other social-service organizations that specialize in helping kids. As children find contentment and achievement in being different, they will surround themselves with friends who complement their image and will be better prepared to say no to questionable activities, and mean it.

Don't criticize fads. Teenagers have a strong need to rebel. In itself, this isn't so bad. However, the rebellion may reach a point where kids will pursue a cause just so that they can continue rebelling. Under such circumstances, their "cause" is merely a signal that they need an outlet for their energy. If you criticize a fad too severely, you risk your child's seeing you as not caring about his or her need to be an individual.

Causes and fads are methods of experimenting with one's individuality. If you handle them constructively, you can help shape the child's personality. But don't try too hard to understand the inner workings of the latest fad. Just about the time you figure it out, the kids change it.

Do stay informed. You will not be able to help your children attain a sense of individuality and self-confidence unless you stay informed about the world in which they live. You must not assume that you automatically know what your children are experiencing just because you were once a kid. The teenager's world is constantly changing. It takes a super effort to keep up with it.

You can do two things to stay informed: First, ask your kids questions. "Tell me about your experiences with drugs. What do you know about the pill and abortion? What does 'trust' mean to your best friends and to you? You say you want to be different. So why do you seem to follow every fad that comes along? How do you cope with your teachers?" Work these questions into comfortable conversations. If the kid doesn't want to talk, don't push.

The second way to stay informed is to read articles and books and attend lecture-discussions. Magazines such as *Psychology Today* and *Human Behavior* are readily available and contain excellent information on up-to-date research and successful application of new techniques.

In the end, there can be no substitute for reliable information in winning the battle against peer pressure.

Don't try to give values. Values are judgments about right and wrong that kids determine for themselves when they reach the stage where they must totally depend upon themselves. Values can't be placed in a child's head like water being poured into an empty glass. Values grow in bits and pieces as kids are exposed to consistent guidelines defining right from wrong. Values, by definition, are habits that have grown up.

Do give information. Even if your kid pretends to be the "coolest dude in town" or the "foxiest chick around," don't hesitate to give him or her information that you have gathered from reliable sources. Reliable information about sex, drugs, diseases, and reputations is as scarce as hen's teeth among today's teenagers. Hearing about the mistakes that others have made can give kids vicarious satisfaction of their curiosity. They may not need to experiment with the real thing.

Don't try to control social behavior. Once your child reaches adolescence, you lose 99 percent of your ability to control whom he sees and where he goes when he leaves home for an evening out. If you push him for all the facts, and he has seen someone he knows you'll disapprove of, then you set yourself up for a lie. Comments like "I don't want you hanging around that slut" or "Why can't you find a friend with a better future?" will turn your kids against you. Save your concern and energy for behavior that you can control.

The fact that you lose influence over social behavior with each year is a good reason to implement my recommendations long before your kids reach adolescence.

Do set realistic guidelines. Realistic guidelines should be established for such matters as help around the house, school performance, and appropriate use of clothes, car, cash, stereo, telephone, toys, and other material possessions. Realistic guidelines are also flexible. Adding a flavor of give and take gives the guidelines an air of justice and promotes the lesson "You earn what you get."

Successful application of these dos and don'ts not only generates self-confidence in battle-weary parents but also provides energy for further refinement of the values relating to individualism.

When parents enjoy this individuality, they are free from the haunts and taunts of the "everybody" ghost that regularly interrupts family serenity. Individuality also brings freedom from self-doubt, from worry about what the neighbors are doing, and from being mentally handcuffed by conniving teenagers. Most important, you gain freedom from the slavery of self-recrimination, which can cruelly punish parents who care.

Several timely questions and answers will help clarify this complicated subject.

You've completely confused me. On the one hand, you use peer pressure to solve school disruption, and now you say that peer pressure is only a ghost. Which is correct?

I hate to say this, but both are correct. Peer pressure exists but not in the way most people think. It feeds on confusion and self-doubt and is eroded by individualism. As for my use of peers in school-related disruption, my stand is purely pragmatic. Peer pressure exists—a fact I don't like—and I think the energy can be harnessed in a positive direction. If kids can learn to pull together in order to find answers to difficult problems, it often gives them the confidence to pull away. You might say they gain enough strength from being attached to a psychological umbilical cord that they can, in turn, cut and gain independence.

Your recommendation on competition goes against everything we teach our children. What do you use as a standard of comparison if you don't compare yourself to other people?

Your standard of comparison should be what your morality and goals dictate. In other words, you compare yourself to what *you* want to become, not what other people *have* become.

I've got the opposite problem. My kid has no friends and likes to stay in his room and draw. What about that?

Don't be too upset about a loner. What's wrong with it, anyway, if the loner wants it that way? From time to time, see that your child is able to display some fundamental social skills, such as saying "Hello," "Thank you," "I'm doing fine," and so on. If he likes to draw and you're worried about his social contacts, give him some exposure to group art classes.

I finally asked my daughter who "everybody" was, and she gave me the names of her best friends. It seems to me that "everybody" is not a ghost but just the kid's best friends.

The kid *thinks* her best friends are "everybody." At any one moment, a group of best friends might actually seem like "everybody." The point is that "everybody" changes depending upon fads and the nature of the kid's request. It's a tool to manipulate authority figures.

The best way for me to explain how "everybody" is a con job is to describe two situations that often occur in the same evening around home.

First you have the situation in which your daughter wants to go to a special all-night party and you don't want her to go. She will use every version of "Everybody is doing it" to get you to bend your rule.

If you survive that hassle, it may be only a matter of minutes before you encounter this: You tell your daughter and her sister that neither can watch TV, because the upstairs bathroom is a mess. The same daughter that minutes before used peer pressure to get what she wanted now says, "Mother, why can't you treat me as an individual?"

No wonder parents turn gray before their time!

One of my son's best friends is a bad apple. He's been arrested, smokes dope, and doesn't have any curfew. How do I keep my son away from this boy?

Be careful not to reject the boy too severely. If you reject your son's best friend, you are rejecting that part of your son that likes the boy.

Then what do I do about this kid who I know will be a bad influence on my son?

If you are that sure that this boy will create some problems, let your son know how you feel and then make him pay an extra price every time he wants to see this kid. For instance, if your son goes out and sees this kid, chop an hour off his regular curfew.

Isn't that blackmail?

Not really. It's a very effective way to let your son know that he is flirting with danger.

Do I have to let this kid into my house?

You just answered your own question. It's *your* house, and you had better run it according to your morality, not the pressure your kid puts on you. If you don't want him in your house, then he shouldn't be allowed in.

That's easy to say, but what if the kid sneaks in?

Then I think you have two options. First, you contact the boy's parents and tell them about this act of trespassing. Second, you may need outside reinforcement or family counseling to help you help your son.

You suggested that I stay up-to-date with the latest information and then pass it on to my child. Aren't today's young people better informed than ever before?

Not from what I've seen. You might say they are better informed as to the problems of the world and therefore have more questions than you and I did when we were growing up. Relatively speaking, then, they have a greater need for answers than you and I did; hence, a greater need for information.

How can this be, what with all the information available and all the educational programs in schools?

Several things happen. Kids are often bored with school, believing they shouldn't have to study anything that's not fun. Also, many kids who are ignorant don't wish to appear so; therefore, they don't ask questions, for fear of being called stupid. Kids pretend to know all the answers, and parents are either fooled by the pose or relieved that they don't have to confront embarrassing discussions. As a result, valuable information never reaches the child.

Why are various types of cults so powerful these days?

That's a tough question. In my view, the reasons are decay of individual morality and excessive permissiveness. These two factors combine to give many kids in late adolescence or early adulthood a sense of being lost. They lack the self-confidence that comes with discipline. They are easy targets for sweet-talking so-called leaders who give them quick answers to life's difficult problems. More hard-nosed discipline early in life would put these cults out of business.

Can't I be proud of my son without feeling peer pressure from other parents? You make it sound like that's wrong.

Pride is very important. I definitely think you should spread it around. Ask yourself this question: "Am I proud of my son for what he did for himself or what other people will say about me because of his achievements?" If your answer is the former, I would agree your pride is genuine. If you think the latter, then I think your pride is false.

Facing the ghost of peer pressure and telling "everybody" to go to hell is an exhilarating experience. It can help make individuals out of the most reluctant parents and children. If more parents were to challenge this ghost, a new fad would develop. We could call it "freedom of choice."

Can't you see it? This fad would be an absolute smash at gatherings all over our land. At barstools, back booths, and kitchen tables, self-confident parents would be boasting, "Why, everybody's doing it."

10

Temper Fits

*Principle #7. Children who display temper fits will be
expected to "cool off" and use their rational senses*

Nothing shocks people like violence. Yet violence seems to
be a part of everyday life. The longest line at the theater often
forms for the scariest movie, and newspapers with gory head-
lines are immediately snapped up. Murder goes steadily
upward, suicide seems to be a popular coping mechanism, and
temper tantrums of every degree and description are as common in our homes as peanuts at the ball game.

The shock of screaming, crying, hitting, and attacking
somebody or something creates a strange, double-edged reaction in most persons. One part of us is horrified and outraged;
we turn our heads away. Yet another side of us draws us inex-
plicably back, watching and wondering, getting some warped
sense of vicarious satisfaction from violence.

Objectively, violence rarely makes sense. However, violence
is strangely justifiable, at least to the guy or gal who is clob-

bering someone else. This is especially true of kids where violence takes the form of temper fits. Haven't you noticed how little Billy can justify his beating up his sister because she called him "stinky"? You try to explain that hitting people isn't right, and he gives you that surprised look of "What do you know?"

This chapter focuses on the violent behavior caused by flares of temper (I've excluded premeditated crimes and included the wild antics of temper tantrums). Though adults get into just as much trouble with their temper as children do, children's need for help is more important, at least for my purposes.

Close inspection suggests that some degree of temper seems to be present in all children. In fact, they act as if fits come naturally. I think that, in part, they do.

An analysis of violent behavior demands that we accept that part of our tendency to hurt others is a result of genetic programming. We are born with a mean streak. Likewise, a child's early experiences in the immediate environment play a major role in how this tendency is shaped.

Temper fits and violent behavior appear to be caused by an intricate combination of genetic predispositions and childhood learning experiences. However, this fact does little to suggest a cure. To say why violent behavior occurs does not stop it. Parents who are confronted with fits of temper want answers, not explanations.

In my view, controlling temper fits, and temper itself, requires optimum use of our free will. We must call on the allies of self-love, logic, authoritative morality, and various disciplinary procedures to conquer the beastly tendency that lurks within. Though nature gave us this beast, it also provided the means by which we can anesthetize the unwanted creature. But we must first willfully determine to use the rational powers at our command.

No matter how your child exhibits temper, there are two things you can do to help him or her control it. First, you must enforce a cooling-off period, during which the child is helped to regain a sense of rationality.

The second step calls for "thinking it over." When talking to young children about temper fits, I like to use the question "What is your brain saying to you?" Children can relate to this gamelike approach. It makes sense to ask a child what his or her brain is doing. The child sees the question as a challenge; it stimulates conversation. It also gives you the opportunity to teach the child the fundamentals of self-control.

I typically follow up this question by asking the child to engage in one of two games. (I don't use the "games" concept with children over age twelve or thirteen.) These games are *role reversal* and the *decision tree* and are illustrated below and in the appendix.

My recommendations for control of temper fits are aimed at three common problems: tantrums, bullying, and sibling fights. I will discuss these three and then deal with other problems by way of questions and answers.

TEMPER TANTRUMS

The most basic show of temper is the tantrum. We usually associate screaming and crying and writhing and wriggling with temper tantrums. These symptoms are characteristic of most childhood tantrums.

Before you look down your nose at kids while I talk about their tantrums, keep in mind that adults also have temper tantrums. In case you're wondering what I'm referring to: Have you ever seen what happens to a forty-year-old aspiring executive who misses a three-foot putt that costs him a golf match? Or have you witnessed the tantrums that occur when fifty women push and shove to get the best bargain at a going-out-of-business sale?

Although everyone loses his or her temper now and then, children have a patent on temper tantrums. Most parents can handle the jumping up and down, the wriggling and writhing, the red face. They aren't even too distressed when their pride and joy says "I hate you. You're nasty." One parent was able to tolerate her child's pretending to vomit. But I've yet to see a parent who isn't extremely upset by screaming. The noise alone is enough to make you want to give up parenthood.

The violence represented by screaming is what typically triggers parental action. In nine out of ten cases, the parent of a screaming, wild child waits too long to do something. Ignoring is a good thing to do if you can ignore the child *until* he or she remains quiet for a minute or two. More often than not, parents ignore temper tantrums until the screaming reaches the fingernails-across-the-blackboard stage. Then the lid is blown off Mom's or Dad's patience and a death threat fills the air: "If you don't shut up right now, I'll spank you so hard you'll wish you were dead!"

Parents don't really mean this; it's just frustration speaking. You might say that when Junior has a temper tantrum, Mom tries her best to control herself until finally, overcome with frustration, she has a tantrum of her own. This battle of tempers is a losing proposition for both parent and child.

When a child is going wild and you don't have the time or patience to ignore him or her, your first move has to be to help the child to cool it. Three useful techniques are removal, startling, and time-out. Here's how you might use these three with a five-year-old boy who's going wild because you told him that he couldn't go out after supper.

Let's say the boy is standing in the kitchen while you're doing dishes and he's whining and complaining about wanting to go outside. You finally warn, "For the last time, *no*. Now, be quiet."

He in turn intensifies his screaming, jumps around the kitchen, and yells accusations through his tears.

Using *removal*, you might say, "Get out of here. Go to your room until you can be quiet, then you can come back and join us." If the child is older, you might say, "Why don't you walk around the house six times and cool down. I don't want to hear your temper."

If this works, then your child is having *minor* tantrums and you have good control. Usually, removal doesn't work so easily. You might have to take the child to his or her room and repeat the directive. If simple removal doesn't help the child cool it, then you might have to add *time-out* to your discipline.

The best way to give time-out to a child is to use Grandma's technique of making him stand in the corner. You use boredom as your tool of control. Thus, you might say, "Be quiet or else you'll stand in the corner." If he doesn't shut up, place him in a quiet corner near the kitchen, set the timer at five minutes, and say, "If you remain quiet until the bell goes off, you may come out of the corner." (Check the appendix to see how to use the timer, what to do if the child won't stay in the corner, and how to select the amount of time he must spend in the corner.)

If the child remains out of control after you've tried removal and time-out, you may need to startle him. If the boy is completely out of control and you're ready to pull your hair out, put two or three ounces of water in the bottom of a glass and, without warning, toss the water in the boy's face. The shock will stop the temper fit so that you can institute some other disciplinary procedure. If the child has reached such a state of tantrum, you probably should use time-out instead of removal, since time-out has a stronger punishment value to it. It may help you avoid a repeat performance. (Make certain you check the appendix for the precautions of startling before using it.)

Once the child has cooled it, you may elect to use role reversal or the decision tree to teach him a further lesson. (These are illustrated in the next two sections of this chapter.) Whatever you choose to do, make sure you take some action before your child's temper tantrum creates a similar reaction in you. If both of you lose self-control, you give the child a lesson in how to raise hell.

BULLYING

It's rare for a child to grow up without encountering a bully. It's even rarer that a child will know how to cope with a bully without parental help. The best time to help a child cope with a bully is *after* the first encounter and during a quiet time at home, but *before* the second meeting. Explanations as to *why* the bully is mean are not as important as is helping the child know what to do during the confrontation.

Since I espouse nonviolence, I advise you to teach your children to avoid physical aggression if at all possible. However, if all nonviolent measures fail, then your child must be prepared to defend himself or herself. I believe in turning the other cheek *emotionally*, but I think it's ridiculous to ask a child to be somebody's punching bag.

Here are a few examples of kids who overcame bullying, following my recommendations:

A fourteen-year-old black kid simply ignored the racial taunts thrown at him by a younger kid who occasionally saw him on the school bus.

The seventeen-year-old son of a minister took boxing lessons for two reasons: to get accustomed to rough physical contact and to let the hallway bully know that he would no longer tolerate unprovoked aggression. When the bully punched him on the shoulder as he passed by, the kid squared off and hit the bully in the stomach. The bully hit the boy twice more but never messed with him again.

A sixteen-year-old who was constantly victimized by a bully and the bully's two friends was taught how to "go nuts." When they pushed him around, he screamed, yelled, bit, scratched, kicked, and fought "dirty" in every sense of the word. The kids decided he was nuts and left him alone. He understood that he was using violence as self-defense.

A fifteen-year-old girl was advised to tell the dean of girls, "If Cindy Green doesn't quit pushing me around during gym class, I'm going to do everything I can to hurt her. So if I'm sent to the office, you've had fair warning." The dean decided to advise the gym teacher to give more supervision.

A gifted art student became the object of several big kids' bullying. I told him to draw cartoons for the school newspaper depicting the football team as tough and crushing the opposition. The football team became his *friend* and he was their publicity manager—a comfortable marriage.

A very bright, diminutive fifteen-year-old solved his bully problem when he made friends with the biggest kid in the school by helping him with math. He used his smarts to barter for protection.

All these recommendations excluded the parents from intervention at the beginning. I've found that if you immediately jump into your kid's problem by calling other parents or pounding the principal's desk, your kid has twice the problem once the word spreads ("Billy has to have his parents fight his battles for him").

Help your child solve his own problems, letting him know that you are backing him all the way. One little piece of street-corner advice you can pass on to your child is this: The biggest, meanest bully of them all will think twice about messing with the littlest guy in the crowd if the bully thinks he might get hurt.

There is one remaining problem concerning bullying that is difficult to solve; that is, how does the kid know which strategy to use in the situation he must face? Once again, my advice is to give your child the means by which to answer this question. Don't answer it for him or her.

Selecting the best coping strategy calls for a simplified procedure I call the "decision tree." Here's how the decision tree worked when Joe Decker was confronted with a bully situation.

Joe fancied himself a lady's man. However, every time he started getting interested in a girl, a big bully named Derrick claimed that the girl was his and that Joe had better leave the girl alone or else he would get hurt. Joe's first and only alternative was to put marijuana in Derrick's jacket and then turn the bully in to the school policeman. Joe and I completed a decision tree for the purposes of evaluating that choice in light of any other choices he might make, looking for the most effective alternative.

I started by drawing Joe a picture of what he was planning to do. It looked like this:

The trunk of the tree represents Joe's problem; he is being bullied. The two major limbs signify the first decision Joe must make: to do something, or nothing. Joe agreed that sometimes doing nothing is the best course of action. The limb on the right represents Joe's doing nothing. The left limb signifies Joe's doing something, but *not necessarily the first thing that came to his mind.*

The diagram on page 189 is an advanced picture of the decision-tree procedure. As you can see, branches have been added to the "do nothing" alternative and smaller branches to the "do something" choice. The branches of frustration and embarrassment were much heavier than those of safety. Thus, Joe rejected the "do nothing" limb and elected to follow the "do something" alternative. The choice process began with this small step and laid the groundwork for more difficult decisions to follow.

The smaller branches attached to the "do something" limb represent all the things that Joe might do, only one of which was his first impulse. In this way, I helped him see that there were other things he could do to get Derrick off his back.

As you can tell, we came up with six ideas: ask Dad for help; plant the marijuana; fight Derrick; warn the dean of trouble; tell the girls about Derrick; and have a rational chat with the bully. I included seven smaller branches because there is always one more alternative—the one we hadn't thought of.

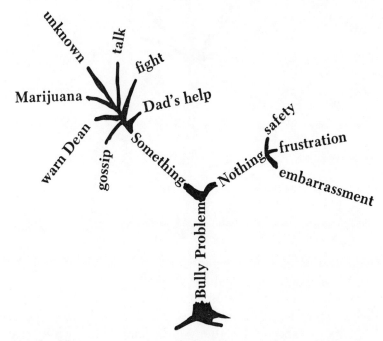

In the blown-up picture of the "do something" limb (page 190), you see the third and final step in the decision-tree procedure. Together, Joe and I projected the probable outcomes of each of the "do something" alternatives. We expressed the outcomes in one word and attached them to the branches as twigs. For example, spreading the word about Derrick, which we called "gossip," would probably result in some revenge, much attention, no blood, and possibly being seen as smart. Asking for Dad's help would probably mean increased ridicule from other students even though it meant getting support

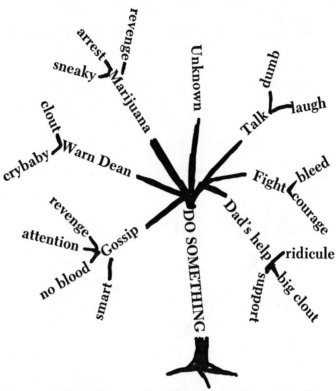

from Dad and considerable clout. (We actually projected many more outcomes than are shown.)

The major task for Joe was to calculate how sturdy each of the branches would be and, thus, which branch would be the best one to stand on. In other words, Joe had to decide which alternative promised the highest payoff with the least cost. This choice brought Joe to the heart of decision-making. He was confused for a while as his freedom to think, project, weigh, and decide suffered some growing pains.

Joe learned several valuable lessons from this procedure. For example: Decisions involve much thought and weighing of evidence; making decisions calls for learning from past mistakes; hasty decisions are almost always poor ones; making decisions carefully causes the person to "think it over" and also aids the cooling-off process, simply because it takes time; and finally, no matter how many alternatives you generate, there is always one more—one you haven't thought of—so keep thinking.

By the way, Joe liked the slickness of the gossip alternative and the fact that he would get to talk to more girls while he was "spreading the word" about Derrick. Still, he never followed through with this plan of action. He told me that just thinking about doing such a crafty thing gave him satisfaction. He also noted that any girl who was fooled by Derrick's possessiveness was not good enough for him. In his own way, in his own time, Joe found the seventh solution.

SIBLING FIGHTS

When brothers and sisters live together, temper fits are inevitable. Learning to live with other people in harmony is difficult, even for adults. You can imagine how tough it is for kids.

I've found that sibling fights are extremely complicated. Do you punish both of them? Do you investigate, find the culprit, and punish only him or her? Do you ignore them until they're about to drive you crazy? How far do you go in demanding peace and tranquillity in *your* home? The answers to these questions are found in a hard-nosed view of life itself.

Disagreements, grudges, jealousies, and even physical fights will occur as children seek the delicate balance between cooperation and competition. While children compete within themselves to achieve, they must also come to grips with the joys and benefits of cooperation, if for no other reason than it will help them improve upon past performance. Thus, don't be too hard on yourself if your children are fighting; it doesn't necessarily mean that they hate one another or will turn out to be bad kids.

The drive for competition and cooperation is healthy. I'm not pleased with a kid whose Little League coach says, "He's a total team man; he never wants anything for himself." I'm also not impressed when someone remarks, "Oh, that boy is wonderful; he's really a good loser." Not wishing to sound overly dramatic, I don't like good losers; they tend to add to our prison population and welfare rolls.

One of the simplest recommendations for handling sibling fights is taken from a page of my personal history. It concerns a sibling fight between my brother and me and how my grandma controlled it.

My brother was a loving child. He stood up for me more times than I can remember. Yet when we went to Grandma's house, he turned into a little devil and liked to pick on me. Most of his actions would be called "teasing." I would holler and scream and try to pinch, bite, or kick him. He, in turn, would end up hitting me on the arm. After thirty years, I swear the bruises are still there.

Grandma had a solution that cut through the complexity. She would say, "Both of you stand in the corner until I tell you to come out. If you start fighting again, neither of you will get any strawberries."

Not wishing to miss out on Grandma's strawberries and thinking that I was being treated unfairly, I would complain. "But, Grandma, he started it. It's not fair that I get punished too."

Grandma had a comeback that I still like to use today. She'd reply, "You're a smart lad, aren't you?" As I was nodding, she'd continue, "Well, then, I'm sure you will figure out a way to stay away from your brother when he's being so mean."

As long as I wasn't being seriously hurt, Grandma stayed out of the way. She had too many things to do to investigate our spat, interrogate the "suspects," weigh the evidence, and come up with the just solution. She didn't know about behavior modification's research on reinforcement, contingency control, and the like, but she knew what worked. With her simple reply, she cooled us off, threatened us with the suspension of a treat, and forced me to complete a simplified version of the decision tree—not bad for a lady who never finished grade school.

It is with this spirit of individualism that I encourage you to let brothers and sisters solve their own problems, provided two conditions exist: Debates and altercations between brothers and sisters must be governed by justice and moderated by tranquillity. If your kids fight in a spirit of justice and tranquillity, let them go.

If one child has an unjust advantage over another and is using it to harm the other, you should intervene by giving the stronger one a handicap. A bigger child who wants to fight with his younger brother should tie one arm behind his back. Better yet, put both of them in a swimming pool. Water is a great equalizer.

As for insuring tranquillity, you are the sole judge of that. If sibling fights reach the stage where the noise interrupts whatever you're doing, make this directive: "You kids keep your fights to yourself or else I'll fight with both of you, and you know who's going to win."

For those of you who have the time, I recommend the use of role reversal in teaching children not to fight. Role reversal is a prevention technique but can be used to settle a squabble, *after* an initial cooling-off period. It works this way:

Say your six-year-old daughter runs up to you and complains, "Joey [your nine-year-old] just called me a baby. I'm not a baby, Mom. I'm not!"

Joey approaches soon after, and you ask, "Did you call her a baby?"

Joey gives you an innocent look and replies, "Not really, Mom. I just wanted to use her glue for a second. I didn't—"

Kathy interrupts. "You took my glue and then called me a baby. He's lying, Mom!"

Joey gets angry and starts screaming, "You *are* a baby. *Baby!*"

At this point, cool them off, even if you send both of them to their respective corners or sit them on chairs. Once they've calmed down, bring them to the center of the room and say, "Okay, let's try this once more. Only this time, Joey and Kathy, I want you to help me play a little game. Okay?"

Once they nod or otherwise agree to play a game with you, which children always like to do, say, "I want you two to pretend to be a movie actor and actress. This is the tough part.

Joey, I want you to pretend to be Kathy, and Kathy, I want you to pretend to be Joey."

If you still have their attention, they will be excited to try this game. Ask them to reenact the scene in which they fought over the glue and Joey called Kathy a baby. Remind them that they must play the opposite part they played in real life. Give them a setting, remind them of the main conflict, and stand back, calling, "Action!"

Chances are you will witness a dialogue with two or three interactions. Kathy, playing the role of Joey, will say, "You're just a big baby." Joey, as Kathy, will respond, "So are you. Baby!" This type of role slippage will break up the game, as Kathy says, whining, "See, Mom, he did it again."

Sit the kids down at the table and ask Joey, "How did you feel when Kathy called you a baby?" Get the message across that it hurts to be put down and called names.

Then ask Kathy, "How did you feel when you called him a baby?" Help her understand that if she would have shared the glue freely, she would have avoided the scene.

If done quickly and in the spirit of a game, role reversal can teach a valuable lesson in empathy and self-control. In case you're wondering, role reversal has application to any inter-personal-conflict situation.

QUESTIONS AND ANSWERS

Why do you call temper tantrums violent behavior?

No offense, but I gather by the nature of your question that you've never witnessed a true-life temper tantrum.

I think your grandma was wrong to force you to deal with your brother. She should have punished him.

Grandma was tough, and she taught me to be tough. In her wisdom, she knew that I could figure it out for myself and gain self-confidence. Anyhow, I didn't turn out so bad.

I'm sixteen years old. You've talked about children's temper fits. What about parents'? They have fits, too, you know, and what are we supposed to do about that?

Parents do have fits. Often the fit is caused by the parent's getting so frustrated at not solving a child's problem that one extreme leads immediately to another. Parents who have temper fits and abuse their children are a special problem. If they seek help, then everyone can work to improve self-control. If they don't, then I encourage kids to seek outside reinforcement. Many agencies are funded to work with child abuse.

What should I do about a bully in the neighborhood who assaults my son almost every day? Nothing has worked. I even talked to the boy's parents.

Call the police.

What should I do with a ten-year-old who started a fire when playing with a candle in the closet?

If you can resist the temptation to put him up for adoption, focus your attention on teaching him a lesson. I will assume that he doesn't respect fire. Have him spend an hour or two with the local firemen discussing the horrible power of fire. Teach him how to start a fire properly in the fireplace or while burning leaves. Explain that fire in the oven cooks food but fire misused can cause awful burns. Try to avoid yelling, screaming, or punishment.

What if he does it again?

You might try a tough penalty, restricting privileges or freedom. You also may consider talking with a family counselor about the problem.

That decision tree looks like a good idea. How old should my child be before using it?

That depends on your child. Using the child's arms and legs in place of tree branches, I've used the procedure with a four-year-old.

My five-year-old hits me, and he isn't joking either.

Make certain the child knows that it is wrong to hit another person unless in self-defense. Then identify one corner of the living room as "jail." Tell him that he will have to go to jail the next time he hits you. If he hits you, tell him that his sentence will be five minutes (or however long it takes to get his attention). Use the kitchen timer.

What can be done about violence on television?

This explosive issue has a simple answer, at least to me. There's an "on-off" switch on the television. If you don't like what's showing, use the switch. You can employ the program selection process detailed in chapter 5.

However, this simplistic answer doesn't satisfy most parents, because it's not their real question. I find that parents who are confused by the TV-violence issue have another question, like this: "Whom do I quote to back me up if my child asks, 'Why?'"

It is unfortunate that parents have lost sight of old-fashioned values and turn to an external source to find a reference point that will give clout to their decisions.

When confronted with "Who says?" parents often reply, "*The New York Times* says," "The minister says," "An article in *Good Housekeeping* says," or "The PTA says."

With reliable information and much self-confidence, parents might say, "Violence teaches people to hurt one another. Violent television shows will not be allowed in this home."

When barraged with "Who says?" parents can simply answer, "I do!"

Why is there such an increase in violence these days?

From my readings and what I've heard sociologists say, it seems to me that there is growing disregard for human life. To many, life is more pain than pleasure, and it's just being spread around. From my view as a psychologist, I think violence is increasing because we all have it too easy. We've come to expect life to be a rose garden, and then we are terribly upset when we learn that sometimes, life is a manure pile.

The teacher complains that my twelve-year-old son has tantrums in class and nothing the school tries has worked. What would you suggest?

With the advance knowledge of only the teacher and principal, visit the school and sit in the back of the room. If your kid suddenly realizes you are watching, he'll shape up. If he sees you and doesn't shape up, suspend privileges or restrict his freedom. You might enforce your own Saturday-morning study session, thereby canceling the cartoons.

My teenage son got so angry the other evening, he ran his hand through a wall. Do I punish him, or just talk?

Both. However, at the moment of the temper fit, stay clear. Then find out what triggered him, but don't be surprised if you hear "I don't know." Whatever his response, let him know that you will not tolerate such outbursts. Give him several hours of work penalties (discussed in the appendix) and make him fix the wall. Don't be afraid to seek family counseling if you're concerned about the fires of discontent that burn within him.

I saw my son horsing around during a baseball game and he almost hit the neighbor's boy with a bat. I whipped him. That'll teach him, right?

Yes, that'll teach him, teach him to hide his recklessness. Then you won't have a chance to teach him caution. Be thankful you saw it, but don't punish him for physical recklessness by assaulting him. Suspend his baseball-playing for a week.

Get this: My fourteen-year-old son beat up on his sixteen-year-old brother, who's bigger than he. How about that one?

I must admit that this is a little unusual. Two things come to mind: First, maybe the sixteen-year-old needs to be a little tougher; if he was, maybe the fourteen-year-old would learn a valuable lesson, even though it might cost him a black eye. Second, try role reversal and see if each boy can empathize with what the other is feeling.

Our sixteen-year-old daughter tried to kill herself. She took ten aspirin and then told us she did it. We took her to the emergency room, but later our minister said we overreacted. What do you think?

This is a confusing situation. On the one hand, any kid who even plays with suicide must be dealt with seriously. However, if you make too much fuss, you run the risk of teaching your child how to manipulate you. My best advice is for you to become concerned, but not panicky. Then take your child to somebody who will make the "fuss" and, in effect, tell the child that flirting with death is serious business. Also, I agree with the hospital trip, *complete with a stomach pump.*

My kid tried the same thing, and I called an ambulance. The embarrassment from the neighbors taught her a lesson.

I have two problems with your action. First, calling an ambulance is overreactive. If you're worried about your child, *you* take him or her to the hospital. Second, the use of embarrassment by way of the neighbors is a painful thing for a teen-ager to overcome.

You've not yet talked about how teenagers get depressed, and that causes temper fits. Don't you believe in depression?

I sure do, but I've found over and over again that teenagers are terrific at coping with pain. They have an amazing ability to find a silver lining in the darkest cloud, and we all know how they can find a dark cloud on the sunniest day. When kids get surrounded with pain and adults think they should become severely depressed, they have a remarkable ability to survive the trauma. As for depression causing temper fits, I don't believe that. Lack of self-control causes temper fits. The stress of depression may result in temper fits, but the person, through poor self-control, *causes* the fit.

My five-year-old bites her older brother. What can I do?

Three things: Expect her to express tenderness toward her brother by way of doing nice things for him and touching him gently; second, you might break the habit by gently but firmly putting the girl's hand in her own mouth and closing her jaws (just be careful not to overdo the bite); third, you might carry a small piece of soap in your pocket and stick it in her mouth whenever she starts to bite. A tiny taste of soap may stop the biting.

My eight-year-old is often involved in fighting on the playground. What can I do?

One article[*] I read recently reported that kids reduce their playground fighting when they are helped to share interesting

---

[*] T. Grieger, J. M. Kauffman, and R. Grieger, "Effects of Peer Reporting on Cooperative Play and Aggression of Kindergarten Children," Journal of School Psychology, Vol. 14, No. 4 (Winter 1976) pp. 307–313.

things with one another. Conversely, when they talk about being unfriendly or share nasty things, they act out their words like a self-fulfilling prophecy. So you might suggest to the teacher that she use more "show and tell" experiences with your child. You might have a few of your child's friends over, encouraging them to do and say things that demonstrate cooperation.

My neighbor told me that my eleven-year-old was shooting out windows in a vacant house with his BB gun. What should I do?

If you believe her, take the boy's gun away. Do not let him have it back until he participates in some program that will teach him to understand and respect guns.

Possibly the most poignant view of the control of violence is paraphrased from an episode of *Star Trek*, the classic science-fiction TV series of the 1960s. When victimized by senseless provocation, Captain James Kirk, the unflappable leader of all "Trekkies," turned to his crew and said, "We must accept the rage that burns within us. But we can use our willpower to say 'Today, I *chose not* to be violent.' If each of us will repeat this every day, we will rid our species of violence."

I'm thrilled when I think of Mr. Spock, that point-eared Vulcan logician, raising his eyebrow and replying, "There is hope for you humans after all."

11

Lying, Theft, Cheating, and Assorted Rip-offs

Principle #8. Children who lie, cheat, steal, vandalize, or commit any other act of deception will be taught a lesson in developing and protecting a reputation

If your kid has stolen a car or stuck up a gas station recently, you won't get much help from this chapter. You ought to see a professional counselor. My comments are aimed at those kids who haven't gone that far, the ones who are just confident and cocky enough to try to get by with a minor rip-off. My definition of "rip-off" includes not only such acts as shoplifting a piece of bubble gum from the local grocery store or banging a quarter out of a vending machine but also vandalism and the theft of trust that results from lying and cheating.

More kids than ever are engaging in all forms of theft. It doesn't seem to matter whether the victim is friend or foe. "Get what you can now and to hell with the consequences" seems to be their motto. If you put much faith in the FBI's crime statistics, then you must conclude that ripping off may soon replace spectator sports as the national pastime.

Living in a nation built on hard work and the golden rule, most of us find it difficult to understand why kids rip off as much as they do. To my way of thinking, it is the result of an exaggerated sense of self-confidence combined with a lack of fear, which says "Getting caught is no big deal!"

Kids who rip off usually brag too much and fear too little. This imbalance of confidence and fear results from a breakdown in the *implementation* of traditional moral values and old-fashioned discipline. Authority figures do not take *action* in teaching kids that stealing is wrong. Consequently, kids learn that ripping off does not result in punishment. As a result, they get the notion that they somehow are more important than the rest of us.

I regularly get kids in my office who have committed some minor rip-off and are surprised when their parents want to make a punishment stick. Time and again they say, "I don't know what everybody's upset about. It's no big deal. I know it's wrong to steal." When asked why they do it, they reply, "I don't know. I really didn't hurt anyone. I won't do it again."

But this pledge doesn't mean what it sounds like it does. What they are really saying is that they have no intention of getting caught again. Still, their fear isn't strong enough to prevent them from trying it again. The reason is that today's kids don't fear getting caught as most of us did when we were young.

Past generations were raised to fear a punishment if caught. Today's kids fear getting caught because of the embarrassment of being dumb enough to have got caught. They're more scared of what their friends will say than of any punishment they might receive. Without a just punishment, the fear is not cemented into their consciences. Consequently, they rip somebody off, but they don't learn a lesson.

This makes a bad situation worse. If kids learned a lesson every time they ripped somebody off, then at least a slashed tire or broken window would mean that another kid would learn to walk the straight and narrow. But that's not the case. In fact, ripping off is almost glamorized in some circles.

I saw a commercial on national television the other evening in which two "macho men" were passing a football around as they modeled the latest fashion in sportswear. The commercial ended as one guy threw the ball through a neighbor's window. Both of these handsome, all-American men picked up their name-brand sports jackets and walked hurriedly away, giggling with some warped sense of delight. With widespread morality of this kind, it's little wonder that our children view ripping off as "no big deal."

I'm delighted that children have the security and confidence to test the limits and see how much they can get away with. But I think authority figures of every persuasion should be smart enough to catch them red-handed and teach them a lesson they'll never forget.

Ripping off is a complicated transgression. It comes in so many shapes and sizes, it's difficult to find one solution that fits all. I intend to give you a viable procedure to use in all instances of ripping off. First, I will discuss three categories of rip-offs: theft, vandalism, and lying and cheating. Then I will outline the procedures for dealing with them.

THEFT

A thief has many messages for his or her victim. Among these are "I don't respect you"; "I'll have excitement at somebody's expense; it might as well be you"; "I don't want to wait until tomorrow to get what I want"; and "You're not smart enough to catch me."

No matter what a crook might be saying to you, getting ripped off is a maddening experience. It's made worse by the fact that you rarely get to speak your mind to the thief. It may not be very nice, but giving a crook a piece of your mind sure helps you feel better.

Theft is simply taking something that doesn't belong to you. We must teach our children that another's property is very valuable and worthy of respect. The best way to do this is to teach them to respect their own property. If they have to earn their own things, they will have more respect for them. They will also be more sensitive to how it feels to lose something one has worked hard for. Teaching the value of property is covered in more detail in chapter 14.

VANDALISM

Snap! Slash! Crush! Smash! Rip! Squish! With these and other agonizing sounds, car antennas, steel-belted radials, street lamps, school windows, convertible tops, prize tomatoes, hand-trimmed lawns, and other targets meet a meaningless death. The perpetrators of this rip-off are usually ten to eighteen years of age, two or three in number, represent either sex, and wander around any territory in the country with more time on their hands than sense in their heads.

Vandalism is the senseless destruction of another's property by someone with an ill will. It's hard to understand why vandals do what they do. It appears to be a crime with no motive. Yet vandals have a very definite purpose in mind when they break the law. They kill a material possession that has special meaning to someone else. In so doing, they express their disregard for the adult world.

I've come to this understanding by talking with kids who have committed vandalism. Their reasons vary. "It turned me on," "I did it for the hell of it," "It makes me excited," "I don't know," and "Nobody caught me" are a few of the most frequent explanations. When I challenge their reasoning, I usually hear some justification that sounds vengeful: "Anyhow, they deserved it."

The hidden meaning of vandalism sounds like this: "I'm fed up with being a kid. Adults don't give a damn about me; they just want their material possessions. They think they can brush me off with a few words, like 'someday you'll grow up.' Well, I got news for them: I don't want to grow up. And I'll show them what I think of their 'grown-up world'."

Since authority figures cannot attack this reasoning directly, and since very few vandals are ever caught, the answer to reducing vandalism is a primary-prevention program. To me, this kind of program leads children into the oldest therapy of all: work. (I will explain my work program in chapter 14.)

LYING AND CHEATING

Most parents get upset with lying and cheating. I don't blame them; I do, too. But too often parents get so upset that they lose their heads and fail to teach the child a lesson.

I'm quite pleased when I hear of a child who tries to lie or cheat. It usually means that the little bandit is very healthy and is just trying to find a shortcut to whatever he wants. Since most kids are lousy liars and cheaters, it doesn't take you long to discover the truth. Then, if you keep your wits about you, you can teach him or her that the shortcut isn't always best.

Lying should be dealt with as a form of self-inflicted character assassination. That is, lying and cheating tears down the trust between parent and child as it damages the child's reputation. If you catch your child lying or cheating, keep a cool head. Find a consequence that will teach him or her to protect his or her reputation. Honesty may not always be the best policy, but every kid must learn not to lie and cheat.

Before I move into a step-by-step discussion of the procedure to use for all forms of ripping off, here are the three goals of the procedure:

First, catching your child is an absolute must. Only through apprehending him or her can you ensure that he or she can be taught a lesson. But this is a risky business. On the one hand, if you "snoopervise" without adequate safeguards, you never give your child a chance to develop trust. On the other hand, believing your child would never do anything wrong is hiding from reality. Somewhere between these two extremes rests the delicate balance of guarded trust that permits you to lengthen the control rope slowly but surely.

Second, you must instill a mental red light in your child's

conscience. This light starts flashing the second that fun turns into potential trouble. The message of the flashing red light is "*Stop!* If I proceed with this act, I will suffer negative consequences."

Third, you must build all disciplinary procedures around the development and protection of reputation. A good reputation, gained by reputable and forthright actions, is like a saving's account. The more you put into a reliable reputation, the more you can draw on it when you need it.

DISCIPLINARY PROCEDURE FOR RIP-OFFS

Following are the seven steps in a disciplinary procedure I refer to as "prosecution." Follow these steps when dealing with all varieties of ripping off. Exercise justice but remain undaunted even when you hear "This isn't prosecution, it's persecution!"

Gather evidence

It's dangerous to proceed with disciplinary measures against a suspected thief unless you have some reliable evidence. If you implement a punishment without considerable confidence in your facts, you run the risk of fanning the fires of rebellion. Therefore, I often advise parents to do nothing if they're not reasonably certain of the facts.

I don't pretend to be a legal consultant, but you should have more than a sneaky suspicion or the bland word of a snoopy neighbor before taking action against your child for any rip-off. You can feel confident if you have two or three reliable witnesses (such as school officials). If you end up with circumstantial evidence, push for a confession (no torture allowed).

With or without sufficient evidence, you can always use the next step when you suspect a rip-off.

Confrontation

Sit down privately with your child and confront him or her with the evidence you have. Keep your comments to a minimum and then permit a response. What your child says to you after an initial confrontation may guide you in further prosecution. For example, if the child hits you with a fabulous alibi, you may have to suspend confrontation until you gather more evidence. If he or she confesses immediately, then you need not waste time with further confrontation.

There is a very important rule you must follow during this part of the prosecution. Many legalists do not agree with me, but I hold firmly to the proposition that when dealing with youthful rip-offs, *you judge the act, not the age.* In short, this means that just because your child is five years old, it doesn't excuse him if he shoplifts a piece of candy. Shoplifting is stealing, and being five doesn't change that fact. If you want to allow for the child's age, do it when you enforce a penalty, not when determining guilt or innocence.

Catharsis

Getting caught is an emotional experience for both prosecutor and defendant. Don't ignore your feelings of disappointment or anger. Likewise, don't get too upset if your child has similar emotions. Accept a moderate degree of disgust, whether expressed by you or your child. But don't institute any further prosecution until you've given your emotions and those of your child their "day in court."

If the child refuses to calm down or you're too angry to continue, enforce the periods of cooling off and thinking it over discussed in the previous chapter.

After you air your emotions and listen to your child's feelings, the next three steps become more time-consuming. They can occur in any order you wish, not necessarily the way I've listed them.

Facing the victim

If at all possible, a child who rips off somebody should face that somebody, be it brother, sister, parent, friend, foe, shopkeeper, or total stranger. This permits the victim to vent some frustration while it forces the child to see first-hand what his or her actions caused in other people. A face-to-face confrontation with a victim can teach a budding rip-off artist to change his or her way of having fun.

Accompany your child when he or she "faces the music." You can make sure the child is properly admonished without being badgered or subjected to undue ridicule.

Punishment

A child should be punished for ripping off. The punishment should be tough but quick. The longer a punishment lasts, the more likely it will lose its effectiveness. A five-year-old might be punished for a day or two; a teenager, a week. Some combination of restriction of freedom and suspension of privileges is best for ripping off. Fines and work details might also be used, especially if done in conjunction with restitution.

Restitution

This step in the prosecution process involves some type of payback to the victim as compensation for the insult of being ripped off. It can also serve to pacify the victim, giving him or her a sense of justice. Thus, if your seven-year-old swipes a piece of gum from the local store, not only should he pay for the merchandise and be taken off television for three days; he should also sweep the aisles of the store (under parental supervision) after closing.

In my book, restitution involves more than just paying for the damage or reimbursing a person for a loss. Restitution isn't complete until the child pays for the insult inherent in being the victim of a rip-off.

Reearning reputation

As the prosecutor, you must find a way to demonstrate to the child that theft of property or trust results in a damaged reputation. Furthermore, a damaged reputation isn't repaired by simple words of reformation. It takes time to build a good reputation, and it takes time to repair a damaged one. Obviously, the time of reparation depends upon the severity of the rip-off and the history of reliability prior to the "crime."

My favorite recommendation for rebuilding a damaged reputation is a form of probation, using curtailment of freedom and the gradual return of standard conditions as the disciplinary procedure. Thus, if your seven-year-old is on "probation" for a minor incident, you may say that he will not be permitted to visit a public place (candy store, movie theater, Burger Palace) for two weeks and then can go to such a place only with adult supervision for four more weeks. If he complies without complaint, he will have reearned his reputation, and then he is free to exercise the freedoms he had before the incident. (For more information and examples of this "probation," check the appendix.)

QUESTIONS AND ANSWERS

I think my son is taking money from my wallet, but I can't catch him. Should I hide the money, or go ahead and punish him?

Be careful about punishing without some solid evidence. Also, refrain from turning your house into a security unit. Let the boy know you suspect something and will be watching him very closely. Also, review his source of income and expenses, looking for unrealistic expenditures. If you make him suspicious, maybe that will be sufficient to stop the theft, if indeed he's doing it.

Isn't that accusing him unjustly?

Such an accusation, if based on some suspicions and evidence (disappearance of money), is just. Punitive action based on such suspicions would be unjust.

If I tried to punish my child and make him pay restitution, he would accuse me of putting him in double jeopardy. What do you think of that?

I think that your son is smart enough to know that he can con you with that junior-lawyer routine. Next time he says that, reply, "Since you're smart enough to know the concept of double jeopardy, then you're smart enough not to rip off again."

The way you talk, you act as if you expect all kids to be thieves.

No, I don't expect all kids to be thieves; I do expect all kids to *think* about theft.

What if you make an accusation or even a punishment and then find out that you were wrong? How can you recover from that?

First of all, make certain you were wrong. I've seen kids who were so smart they could convince their parents of anything. If you were wrong, admit it, give the kid an apology, and make restitution. For example, give the kid an extra hour out the next time he wants to go somewhere.

You said that all kids are showing contempt for the adult world when they vandalize. I remember doing some stupid things just to have fun. I don't remember wanting to get back at the world.

I'm sure you did have fun. So did I when swiping watermelons from a farmer's patch. So do all kids who destroy somebody's property. Just because we have fun and aren't aware of the gravity of what we're doing does *not* make it legal and right. It is illegal and wrong. I make the "mad at the world" comment because I believe that vandals are rebelling against adult guidelines.

You say work is the primary prevention for vandalism. Does that mean that kids who work don't vandalize?

It means that they will vandalize less with less destruction than kids who do not respect the value of work and of earning what you get. We'll never stop vandalism altogether. I would like to see the intensity of vandalism return to the less severe forms in vogue thirty years ago.

My husband shares his past acts of vandalism with our teenagers. I don't want them to get the wrong idea. How can I stop him?

I'm not sure you should stop him. First of all, teenagers already have their own ideas of raising hell. If the children were younger, I would probably not want him to share his past. But if he does share his memories, encourage him to include the fear he had as he committed his acts. Likewise, you can comment about how you would feel if somebody vandalized your car, yard, or garden. Also, ask the kids how they would feel if somebody busted up their stereo. That should get the point across.

I keep a close eye on my kids. They don't have time to vandalize anything.

That is a side benefit of work; you're too busy to have extra time on your hands. Kids who vandalize wander aimlessly around looking for something to do. When kids have too much time on their hands and a streak of revenge in their hearts, something somewhere will get busted up. But even if you could account for every minute, which you shouldn't even if you could, you still won't stop the kid from taking a chance with hell-raising.

Are you saying that all kids have this "killer" instinct? I remember tipping over an outhouse, and I wasn't a bad kid.

I didn't say that vandals were bad kids. I said they committed a bad and illegal act. Those are two different things. A majority of kids experiment with expressing their displeasure with the adult world. That doesn't make them bad.

Isn't it true that only poor kids vandalize?

Absolutely not. In fact, most vandals come from middle- or upper-income homes. I have learned that poor kids rarely destroy something just for the fun of it. They may steal your car and drive it all over hell and back, ruining the tires and engine, but they will enjoy their ride. They steal to use, not to abuse.

How do I know whether or not my kid is a vandal?

You never know for sure. Of course, you could ask him, but I doubt if he'd come clean. I think you can be certain that he will at least consider vandalism sometime during his teenage years. Just keep your eye on his work behavior and his respect for his possessions. That's the best prevention of all.

You keep using the word "he" when referring to vandals. Am I to assume that girls don't vandalize as often as boys?

I don't know about actual frequency when it comes to the sexes and vandalism. But in terms of who's arrested, the FBI reports that males outnumber females almost ten to one in being arrested for vandalism.

How does work fight vandalism?

It gets to the heart of the two causes of vandalism: time on the hands and revenge in the heart. If kids must work in addition to their duties at home and school, they will have much less time on their hands. Likewise, they will feel more a part of the grown-up world, which demands that we all work in order to survive. In turn, they will have more respect for material goods and be less inclined to destroy the objects that they, too, hold in esteem.

You sound like you want kids to join the rat race for acquisition of material goods. That doesn't sound right.

One doesn't have to be in a rat race to have material things. Possessions are very important in today's world. Kids need to learn that. However, without love and compassion, kids can get the notion that money is more important than family, children, and trusted friends. That's just not true. But when considering the real world of survival, I take my father's stand: "Money may not be everything, but it's way ahead of whatever is in second place."

You just contradicted yourself. Which is more important—love, or money?

Since you've asked the question, you've missed my entire point. If you'll recall the outline given earlier, you'll remember that money and love are in two separate classes. Money is conditional, just as approval and disapproval of behavior are. Love, on the other hand, is unconditional: You give it without some design on getting love in return.

Money is one of the conditional aspects of living; as such, I view it as occupying the number-one place of honor. But without the power of love, life could easily be reduced to our throwing dirty pieces of green paper at one another—not a very pleasant prospect at all.

I snooped in my daughter's room and found more than I ever expected. I discovered dresses, blouses, and sweaters with the original tags still on them stuffed in the bottom of an old cedar chest. Now what?

You've just described one of the toughest situations for a parent to handle. You really shouldn't have snooped to that degree, but since you uncovered the possibility of a serious rip-off, you can't look the other way, pretending you didn't see it.

My suggestion is that you do two things: Explain why you were snooping in the first place. You had some reason to be suspicious; tell her. Second, tell her what you found and that you suspect she has been stealing. If she doesn't explain the clothes away to your satisfaction, let her know you will pursue the truth even if that includes going to the store.

I couldn't do that. She'd blow up!

Then you need outside help. The problem must run deeper than discipline. You probably need family counseling.

You seem to rely on family counseling a lot. Is it all that necessary?

If people seek consultation about hairstyles, dress design, and income taxes, then complicated family situations that call for more than discipline certainly qualify as needing outside advice.

I found out that my son stole a small radio from a discount store. I'm not sure how to handle it. He's twelve years old.

Take the boy and the radio to the store manager and have the boy admit his theft. Then follow the prosecution process outlined earlier.

My sixteen-year-old daughter was arrested by the police after shoplifting a ham sandwich. I didn't know what to do.

I am assuming that your daughter was experimenting with a minor rip-off and hasn't made a habit of shoplifting. However, she has probably tried it before and figured it was "no big deal" since she'd never been caught. In this situation, I would get the police out of the picture as soon as possible. I would implement some degree of "probation," gradually permitting her to return to normal privileges over a period of five or six weeks. By the way, forget the "Be a good girl" lecture; she'll learn her lesson without it.

I used a type of probation, and as soon as the probation ended, my daughter committed another rip-off. Why?

It could be one of several possibilities. First, she may want to get caught in order to get your attention. Second, she may be seeking revenge toward you for some reason. Third, she may fashion herself to be a junior Ma Barker. Fourth, the home probation you did the first time may not have been properly executed and may need to be done again. Finally, it may be a combination of two or more of the above. My best suggestion is that you implement the probation program again and increase the degree of grounding you enforce. If she keeps ripping off, you may need outside reinforcement or family counseling or both.

My eight-year-old stole a dollar from his sister, and I had no idea what to do with him. What would you suggest?

It's a perfect time to teach him a lesson in "Life is tough." The next time you take the family to a carnival, a roller-skating party, or some other outing they all enjoy, make the boy sit on the sidelines while everyone else participates. Don't permit any sarcasm from the other kids, and remind the boy that if he's gonna play, he has to pay.

That's being awfully mean, isn't it?

Tough, yes; mean, no. I never believe in being mean to a kid. "Tough" includes love; "mean" does not. Theft is a tough topic, and many kids spend time in jail for getting into the habit of stealing. And jails *are* mean.

What can I do with a brother and sister who squabble about borrowing? One says he borrowed; the other says he stole.

Kids have a strange way of turning a simple situation into World War Three. "You took my radio, you thief!" "I did not! You're a liar. You said I could borrow it." "I did not! You're a thief." "Am not!" "Are too!" "Am not!" "Are tooooo!"

If you get in the middle of this argument, you'll just make matters worse. Solve this one by making a rule that there will be no borrowing unless there are signed agreements given to you first.

What about trading? My fifteen-year-old traded his new record album to his seventeen-year-old brother for an old, beat-up hat. Then the younger one comes crying to me saying his brother stole the album.

Wow! Two teenagers in the same home. You have my understanding. You also have a sticky problem. On the one hand, the seventeen-year-old took advantage of a younger kid's excitement. On the other, the fifteen-year-old has got to learn how to handle con men. Use the role-reversal procedure discussed earlier. In the end, maybe the younger one could pay a buck to get the record back.

My twelve-year-old lies about where he goes and whom he goes with. I want to know these things. What can I do?

Agree on a list of places and people he can visit. When he goes out for a few hours, you will have given prior approval to the people and places on the list. Add one name of a place or person that you consider to be potentially troublesome. Let the boy know that if he doesn't lie, you will continue to add persons and places that are questionable. Find ways to build trust in your son's ability to protect himself. Two or three years from now, you'll never find out that he's lying.

You seem to pick on children: Kids vandalize; kids rip off; kids lie, cheat. Don't you realize that adults are just as bad, if not worse?

I'm not certain about that, but I accept that adults rip off to the tune of millions if not billions of dollars a year. I'm just not that concerned in this book about adults' ripping off.

Why? They set such a bad example for our children.

Because kids have their entire adult life ahead of them, and they're still not totally set in their ways. In short, there is still hope for them, whereas adults who habitually rip off others are too far gone for me to correct them.

That's an awfully cold attitude from someone who's supposed to help others. It's also not fair to expect the kids to shape up but not worry about the adults.

If any adult asks me for help, I will give it. But since they don't, I can't make them change. But authority figures still have control over children, and we can use whatever clout we can manage to encourage them strongly to stop their ripping off. As for "fair," adults have more power (by way of money) than children: That's not fair. Adults can hire a good lawyer; kids can't: That's not fair, either. Thus, with children not being equal to adults, they have to be helped ten times more than do grown-ups. *That* seems to be fair.

Getting ripped off is maddening. It's easy to get angry and seek revenge. Whether you have been a victim of a rip-off or the parent of a perpetrator, the steps of prosecution outlined above will help you channel your energy in a constructive direction. This action teaches children a valuable lesson as it helps you avoid the buildup of frustration that often results in persecution rather than prosecution. One last thing to remember: We all have larceny in our souls, and sometimes it comes out in a poisonous tongue or sticky fingers. So when you implement the steps of prosecution, follow one rule: If you've never made a mistake, then you are free to belittle the ones who have.

12

Sex and the Single Kid

Principle #9: When dealing with sexuality, parents should focus attention on the circumstances surrounding sexual conduct rather than the conduct itself

Sex is a private affair. We don't want others looking over our shoulder as we indulge our passion, lust, and biological urges. The fact that our children are younger and inexperienced doesn't lessen their need for privacy. In fact, being inexperienced, they are prone to more insecurity; consequently, they have a stronger need for privacy than we do.

The easiest path in handling sexuality is to be open, frank, and honest right from the start. That way, sharing insecurities, talking about scary experiences, and discussing dreams and disappointments gives you the best chance to prevent any problems. But sex is a powerful part of us all. It can cause us to lose our heads quickly. Thus, the development of trouble, conflict, and confusion concerning sexuality often faces the best of parents.

The goal in disciplining sexual conduct is the growth of a

219

sexual morality within the child. We should help our kids develop a sexual morality that they in turn can use to control sexual activity. In addition to the need for privacy and the child's tendency to protect that privacy with lies, half truths and other defenses, the irrationality of passion makes disciplining sexuality infinitely more complicated. We all know that once biological urges surface, rationality goes out the window. If we don't think about what we're doing before we let our passions go, we are left with memories about what we should or should not have done.

Because of the passion and privacy of sexual conduct, disciplinary procedures relating to sexuality must be indirect in order to be effective. If you try to control your child's sexual activity as if it were a temper tantrum, you'll face frustration, never-ending worry, and a sense of helplessness that can all too easily result in using guilt as a weapon of control. That's why I say that disciplining sexuality is the toughest issue facing parents.

Here are four guidelines that will help you deal with sexuality.

1. Focus on the circumstances associated with mature sexual conduct rather than on the conduct itself

Sex is typically seen as an adult function. Most of us have a difficult time thinking of our kids as sexual creatures. But when our children reach the teenage years, biology disagrees with us and calls them adults.

My old-fashioned notion is that if and when kids want to engage in sexual activity, they must be prepared to demonstrate proficiency in key areas of living. That is, if they want to play with passion, they should approximate adult behavior in their daily life. When you decide to intervene in your child's sexual conduct, focus your attention on the basics of adult behavior. I summarize these by giving a rebirth to the concept of the three R's. Maturity is measured by Respect, Responsibility, and Reciprocity.

If your sixteen-year-old daughter wants to go steady, then you expect *respectful* language, or you don't permit her dating privileges. You expect considerable *responsibility* when it comes to household chores, careful use of the car, good school performance, or you begin to set stiffer curfew regulations. You expect her to demonstrate *reciprocity* by engaging in compromises with her brother and with authority figures, or you supervise her phone calls and demand that all dates be chaperoned.

If your child demonstrates a working knowledge of the three R's, you can be more confident that the maturity exhibited in those areas will carry over into the development of a sound sexual morality. If he or she has a bad day or two, reverting back to childish temper tantrums or irresponsible messiness, then you can pull the reins a little tighter on dating privileges. As such, you remind the child, "Behave like an adult, and I'll treat you like one."

2. There's much more to sexuality than touching

Sexual activity begins when people talk to, not touch, one another. Sex education must begin with how to talk to another, not how to touch.

Focus your information on social and emotional factors first. Then talk about physiology. Without knowledge of how to talk to another person, kids have no avenue by which to approach the sexual situation calmly and confidently. When a state of ignorance prevails, crude talk, misuse of pornography, and aggressiveness dominate the sexual scene.

Kids who know a lot about sex are often interpersonal morons. They know what lies beneath another's clothing and how to touch another person's body, but they don't have the foggiest notion of how to touch another person's soul. Once kids understand the elements of worry-free, honest, and spontaneous communication, they can concentrate on trust and friendship, and *then* move on to the "good stuff."

3. Separate your morality from your hang-ups

If you read pop psychology or put much faith in talk shows, it'll come as no surprise that many adults have sexual hang-ups. Guilt, fear of rejection, and a poor sense of self-esteem are leading contenders for causes of these problems. If you have sexual hang-ups and you discipline sexuality, you run the risk of passing the hang-ups on to your children. For this reason, it is important to distinguish hang-ups from morality, ridding yourself of the former as you strengthen the latter.

Hang-ups are easily disguised as morality. To tell the difference, you must carefully examine your conscience, using honesty to pierce the protective wall of defenses. If you honestly examine your beliefs, you'll separate fact from fiction. When you do, fear, guilt, and other causes of sexual hang-ups tend to disappear.

Here are a few popular hang-ups paired with statements reflecting morality. Use these as guidelines in examining your beliefs.

Hang-up: "My kid will not look at dirty pictures."
Morality: "Erotic pictures will be subjected to authoritative scrutiny."

Hang-up: "Sex is bad unless you're married."
Morality: "Sexual activity outside of a lasting relationship will be discouraged."

Hang-up: "Provocative clothing is disgusting."
Morality: "Parents will enforce an appropriate dress code."

Hang-up: "Sex on TV and in the movies is absolutely repulsive."
Morality: "Children will not be exposed to sex on TV and in the movies without close supervision."

Notice the harsh and judgmental nature of the hang-ups, particularly the words "dirty," "bad," "disgusting," and "repulsive." You can see how disciplinary actions flowing from such hang-ups would tend to create fear, guilt, or poor self-esteem in children. Furthermore, a kid disciplined in this manner would be so busy feeling bad that he or she would miss the point you're trying to make. This is another situation in which a focus on behavior can save you countless arguments, revengeful feelings, and nagging headaches.

4. Develop trust in your child's ability to handle sexuality

Nothing brings out the need for trust between parent and child as do the issues relating to sexuality. You need to be able to trust your son or daughter when it comes to his or her exploration of sexual passion. You can take the first step toward the development of this trust by being honest about your concerns.

I've heard thousands of parents confuse themselves and their kids by camouflaging their real concern. They say "I don't want you going to that movie at the drive-in" when what they really mean is "I'm worried that you won't be able to control necking and petting." Or they say "You're not to stay at your girl friend's house past midnight" when an honest warning might be "I don't trust your sexual urges when you're at your girl friend's house and her parents go to bed."

Many parents make the complaint "You never bring your dates over here. Can't you hang around here some Saturday nights instead of always going to a party?" when they want to say "When you go to parties, I don't trust you to control yourself."

You'll never develop trust in your child's ability to deal with sexuality if you aren't first honest about your concerns. If you state the truth, give your kids sufficient opportunity to prove themselves, and then keep your eyes and ears open (as suggested above), your kids will have a chance to demonstrate mature behavior. Then you can begin to trust them. But don't wait for your kid to express the core problem. If you don't introduce the subject, you'll continue to pursue problems that are simply mirages.

After many heated discussions with parents concerning sexuality, I've concluded that the best way to explain my position on disciplining sexual conduct is by way of answers to popular questions.

I found my eight-year-old reading Playboy. *It didn't upset me too much, but I wondered what you thought.*

I don't like it very much. I'm not against proper use of pornography, but I think eight years of age is too young for any child to experiment with pornography. At this age, children could easily get the notion that there is something "bad" or "dirty" about the human body. Don't let that happen. *Playboy* magazine isn't intrinsically bad, but what an eight-year-old reads (or looks at) needs to be monitored.

My oldest son gave some "dirty" pictures to my ten-year-old. What should I do?

Try to refrain from using the word "dirty." You and I know what you mean, but will your child? Warn your oldest son to keep such property to himself; otherwise he won't be allowed to keep it. Stay away from instilling fear, guilt, or disgust. These things are devastating to the growth of a healthy sexual identity.

It sounds as if you're condoning the use of pornography by the oldest son in this case. Is that true?

It's not my place to condone or condemn pornography for somebody else's child. I *am* saying that no picture is intrinsically evil. We have a free will to help us decide what is evil *for us* and what is not. It is a parent's right and responsibility to help a child develop that free will.

Are you saying that a child can do as he pleases, then?

No. I hope that every parent assumes the authority role, using the control rope to influence how the child exercises his or her free will.

What if I find out that my daughter went to an X-rated film?

Ask her if she wants to discuss it. Then, you may want to forget about it, especially if you trust her. If not, confront her with the way you found out, suggesting she be a bit more discreet. Explain that many people might hold it against her, that it could damage her reputation.

That sounds like you're teaching the girl to react to peer pressure.

She's not reacting to peer pressure to be concerned about her reputation. This girl could suffer much prejudice if certain key people in her life find out she went to an X-rated film. She can accommodate the reality of peer pressure without giving in to it. That's why I suggest she be discreet.

You make it clear that you approve of filth in film.

Hold on, now. People hurting one another is filth; people loving one another is fantastic. I do think it is a private affair to be supervised by parents.

Are you saying that you'd let your son go to an X-rated movie?

Only if I went with him to find out what he was seeing and whether or not I thought it was correct. Much of the action in these films is designed simply to give people an unrealistic thrill. I would like to see that my son gets reliable information about sex. In the last analysis, I can't stop him from going to those films.

What's your opinion about homosexuality?

This issue has been blown out of proportion. I do not believe that homosexuality is a mental disorder. The homosexuals I've worked with have had more problems with social prejudice than with their sexual desires.

Then you believe in the rights of "two consenting adults"?

Yes.

Your statement that kids should be taught to talk to, not touch, one another goes against the main emphasis of sex education in our schools.

Darn right it does.

What is your professional opinion about teenage girls' using the birth-control pill?

If the girl is mature in the three R's, then she should have the opportunity to review the use of the pill, both the pros and the cons.

Isn't that giving approval to her having sex?

As I pointed out before, you cannot directly affect your child's sexuality. It's a *very* private thing. You cannot give your approval. By giving the kid access to birth-control information, you are coming to grips with her maturity.

How old should a girl be before she can go to a birth-control clinic without parental permission?

That's a tough question. Some girls are mature at fifteen (although very few) while others are still unable to handle sexuality at age twenty. I would think that any girl under the age of fifteen who seeks birth control should be counseled to involve her parents. If she resists, then some provision for approval by a social agency should be made.

I found porno magazines in the bottom of my son's dresser. What should I do?

First, ask yourself what you were doing in the bottom of the drawer. If you don't trust him for some reason, discuss that issue with him. It sounds as if you had no reason to snoop, and therefore you shouldn't do anything about the magazines.

How can you approve of porno pictures when they lead to rape?

There is no evidence that porno magazines lead to rape. Rape is an exceptionally violent act and, as such, is caused by factors much more complicated than a person's reaction to nudity. In my experience, men who look at pictures of nude girls seek normal outlets for their passions.

What about the impact of pictures of so-called unnatural acts; say, acts involving animals?

I have found that kids rarely if ever pay much attention to such pictures. If kids want to see animals, they go to a zoo, not to a pornography shop.

Then where do I draw the line? Do I let my son look at two guys in a nude homosexual picture?

I think you just answered your own question. Most parents will accept heterosexual pictures but refuse to tolerate homosexual pictures or magazines featuring "unnatural acts" or acts depicting violence. I agree with this standard.

I agree with you partially. But I can't agree to let my daughter look at Playgirl.

Why not? The double standard of sexuality has gone on long enough. The myth that girls don't have lustful desires and passions is ridiculous. If you permit porno pictures for your son, then your daughter should have the same privilege if she so desires. If you don't give the permission, you run the risk of teaching your daughter that sex is bad.

It's high time we all take a long, hard look at the contradiction in our sexual morality. We want our sons to be experienced and our daughters to be virgins. And we think our kids are confused!

You don't seem to think that sex is that important. Haven't you heard that marriages start to go bad in the bedroom?

Yes, I've heard that myth. I've also heard about little green men from Mars. But I don't believe either one. Sex is powerful, but not powerful enough to replace trust, sharing, and the other things that love should bring to a marriage. If marriage is based on erotic pieces of fat and muscle, tissues that fill with blood when excited, and a delightful ten-second muscle spasm, then it went bad long before sex even started.

I think my sixteen-year-old daughter is sexually active. What can I do?

Confront her with your suspicions. Say to her, "We're going to talk." Follow the four guidelines I introduced earlier. In addition, direct her to seek out a physician for the purpose of examination and consultation. Make certain she is exposed to birth-control information. Finally, make clear to her that if she continues steady dating, you will expect her to exhibit the three R's consistently.

Could you say the same thing if it was your daughter?

Yes, except first I would lament, "Why me, God?"

I tried to be honest with my daughter and she just said, "Oh, Mom, don't be so stupid. I know all that already."

Tell her to be quiet and listen. Don't be fooled by her statements, be they real or pretense. You are perfectly justified *not* to trust her knowledge. Many kids pretend to know the facts of life but seriously lack reliable information about sex.

How can this be, with so much explicit information floating around?

First of all, the so-called explicit information is designed more to excite than to inform. Also, many kids still learn about sex in alleyway gossip—notoriously unreliable. Finally, kids are afraid to look stupid by asking a serious-minded adult for reliable information.

What about health classes in school?

My experience suggests that they are nothing more than simple physiology revisited. They're boring, and kids don't pay any attention to them.

How should I treat my daughter's boy friend? I know they've been intimate, and I just can't stand to be around him.

You might consider that some of your reaction is due to a hang-up rather than to morality. Try to figure out what the hang-up is, and at least be cordial to the young man. If you absolutely can't do it, tell your daughter the truth, and ask her to keep the boy out of your way. Hang-up or no, it's still your house, and you have a right to say who visits.

I don't think my daughter is sexually active and I want to keep it that way. This boy she's dating has flipped over her, and if I don't stop them, I'm certain they will have intercourse.

First of all, you should tell your daughter what you're thinking. Then find a way that she can repay you for your concern.

You must accept that you *cannot* stop her from having sexual intercourse. You can only find indirect means with which to drive home the point that sexual activity is serious business. This might mean that you expect her boy friend to spend more time with you and your husband. Or you might tell her that she will have to be more responsible for her own money and, hence, must find a part-time job.

Does that mean I can't stop this nineteen-year-old from dating my sixteen-year-old daughter?

If you really wanted to, you could make life very difficult for the boy by seeking outside reinforcement through legal sources. In short, you could find a way to threaten him with contributing to the delinquency of a minor if he persists in contacting your daughter. I would prefer that you first try to work with, not against, them. If you decide to absolutely forbid her to see him, I suggest you do it with the consultation of a professional counselor.

My daughter is fifteen and dating an older guy who's known to have fathered an illegitimate baby. What should I do?

Cut off all dating privileges (not just with this guy) for a month. If she has to think it over, she might realize she is in over her head. This "time-out" will also encourage the young man to look for an older girl to date.

You just contradicted yourself. You say you can't stop a girl from dating, and then you tell us how to do it. What gives?

You must draw a line somewhere. I draw the line at age sixteen. You can't stop her from seeing this guy, but you can stop all dating.

Aren't you taking away a kid's right to make a mistake when you run interference like that?

If you were reasonably certain that your child was about to make a serious error, could you stand by and watch and only say, "Well, the kid will learn from hard knocks?" I think there comes a time at which you jerk the control rope, reminding the child that he or she has finally strayed too far. The trick, of course, is when to jerk the rope. I hope I'm helping with that decision.

I caught my thirteen-year-old son masturbating. I didn't know what to do.

First of all, relax, there's nothing to worry about. Then ask yourself how you found out. Were you snooping needlessly, or was he being careless, or was it just one of those things? If you were snooping, maybe you need more information about how your son is developing. Ask him. If he was being careless, tell him to keep his private affairs to himself. If it was an accident, apologize and move quickly on.

But what if he is "careless" again?

Then you probably have a bigger problem. The boy might be trying to tell you something. He might be having problems with sexuality or seeking revenge by embarrassing you. Maybe you ought to talk with a professional.

Should I let my son make out with his girl friend in my house? I know that when I go upstairs, they neck.

You are providing a safe environment for their kissing. You might want to interrupt them more often than you do. But keep in mind that they will probably neck someplace. Why not under your nose?

Just about the time I figure you're tough, you turn around and say something that sounds permissive. Which are you?

I advise being tough. But "tough" is neither punitive nor permissive. It's doing the more rational and realistic thing that will prove most beneficial for the child in the long run. It also means enduring arguments, innuendos, and nasty comebacks about "unfairness." I call it "tough" because that's what you have to be to complete the job successfully.

The neighbor's boy's girl friend is pregnant. I don't know what I'd do if that happened in my family.

The first and most important thing you should do is seek professional help. With advice and guidance, seek the best alternative given your morality and the girl's wishes.

Do you approve of teenage marriages if the girl gets pregnant?

No. I strongly advise against them.

I think my daughter is overdoing her experimenting with sex. She wears provocative clothing and teases the boys needlessly. I'm worried that some guy might attack her.

I'm delighted you have observed this trend. Now, put an end to it. Set dress-code standards and *enforce them.* Ground her or restrict her use of the telephone if she doesn't back off her teasing. She'll have enough problems with unwanted sexual advances without asking for them.

My husband and I are worried about our son's lack of interest. He's eighteen and has never even had a date. Should I do something about it?

I'm not sure what you could do. If he demonstrates social skills and doesn't fall apart when girls are around, then maybe he's just waiting till his hormones catch up with his age.

My son is like that, and I'm worried that he might be homosexual.

If the boy is well adjusted in school, around home, and in general community settings, don't worry about homosexuality. I don't think there's much you can do about it. You and your spouse may want to seek counseling to calm your fears.

Should I let my husband take our son to a prostitute to introduce him to sex?

I'm not going to touch that one with a ten-foot pole. That's a totally private affair for you to decide within the confines of your home.

My daughter is coming home from college for the weekend and wants to bring her boy friend and sleep with him. I'm dead set against it, but my best friend says I'm too old-fashioned. What do you say?

I say that you still run your house, even if your daughter comes home for ten minutes. If she violates your morality, then she knows it. Remind her that your values still haven't changed and the boy friend can sleep on the couch at the other end of the house.

Should I let my children see my husband and me naked? If so, at what age should I stop it?

You must answer this one for yourself. There's nothing wrong with nakedness. Yet it can stimulate more questions than you are ready to answer. Since you asked the question, I suggest you watch your nakedness once your children reach three or four years of age.

My child is thirteen and still hasn't asked "Where did I come from?" Should I forget it and assume that he already knows?

No. Sounds like *you* need to know how much he knows. Ask him. If he doesn't know, tell him.

My son and daughter have always taken baths together. Is there anything wrong with this?

Not really. But it's probably a good idea to make them take their own baths once the first child starts kindergarten.

I'm divorced. Should I let my boy friend spend the night?

That depends upon your children. My personal recommendation is that you allow this to happen after your children get to know the man as a person. They can accept his being there as your special friend, if that's what he is. If he is a casual lover, make him leave before the children wake up.

Our only child likes to sleep with me and my husband. He's only two. Should I make him sleep in his own bed?

Yes.

Much of our sexuality occurs above our shoulders, not below. Our wildest parties often occur in our imagination, not in reality. Our own hang-ups about sexuality feed our fear, and in turn we try to overcontrol our children's sexual activity. We say, "Oh, my gosh! I raised my children to be less frightened of sex than I was, and now they are more free to act out their fantasies." This double bind isn't necessary.

If you have helped your children accept the reality of sexual conduct without fear or guilt and have given them a sense of the terrific responsibility that goes with sexuality, then they are more likely to have fewer fantasies about unreal pleasures and a better idea of what is right and wrong for them.

Think about it for a minute: The pursuit of sexual fulfillment is not a ticket to personal satisfaction; sexual activity is the dessert of human interaction, not the main course.

13

Leaving Home

*Principle #10. When it is time for them to leave home,
children will do so in a responsible manner*

Most of you are familiar with the problem of runaways.
Kids sneak out of their bedroom window in the middle of the
night because they are grounded. Children fail to come home
from school because they're afraid of being beaten for a bad
grade. Many kids hide out at a friend's house for a day or two
in order to get revenge on or otherwise manipulate their parents. Runaways occur for different, sometimes opposite reasons; they always prove difficult to cope with.

Many of you are also acquainted with the kid who is an
absolute terror around home. He disregards rules, flaunts his
disdain for authority, remains undaunted by any disciplinary
procedure, and pushes his parents to the end of their rope.
Parents often want this kid to leave home, but he won't, or he
isn't quite old enough to be shoved out of the front door. He
or she hangs around and enjoys driving his or her parents nuts.

Very few of you recognize an equally disturbing problem. I'm referring to the young man or woman who is very pleasant to have around but who doesn't seem to want to leave home and make a life for himself or herself. There's the nineteen-year-old who fails at college, returns home, and settles into the same routine he followed during high school. Then there's the twenty-two-year-old who appears lost, uncertain of career plans, and vows to pursue independence "any day now." That day never seems to come. These kids pick up a nickel-and-dime job, accept a dead-end pattern of daily living, and never understand why they feel that life is passing them by.

The problem of the kid who wants to stay home forever is increasing. It's caused by a combination of fear, laziness, and excessive nurturance on the part of parents. The kid is afraid of failure, expects the good life without working for it, and his or her parents justify continual support by saying that the child needs more time to find himself or herself. These parents are often fearful of pushing the kid too hard. As a result, they don't push him or her at all.

This chapter deals with three problems of children's leaving home: the child who runs away; the kid who lingers on longer than he or she should; and the child who is so disruptive that his or her parents wish he or she would run away. Though these problems must be handled differently, they do have some things in common.

PERMISSIVENESS

All three problems are related to a permissive attitude in which parents believe that talking is the key to their kids' behaving themselves. Runaways who try to manipulate their parents have lost sight of who's in charge. They think they can frighten their parents into submitting to their whims. Kids who run away in order to avoid abuse are taking such drastic action because their parents frequently explode in frustration. The horror of child abuse usually starts out with parents being mean instead of tough.

The incorrigible child is the result of years of permissiveness during which the parents look the other way as the child does what he or she pleases. The child's presence around the home is a painful testimony to what happens when a child is raised with a do-nothing attitude toward discipline.

The kid who doesn't want to leave the nest thinks of his or her home as a haven where he or she is protected from the demands of the world by Mom's and Dad's soft hand of reassurance and their never-ending supply of financial support.

EXTREMES OF CONTROL

The extremes of too much or too little control weave a common thread among the problems of leaving home. Gripping the control rope too tightly results in a child's never learning to be self-sufficient or openly rebelling whenever possible. Permitting too much slack gives the child a feeling of excess power that can result in many forms of manipulation. If you face a "leaving home" problem, you should face the possibility that you overdo or underdo disciplinary measures.

LATE DEVELOPMENT

The problems noted above develop later on in a child's life. If you sit there looking at your preteens and wonder if they will present a "leaving home" problem, you may create a problem where there isn't any. If you follow the disciplinary measures outlined in this book and adhere to my principles of prevention, chances are this chapter will *not* apply to you.

PARENTING CHANGE

Problems in leaving home call for parents to make fundamental changes in their parenting. More control may be needed. More growth space could be called for. Less nurturance and more confrontation might stimulate the needed changes. The difficulty with these and other changes is that guilt can rear its ugly head overnight. You thought you were doing a great job, and *bam!*, out of the blue, you have a kid who has run away.

Parents are quick to condemn themselves when something goes wrong. They think they've marred their children for life. Parents react with guilt when facing such problems, and in effect they do nothing because they're fearful of doing something else wrong.

When there is a manipulative runaway or a child reacting to abuse, poor control, or overnurturance, there is a leaving-home problem, and parents have to face up to their mistakes and make changes.

SYMPTOMS OF DEEPER PROBLEMS

Running away, refusal to live within guidelines, and an unwillingness to leave home are all symptomatic of deeper problems. If a child runs away, it doesn't automatically mean that he or she is abused or is being manipulative. The cause of incorrigibility is not always immediately obvious. A malingering young adult may have a unique set of circumstances underlying his or her fear. There's a good chance that the first or most obvious reason for a leaving-home problem is not always the most accurate one.

PROFESSIONAL HELP

Since the inability to leave home appropriately is sometimes symptomatic of deeper conflicts, and since parenting changes will have to be made, professional help should be sought. The best remedial measure can be determined only after careful evaluation of the unique family characteristics and the specific problem underlying the situation.

I will continue my review of this complicated issue by

answering questions that strike at the heart of the problems raised above.

My thirteen-year-old son regularly gets home ten or fifteen minutes later than I've told him to. Is he becoming incorrigible?

He has a start. In pushing your curfew regulations so consistently, he is slowly but surely moving his way toward a firm foundation of disruption. The fact that he does it regularly means that your disciplinary measures aren't working. Check chapter 6 again for a review of the importance of curfew. Then find a disciplinary measure that works.

How soon should I start enforcing some rules about kids' leaving home?

As soon as the child is old enough to want to go outside and play.

My five-year-old always seems to leave the yard and end up several blocks away. I haven't got time to chase him all the time.

Even if you had the time, I don't think you should chase him. The scene could turn into a fancy game of cops and robbers; then the kid will look for bigger issues over which you might chase him. Use time-out to enforce your restrictions. The amount of time you use will depend upon how far he went, how long he was gone, and how often he leaves without permission.

My fifteen-year-old tells me when he's leaving and pays no attention to my warnings. What can I do?

You're facing one of the problems I noted earlier. You've lost control and are heading for big trouble, if you're not already there. Talk to a family counselor or some other professional who can help you rediscover your clout. Then dedicate yourself to getting the kid in line, no matter what the cost. A visit to the juvenile officer at the local police station might be a good idea. (Check the appendix under "Outside Reinforcement.") Remember, if you don't stop the young man from doing what he wants, someday, somebody else will.

But what if I fail? I know him, and he'll just get mad that I talked to somebody. Then he will run away and get into bigger trouble. I don't want to push him to that extreme.

Your kid is already flirting with an extreme that could have disastrous results. Remind him that you are taking such drastic measures *because* he is failing to control himself. If he shapes up, you'll be more than happy to drop your plans. If you're worried about "losing him," keep in mind that if you can't get him back in line, you lost him some time ago.

My kid would threaten to hurt me if I talked to the cops. I wouldn't dare do such a thing.

If and when a kid threatens to hurt a parent, he or she has sunk to an all-time low. If you buckle under to his threat, you might as well turn the key in the jail cell, because someday, somebody will. You definitely need family counseling and outside reinforcement. Talk to a counselor about the best way to proceed.

How serious is a runaway?

Runaways are very dangerous children. They typically make mistakes, thinking that they are capable of dealing with the world. They are too quick to trust strangers and too slow to get away from a potentially troublesome situation. They often end up in serious trouble without realizing it until it's too late. More than a million kids run away each year, and many of them don't return. They end up in prostitution and drug addiction, sometimes they end up dead. Therefore, I think runaways constitute a very serious situation.

I've heard that runaways are mixed-up kids. Is that true?

Sometimes. Often, however, kids run away because they don't know how to handle stress in the family or in their personal lives. There are many cases in which kids run away in order to escape physical or mental abuse. These kids are probably doing the best thing at that moment. I just wish they would seek out a responsible adult to help them rather than following their first impulse, which can lead them from the frying pan into the fire.

What should I do if my kid runs away?

First, give him some leeway in returning. For example, if your child has been talking about running away and then disappears, give him fifteen minutes or a half hour to return. Then call all known friends asking them to give you the latest information about your child. Call his best friends first; they probably know all about the run. Express your concern and ask them for their help. Do not threaten them at this point. If your kid's best friend is missing, too, it's an excellent sign that your child is actually gone.

Once you're fairly certain that he is gone, call the police. Give them reliable information, including a description, known associates, and possible direction he would go. Police often spot-check young kids who seem to be going nowhere. Finally, you might go looking for the kid yourself. You probably won't find him, but it'll make you feel better to look; at least you'll be doing something.

I don't want the police involved in my personal business. Why should I call them?

When a kid runs away, it's more than your personal business; it's the community's business. And the police, as representatives of the community's welfare, are best suited to help you with your personal problem that has spilled over into the community.

Won't running away cause my child to have a police record?

No, it won't; not officially, anyway. Juvenile laws typically prohibit any formal records from being made public on any juvenile offense. In addition, running away is not a serious crime, and police have no reason to make a big deal out of it; that is, unless they're excited by gossip.

I live in a small town, and if I get the police involved, they'll spread my business all over town. What then?

Go to your local state's attorney or district attorney and swear out a complaint against the police for breaking the law.

If I make a big deal out of my kid's running away, he'll just use it against me in the future. I don't think I should chase him.

I didn't suggest you chase him; I suggested you *find* him. You'll also remember that I advised you to get to the heart of the problem and make some fundamental changes in the way you conduct family business. If your child is using running away to seek revenge, then there's got to be a reason. Find it.

How do I handle the threat of a runaway?

I suggest you take all such threats seriously. However, that doesn't mean you rush out and find a counselor or immediately call the police. Many parents have been successful in using the ploy "I'll help you pack your bags," combined with statements of regret and "I'll miss you." Don't use this light-hearted comment if you think the child is experiencing any serious problem; it could backfire if the child thinks you don't love him or her. If a teenager has self-doubts, a threat to run away could be a way of seeking reassurance.

If you face a threat to run away, try to get to the bottom of it; discussion is your best avenue. It's a myth to suppose that a kid won't run just because he or she threatens to. Let the kid know that you love him but will do everything in your power to stop him, including calling the police. As I mentioned before, looking at what you might be doing incorrectly is very important.

My son threatened to run away and then wanted to go out later that evening. I said no, but he said it was unfair. Was I wrong?

I don't think so. If you are going to take such threats seriously, then you have to back up your stand with some discipline. As long as you're willing to look at your mistakes, then I think you can take a disciplinary stand that will encourage the kid to look at his mistakes.

You need to get the message of trust across. A kid who threatens to run away cannot be trusted, at least for a week or two. You might say, "For the next week, you'd better be home on time. If you aren't, I'll be looking for you." If the kid respects his privacy, he will find another way to work out his problems rather than threatening to run away.

My kid has run away twice, and her friends hid her. What can I do about that?

Several things. You can talk to the friends' parents as well as to the kids themselves. Explain how important it is for them not to become involved in a family situation. Most important, get to the bottom of the problem so that the running away does not occur again.

What is the best punishment for a runaway?

After getting to the bottom of the problem, some type of restriction of freedom and/or suspension of privileges is best.

Is it absolutely necessary to punish? Why can't we just talk it over and then forget it?

Talking about it is crucial, but you must also flex your muscle by way of some penalty. If you don't, you run the risk of giving your kid the idea that he or she can come and go whenever impulses rear their head.

How can I punish and also admit to making a mistake? It seems contradictory to say that I may have contributed to the problem and then have the right to turn around and punish the kid because he did wrong. Shouldn't I punish myself, too?

If you want to, you can; but it won't solve the problem. You must assume the role of disciplinarian when punishing your child for running away. But that doesn't mean that you can't admit to being a person, too—a person who makes mistakes and is honest enough with a child to admit it.

I hear you saying that you have to be "fair" in treating yourself the same way you treat your child. Remember, your child needs a parent in order to grow up responsibly. Have the courage to be a parent, not a friend.

My seventeen-year-old is totally disruptive. He bothers his brothers and sisters, disappears for hours, doesn't get the car back on time, misses school, and rarely does what I tell him to do. He says he wants to leave home, but I don't think he's ready. What now?

Consider the idea that maybe your job is finished; maybe you've done all you can; maybe there's no future in permitting him to do as he pleases. It's time for him to leave home.

I agree that it doesn't sound like the young man is ready to "make it" in society. He certainly won't be able to hold a job, pay his bills, and keep a house or apartment if he can't follow some of your basic rules and regulations. However, he may have to learn this on his own. It sounds as if it's time for the school of hard knocks to take over where you left off.

If he won't talk with you about it or see a professional counselor, then support his idea of leaving home; in fact, if he doesn't shape up, help him ship out.

But he's so stubborn, he probably won't go, just because I asked him to.

I agree. But, in my experience, he probably won't go because deep down inside he knows he's not ready. He's scared. I doubt if he will admit that. Unfortunately, he will probably try his best to prove to you how cool he is, and after the dust settles, he still won't help you to help him. Your only recourse is to give him your best shot of honesty and unconditional love and let him know that you will no longer participate in his delinquency.

I don't think I can make him leave home.

I didn't say you have to *make* him leave. I'm suggesting that you give him a choice: Either he shapes up on the things that you just mentioned or else he has to leave.

But I can't just kick him out.

You have to take some action; you can't just sit there as he heads for a nasty fall. If he won't work with you to change things, then your only other alternative is to force him to choose between his home and his deviance.

I couldn't live with myself if something bad happened to him.

Something bad *is* happening to him, right under your nose. Deviance is becoming his way of life. Disrespect is his strong point. As far as I'm concerned, that's pretty bad.

Can you assure me that he won't get hurt, that he won't die?

No. But I can assure you that if you continue to do nothing, your son will become an emotional cripple, unable to control himself and to do the things necessary to make a good life for himself and his loved ones. That reality gives you a choice more difficult than the one you must give your son. You look the other way as he continues to make a shambles out of your home and standards of decency, or you take "Shape up or ship out" action, with the risk that he will make big mistakes. Now you know why I insist upon professional counseling.

I still can't understand how you can support kicking a kid out of his home when he's not able to survive in society.

First of all, kids are tougher than you give them credit for. A kid dedicated to disruption isn't totally incapable of survival. Second, I wouldn't advocate kicking him out if there is any other viable course of action. Finally, a meaningful threat can be a sobering experience for a kid, one that might make him decide to shape up.

Can I make the threat even though I wouldn't really do it?

No. You'd just make matters worse. If the kid doesn't think you mean it, he'll punish you for making such a bluff. If you're not prepared to do it, then don't threaten it.

Why do kids run away in the first place?

I don't think there is a singular, satisfactory answer. It depends upon the individual child. Some of the causes I have found are the belief that the grass is greener in someone else's yard, revenge against real or imaginary parental transgressions, testing the limits of parental tolerance, and the threatening conditions of abuse—emotional, physical, and sexual.

Running away is a movement away from a bad situation at home, or toward a situation that the child thinks will be more fun. Whatever the cause, I think runaways should be returned to their homes and the problems worked out through family involvement, where possible.

Don't all kids who run away do so because of abuse?

From my experience, I would say that all kids who run away have done so because they *interpreted* that they were being abused. Many times, the abuse is a product of their wishes to be free from discipline. Other times, parents are so lenient that when they finally crack down, kids feel that they are now being abused. Unless there is clear physical or emotional evidence of abuse, the interpretation of abuse must be taken with a grain of salt.

After two years of hell, I kicked my eighteen-year-old son out. He broke in, I changed the locks, and then he broke in again. I gave up and let him stay, but he hasn't changed. Now what?

Do the same thing all over again, only this time, call the police and have him arrested for breaking and entering. You may wish to warn him before you do it.

But he'll have a police record. He's already got enough going against him.

He should have thought of that before he chose to be disruptive. Anyhow, after he sits in the cell for a day or two, you can encourage the state's attorney to drop charges, and your son will have no record. But he will have a clear impression of your clout.

Should I let him come home again?

You might, if you're ready to discipline him and he's ready to be disciplined. If you do, make it a probationary situation in which you will kick him out if he violates any major regulations. You might make it a condition of this probation that he talk to a counselor of his choice.

You left me with the impression that if my college kid quits school and wants to come home, I shouldn't allow that. Is that right?

No. What you shouldn't allow is for this kid to come home and *have no goals.* You should not support a dead-end lifestyle. If your child faces a major change in living, and wants your help, I would expect you to help him or her. This help, however, should be contingent upon the child's helping himself or herself. Thus, give your child all the help you can with the stipulation that he or she move toward a new goal. That goal should be a return to independent or semi-independent living.

If your nineteen-year-old daughter returns home from college, she should be talking about jobs, apartments, careers, and other things that reflect a drive for financial and emotional security. She should not be preoccupied with "cruising," football games, hot cars, the latest "jock," and gossip with high-school buddies. If she is, then start squeezing her to leave.

How long should I support her search for new goals?

It's hard to put an exact time limit on this. I would think that the girl should be finding a new direction within six months.

If my kid returns home after "leaving home," should I make him start minding rules again?

Absolutely. You might say, "I want to help you out, but I don't want to treat you like a baby. So let's agree on a curfew, some ways for you to help around the house, and other things that might create a problem."

Without being too boisterous, you let the young man know that it's still your house and you still have rules.

My kid is twenty, still at home, and says he will move out soon. I make him pay twenty-five dollars a week. Is that wrong?

No way. In fact, I think you're letting him off cheap. I hope he appreciates the cut rate and realizes that it won't be that way when he finally moves out. If he doesn't move out within a few months, up the rent to fifty bucks. That'll give him some idea of reality. Don't be surprised if he decides that since he has to pay that much money, he might as well enjoy the freedom of having his own place.

I have a special problem. My daughter married young, at nineteen, had a child, and when her husband left her, she moved back home with me and her father. How long do I support that? I can't just kick her out.

You have a tough problem. You don't want to kick her out, yet you don't want to give her the notion that she can stay there forever with a built-in babysitter. I suggest you try discussing the problem, pointing out your dilemma. Then let her know that you won't always babysit, do her laundry, cook her meals, or take her with you to run errands. Do as much as you think you want to, but don't forget to encourage the girl to make a new life for herself.

How far do we go in supporting her?

Absolutely no more than halfway. Once she gets settled and starts working, expect her to increase her financial contribution each paycheck so that within six months she is able to support herself in an independent setting.

What if she wants to return to college? Should we support her for that long?

You may want to invest substantially in her future. As long as she contributes something, doesn't run around as if free of responsibility, and continually moves toward a realistic goal, then support her to the extent of your financial resources. However, I wouldn't suggest that you suffer so that she can have a rosy future. You've paid your dues; now it's her turn.

Are you saying it's wrong for a son to live with his mother for the major part of his adult life?

I can't say it's "wrong," but I also can't encourage it. I take a strong position in favor of people living independently of their parents. I think that that is what "growing up" is all about. I believe people will be happier if they make a life for themselves. However, if a child wants to live with his mother for forty or fifty years, I can't automatically say that he is disruptive or unhappy. He is, to my way of thinking, not independent. If he's dependent and happy, then it's none of my business.

Defining what I mean by "Leaving home in a responsible manner" could take forever. There is no easy answer to this challenging issue. Certainly the questions and answers included above are, at best, incomplete. I sincerely hope that each of you, when the time comes, is able to say that your child left the nest in the most mutually enjoyable way possible.

If the problems outlined in this chapter apply to you, or if you have a situation that could become a problem, permit me to repeat my most important recommendation: Seek professional counseling. Parenting is the toughest of all jobs, and it makes good sense to seek consultation when you don't know what to do.

Even with the best consultation, you still won't have all the answers. A piece of you will remain untouched by objectivity. You must accept that this piece developed when you took your baby into your arms and accepted parenthood. You experienced a feeling that changed you forever. Even if your child kisses you good-bye and leaves home with all hearts warmly satisfied, you will never let go of the unconditional bond of love that holds you to your child. That is why I say, "No matter how your child leaves home, you'll never quit being a parent."

14

Work, Money, and Possessions

Principle #11. Children will learn the work ethic early in life

Principle #12. Children will begin a program of financial independence as soon as possible

Principle #13. Children will be permitted to enjoy possessions as long as they use them appropriately; this is especially true of the car

Work, money, possessions—the three most important words in the disciplinary dictionary. In fact, these are the three most important words in any survival manual. If you can't acquire legitimate money through work, spend it wisely, and protect the possessions money can buy, you are in for a very difficult time during your stay on this planet.

Many social critics would be upset with this view, saying that I'm turning my back on love and making money my god.

But that's the same as saying that because I love fruit, I can't eat anything else. A well-balanced diet of survival strategies includes the satisfaction of my tastes—the two most important being love and money. It's ridiculous to say that money isn't important. It is, and our children had better learn how to earn and spend it properly.

Love and money don't work against each other. We can love others and still strive for a bigger paycheck. We can be rich and still care for our fellow humans.

Though love and money aren't comparable, they are compatible. In the world of the soul, love is number one; in the world of the body, money ranks the highest. You can't get along without either one. If you accent love and forget about money, you can't support your loved ones. If you adore money and shun love, you won't have any loved ones to spend your money on. Which is most important—love, or money? That's a pointless question. You need both.

This chapter accentuates materialism. I like materialism. I hope you teach your kids to want and enjoy material things. It gives them greater ability to make their way in this life and gives you more clout when they go astray.

In discussing money, how to get it, and what to do with it, I continue to assume that you have unconditional love for your children. If I'm wrong, then you might as well quit reading right here. If you thought love provided all the answers to the challenges of parenting, you wouldn't be reading this book. Nobody can teach you how to love. If you think that only money is important, then you wouldn't bother with a book about being a better parent. Since you've got this far in the book, I conclude that you love your kids but want to teach them how to put materialism and morality in proper perspective. You're trying to put your body and soul together.

Money is a means to an end. In itself, it is meaningless. It is a token, a ticket to be traded for something else. However, when viewed as a means to an end, money becomes the number-one token in life, linking the work ethic to the proper use of possessions. Hence, you cannot talk about enjoying life if you don't put money in the middle. I encourage you to teach your children this lesson.

The three principles stated at the opening of the chapter reflect the interdependence of work, money, and possessions. It is misleading to talk about one without discussing the others. In outlining the tough approach to this interdependence, I have three goals.

First, I hope to guide you in reawakening the work ethic. Children must accept that work is a necessary tool for survival. If made part of life from the very beginning, it can become a source of personal satisfaction, an avenue of expressing one's self-esteem, and a way of making love more enjoyable.

My second goal is to suggest a program of financial accountability that starts out very early in the child's life and moves him or her toward financial independence. Even if you're independently wealthy, I encourage you to consider my plan, since your children will have to adjust to a world where the majority find much satisfaction and a sense of belonging in the pursuit of money.

The third goal is to teach children to respect the material goods that money can buy. I will suggest that you institute a hard-line attitude that says "If you respect it, you'll use it; if you abuse it, you'll lose it." I have singled out the automobile as the possession that demands the strictest of supervision. Too many kids are destroying themselves by not respecting the automobile as the death machine that it is.

The first two goals are reached by following one of two programs for controlling work and money. Both focus on how money is the outcome of work. The first program outlines the ideal program you can use to start early and to avoid problems later on. The second is for you who think you've been too permissive and want to regain control. Throughout these programs you'll see that I believe in the old-fashioned value "If you want it, earn it!"

DEVELOPING CONTROL

You can teach your children the value of money by starting when the child is old enough to walk into a store and want one of everything. I offer a four-stage process that begins at age two.

Stage One: *Payment for Specific Acts (2 years of age)*

On or near a child's second birthday, keep your ears tuned for opportunities to teach the value of money. "I want" is the introduction you'll hear that tells you it's time to begin. During this stage, you should go out of your way to explain the relationship between earning money by working and enjoying it by spending. Find various ways to demonstrate the definition of money. It is a token; it's used as an exchange for a possession. Its value is fleeting; it should not become an end in itself.

Using this notion of the token, you can teach your children that specific acts called "work" earn the token called "money," which can be turned into fun through "spending." Thus, when a youngster wants a possession, help him or her see that a specific act, clearing the table, can be traded for a token—say, a dime—which then can be used to get the desired object, candy. Make certain your explanations are always related to concrete work tasks, a reasonable sum of money, and a specific desired object.

Three precautionary steps taken during this stage make later stages easier to implement. First, separate love from money. Let children know that clearing the table in order to earn a candy bar has nothing to do with the fact that you love them. Second, instill the lesson regularly. Make a habit out of demanding a concrete work task before the child earns the specific goodie. Refrain from giving the child a treat whenever he or she asks for it. If you do give a treat without the child's earning it, label it a "special treat" that you are choosing to give. If the child starts to expect special treats, then you're doing it too often.

The third precaution is to start your child on some program of savings at this early age. You may want to give the child a penny for each time he or she clears the table, helping him or her save the pennies until the sum needed to purchase the desired object is reached.

Stage Two: *Weekly Allowance and a Checklist (5 years of age)*

Once the child understands the relationship between working and spending, move away from specifics. Start stringing out the time between working, acquiring the money, and spending it. This can be done by posting a responsibility checklist in a well-traveled area—say, the kitchen. The checklist should contain four or five major responsibilities for each child and columns and rows that permit marks to be made indicating success or failure for each responsibility on each day.

Each time a responsibility is completed on time (barring excessive reminders and warnings), a check mark should be placed in the correct column and row. Add up the check marks on Friday evening and award an allowance based on average performance. You probably will decide to award two dollars for 90 percent completion, a dollar and a half for 80 percent, and so on, until you award no money for performance below 60 percent completion.

In this way, you begin to teach the school-age child that money is usually delivered at least a few days after the work is completed. The child must learn to work and wait, not to receive money as soon as the task is completed. For those children who complain about this fact of life, explain that you, too, must work and wait. Let them know that you are preparing them for the real world of grown-ups.

Stage Three: *Reality Closer to Home (9 years of age)*

The real world expects people to perform certain routine tasks without compensation. Household chores and personal cleanliness are prime examples of this. During this stage, you continue to give your children an allowance, but you do not relate it to weekly tasks quite so directly. You suspend the checklist, expecting children to continue their responsibilities without daily review.

During this stage, your children hear this message: "There

are certain things you will do *without compensation.* I expect you to take care of yourself and help around the house simply because you live here."

Examples of duties that you may have paid for during stage two but that you now do not pay for are cleaning up the bedroom, keeping the bathroom orderly, helping in the kitchen, and maintaining personal hygiene.

As you suspend daily review, you may wish to institute a system of fines as a way of controlling disruption and ensuring that the jobs are done. (Check the appendix for further information on the use of fines.)

Your money policy during this stage should emphasize that a weekly allowance is to be protected, not taken for granted. You may also want to prepare the child for the fourth and final stage by instituting a program of loans, permitting limited work, or making special deals with the child for extra money by assigning work tasks that are over and above the expected. Washing windows, scrubbing floors, and doing the laundry are examples of these work tasks.

Do not be reluctant to explain this weaning process, noting that this is just another step in learning how to adjust to the real world.

Stage Four: *Earn Your Own Way (13 years of age)*

This stage separates the permissive from the tough-minded. At least a year before the child's thirteenth birthday, you have a long talk with your budding teenager. Say something like this: "Your allowance is an artificial means that I'm using to teach you about the value of work and how to spend money wisely. It is meant to self-destruct. Next year, on your thirteenth birthday, you will receive no weekly allowance. You will earn whatever money you wish to spend."

During that year, guide the child in exploring alternative sources of income. Help him or her develop babysitting skills and clients, promote the idea of getting a paper route, and search out odd-job possibilities in the neighborhood. Inform him or her about the jobs available around your house. Point out that he or she can earn money by washing windows, scrubbing floors, doing laundry, cooking, ironing, and doing other jobs that are above and beyond his or her daily tasks. When a teenager is expected to earn his or her own way, there's no reason he or she can't work for you.

Here are some other rules I advise you to implement during this stage:

1. Be willing to advance a loan.

2. Demand that 20 percent of *all* earnings be saved.

3. If you help the child earn his or her money—for example, buy gas for the lawn mower—deduct an appropriate amount from his or her earnings.

4. Crisis money can be taken from savings, not from weekly earnings.

5. Try to help the child work for someone other than family. That may mean that your child will work for your neighbor and your neighbor's child will work for you.

6. Remind the child that even though he or she earns his or her own money, you still will supervise the expenditure of it.

Menial work assignments are good disciplinary measures to be used if and when a teenager "goofs off." (Check the appendix for this powerful and effective procedure.)

If you wish to modify the action outlined in stage four, keep in mind that your approach should be designed so that your children will be shaped to enter the real world successfully.

Regaining Control

If you wake up one morning and realize that your child doesn't respect work or money, or if I have shaken up your notions about get-tough discipline, you'll need a program to help you regain control.

First, ask yourself these questions about your fifteen-year-old son. Who controls the flow of money to him? How much money does he get a week? How much does he spend? If he earns his own money, do you still monitor how he spends it? Does he receive an allowance? Is he saving for a "rainy day"? Does the child work for his money? Is he still responsible for household chores?

You need to regain control if your answers vary considerably from these guidelines: The boy should earn his own money and demonstrate a sense of budgetary restraint. Five dollars a week in "goofing off" money is more than sufficient for a fifteen-year-old. Without being snoopy, you should keep an eye on major purchases and be aware if he starts spending large sums of money. He should not be receiving an allowance and should be saving 20 percent of his earnings. Finally, he must maintain a sense of responsibility for the little things around the house.

If you've let things get out of hand, follow this four-stage program of regaining control.

Stage One: *Explain the Change*

Take your son or daughter aside and have a heart-to-heart talk. Explain that you have made a mistake by allowing him or her to take money and your support for granted. Outline a timetable of change using the four-stage program outlined earlier as your guide. You can make modifications to suit your needs.

As you explain what's going to happen, don't expect your child to be happy about it. In fact, as you will see, you must allow for the fact that he or she will be expected to give up the good life—certainly not a happy event. Finish your remarks by saying, "I'm shaping up my end of parenting, so I expect you to shape up your end of being a kid."

Stage Two: *Cut Them Off Slowly*

Once you're convinced that you have to shape up, take your time. Taking into account the child's age, you should implement a work, earning, and spending program over a period of at least several weeks. If your kid is ten years old, use the day-by-day-task stage for two weeks and then a checklist for a month before putting him on the "floating allowance" covered in stage three of the first program.

If you give your fourteen-year-old five dollars a week, shut her off over ten weeks, fifty cents per week. This gives her a chance to see that you mean business and that she had better find another source of money, because her free ride is over.

Keep reminding yourself and your child that you are moving slowly because it takes time to change bad habits. If you start to feel guilty, repeat to yourself, "If I behave like a money dispenser, my kid will treat me like a machine."

Stage Three: *Find a Replacement Source*

After you've begun the conversion process, assume an advisory role whenever possible. Be available to give out free advice on how the child can find a new source of money. Tell the kid about youth-employment agencies, ads in the newspapers, how to approach the manager of a store. Don't expect kids to be happy about working at the kind of job they are best qualified for—dishwashing, being a busboy, serving joyburgers at the local Burger Palace. If you've raised your kids to have expensive tastes (which is perfectly fine), they will want a "position," not a "job."

Do not *get* the kid a job. Allow him or her the pride and disappointment of finding his or her own job. Permit the school of hard knocks to have its turn with your children, no matter how much you want to protect them. If you absolutely must stick your nose into your children's business, give them a few names and make some quiet calls. If you take this step, tell your acquaintances to hire or fire the kid based on his or her ability and merits, not the fact that it's your kid.

Stage Four: *Do Not Weaken*

Your kid will undoubtedly raise a fuss the first few weeks after his or her source of cash has dried up. He or she may not even get a job, figuring that you will weaken, change your mind, and start the money rolling again. Don't do it!

You'll have to remain strong even in a situation like this: Your sixteen-year-old son comes to you and says that he finally got a date with the homecoming queen but that he spent all his money and desperately needs ten bucks. In a gentle voice, you say, "I'm really sorry, Son, but I told you no and I meant it."

You might feel like a heel, but someday the boy will thank you for sticking to your guns. He'll raise your grandchildren with the same loving toughness.

If you're lucky and/or skillful enough to implement a realistic program of earning money, you still have one more goal to achieve. You must regulate the expenditure of funds without over- or underprotecting your child from learning responsibility. Supervision of the acquisition and use of possessions by kids calls for a delicate touch on the control rope.

The happy medium between too much and too little control is a tight rope strung between dependent and independent living, and is loaded with tough questions. Do you make a teenager account for every dime spent? Do you stop a kid from making a foolish purchase? What's foolish, anyway? How far do you let the school of hard knocks bounce your children around? Is stopping an outlandish purchase too much control? Do parents have a right to take away a possession that a child earned? On what grounds?

I can't give you a foolproof program for dealing with these questions, because the answers depend upon the overall maturity and behavior of the individual child. If your fourteen-year-old earns twenty dollars a week on a paper route, saves four dollars, does his chores around home without complaint or reminder, complies with special requests without hesitation, gets home on time and keeps his school grades at an acceptable level, then I can approve of your permitting him to spend his money on something that otherwise might cause you to shudder—say, a BB gun. He demonstrates tremendous responsibility and should engender trust that he will protect the freedom he has earned.

On the other hand, if your teenager does poorly in the areas mentioned, you would be justified in *not* trusting him to use possessions responsibly. Responsibility is contagious; so is sloppiness.

Following is a chart you can use to measure the degree of control you should impose on your children's use of possessions. At the left are listed six of the most important responsibilities in a child's life. To the right are numbers one through four, reflecting frequency of behavior from "never" to "always." Circle the number that best reflects your child's performance on each of the responsibilities and then add up the score. If you're rating a younger child and "earning" and "saving" do not apply, circle the other four and add up that score.

	Never	Sometimes	Frequently	Always
Earns his/her way	1	2	3	4
Saves 20%	1	2	3	4
Does chores	1	2	3	4
Keeps curfew	1	2	3	4
Complies with special requests	1	2	3	4
Keeps grades up	1	2	3	4

If your child is thirteen or older, a perfect score would be 24. The closer the total is to 24, the more you can relax your supervision of possessions, realizing that responsibility in these six areas will probably generalize into the proper use of material goods. If the total dips below 16, keep a close watch on how the child uses possessions. Also, you should be instituting responsibility programs in the problem areas.

For a child who's not expected to earn his or her own way, a perfect score would be 16 or 20, depending on whether or not you expect him or her to save part of the allowance. The same rule of thumb concerning supervision of possessions would apply; that is, the higher the score, the less you have to supervise.

There is one critical exception to the use of this chart in supervising kids' acquisition and use of material possessions. That exception concerns the automobile.

When kids get behind the wheel of a car, a death machine has been activated. Many parents shudder at the thought of what could happen. They know how dangerous a car can be in anybody's hands, let alone those of an irresponsible, joy-seeking teenager who thinks that he or she is indestructible.

You should worry about insurance rates, deadly accidents, and devastating lawsuits. You're a fool if you don't. As far as I'm concerned, the above chart applies only marginally to the teenager's driving a car. Rather than have a nervous break-down, use the car to your advantage. Realize that the govern-ment has given you a tool of disciplinary control that equals the strength of adolescent rebellion.

Controlling the car is the last frontier on which parents can exercise power, even if they've lost control in other areas. The power should be unilateral; that is, you approach issues involv-ing the car as a benevolent dictator. In effect, you say, "I love you, but what I say about the car goes!" No matter what argu-ments you hear, you must maintain absolute control over the car. Period! There is little or no room for compromise in this area.

If kids respect the car, drive carefully, and give solid evi-dence of maturity of character and judgment, you can allow them to drive. Returning the car on time, showing considera-tion for taking younger kids on outings, running family errands, cleaning the car inside and out, and filling the car with gas occasionally are signs of such maturity.

Your teenager gets a speeding ticket, allows a friend to drive the car, has an accident; you receive substantiated complaints about his or her poor driving; he or she leaves the car nearly empty of gas, fails to run an errand, leaves evidence of illegal activity (beer-can tabs, bittersweet smell of marijuana): These circumstances should result in curtailment of car usage *no matter what the explanation.*

Requiring that he or she wash the car, pay for gasoline, and reimburse for damage and suspending his or her driving privileges are effective punishments. Whatever penalties are imposed, it is imperative that your child receive one message loud and clear: "Just because you've got a license doesn't mean you automatically get to drive. The state gave you the license, but I've got the keys."

This dictatorial stance must be tempered with the gentleness of love and an understanding of what it's like to have the source of freedom and popularity sitting in the driveway. In short, you need a balance in attitude to offset your strict action.

When it comes to driving a car, kids must accept the reality that they are *not* equal to adults, even if they have an excellent driving record. A speeding ticket for Dad or a fender bender for Mom is not as bad as it is for a kid. If you don't give your child this lesson in reality and help him or her deal with the "unfairness," the courts or the insurance companies will.

Here are a few of the many questions that arise when I discuss work, money, and possessions.

I don't agree that my grown-up college son should have a curfew when home for the summer. He is mature enough to handle his own affairs.

If he's mature enough, make him pay at least thirty dollars a week in room and board.

But he can't. He's saving for college.

Fine. Be willing to negotiate all sorts of exceptions to your curfew. But remind him that you are supporting his drive for a higher education *and* that you expect some considerations in return.

I've never paid my kids to help around the house. Was I wrong?

Not if they know the value of a dollar and respect the fact that they must earn their money. Allowance is only a means to an end. Many parents use their own example of thrift to teach the same lesson that an allowance does. If you need a program, I've given you one. If you don't, great!

Isn't your position on the car too strong? Aren't you inviting rebellion?

I don't think you can be too tough on supervising the use of the car, especially when driving is the least bit tainted with use of drugs, including alcohol. I want all kids to have a reaction of rational fear when they step into a car. I hope they feel the presence of your supervision over their shoulders. If more kids had red lights going off *inside* their heads when they started to get reckless, there would be fewer red lights going off *outside* their heads, which would mean fewer accidents and fewer deaths. If that stimulates rebellion, so be it.

Just how tough should I be if I find out that my kid was drinking and driving?

When a kid has been driving and drinking, I think you should punish him or her to the maximum. You should restrict all use of the car for two weeks. There should be total grounding, with no phone, stereo, friends' visits, snacks, and television, as well as suspension of all other freedoms and privileges for two weeks. Teach him or her a lesson that will not be forgotten.

What should I do if I find out that my daughter was riding with others who were drinking but that she wasn't?

I would punish her almost as severely as if she were.

But that's not fair. What if she couldn't get out?

Then she'd better learn ways of identifying a troublesome situation before it goes too far and practice ways of excusing herself.

But other kids will make fun of her.

Not necessarily. I've taught many kids to excuse themselves by saying, for example, "Hey, I forgot. I've got this really neat guy (girl) that I have to call. Let me out here so I can take care of business." If the kid plays it right, the other kids will think that he or she is going to call a boy friend or girl friend. In actuality, the neat guy or gal to be called is a parent, to whom he or she says, "Come get me."

You didn't mention the importance of communicating with the child who comes home after drinking and driving.

I don't think talk is a good idea when faced with this situation. I think you can communicate, all right: Communicate that the kid really blew it. The hard-nosed punishment should communicate that very clearly.

Hold on just a minute. I'm talking about sitting down with the kid and talking about things before *you discipline.*

I'm sorry to disappoint you, but that's a waste of time. First of all, you never try to communicate with a drunk. Second, you needn't talk about the whys or wherefores of the act. The kid knows he or she was wrong and a penalty is in order. Finally, you have to remember that parents don't start communication with teenagers; teenagers start it. Parents must listen for an opening and pick up on the fact that the kid wants to talk and share. If the kid wants to communicate about the situation, he or she can do so *after* the punishment has been given.

What you're saying goes against everything we've read in the past few years about the importance of communication. Are you saying that communication isn't important?

My position does vary with many expert opinions concerning the relevancy of communication. I do think that communication is important, but only *after* discipline has been handled. In fact, I don't view a heart-to-heart, sharing talk as discipline. It really has nothing to do with exercising power and maintaining order. As for those who would say that communication is most important between parent and child, I simply disagree.

But isn't communication more important the older a child becomes?

No. To my way of thinking, communication decreases in importance the older a child becomes. Enforcing your morality grows in importance with each year, as the child struggles to adjust to reality. If you provide stability through maintaining order, you increase the chances that your child will reach out to you to seek consolation and advice. Think about it: When you feel weak or confused, you don't turn to someone whom you view as weak also; you turn to someone you see as strong and self-directed. Your children will do the same thing.

I want to get back to money. What about inflation and savings? You say the kid should save 20 percent of his earnings. With the inflation rate the way it is, he will lose money if he saves it. What about that?

I hate to get on my soap box, but I lay many of our problems of irresponsibility at the feet of the permissive, spending-oriented way we treat our children. Saving 20 percent of earnings would teach our kids a great deal of self-control and responsibility. We must change the popular notion that money is good only if you spend it.

At the first stage of developing control, you said to help the child earn task by task, in a specific way. When I do this, do I give my three-year-old the dime, or do I keep it until he wants to spend it?

I prefer you give it to the child at the time he earned it. This teaches him the connection between work and money. Likewise, he has to learn to protect his token until he wants to trade it for a goodie.

But what if he loses it?

Life is hard sometimes. Don't give in and give him another coin. He will learn how to be more careful next time.

Aren't you overdoing this money thing? Why start so young?

I'm not suggesting that the kid read the *Wall Street Journal* by the time he's six years old. Nor am I suggesting that you have to make him earn a nickel or a dime every day. Starting young gives him a head start on the problems that can surface during the preteen years.

Should I expect my ten-year-old to save part of his allowance?

Yes. However, you might permit him to spend it within a week or two of saving it. When he's thirteen, during the fourth stage, the savings should be put into the bank.

How can I stop my teenager from spending the savings?

Put your name on the savings account along with his so that he can't get it out without your signature.

I trust my kid's driving, but I don't trust some of the friends he might pick up. How can I control what his friends do in my car?

You can let your kid know that *he* had better control what *his* friends do in *your* car. I worked with one kid who had a standing rule for all his friends: "If you bring beer or other drugs into the car, I stop, and either the drugs go or you do."

At first, this kid felt embarrassed about doing this, so he'd blame his father by saying, "If my father catches me, I can't have the car for three weeks." Later on, however, he simply made the statement without referring to his parents.

How can I check to see if my kid is breaking any laws while driving?

If you don't trust him, tell him. Then let him know that you will institute a program of "snoopervision." This might include checking the mileage, searching the car for evidence of illegal activity, or following the kid on a random basis. "Snoopervision" is a strong disciplinary measure and must be used carefully.

If I tried to follow my kid, he'd know it was I following him.

Use a friend's car to follow him.

Isn't that sinking pretty low?

Not if you want to protect your kid from the dangers of reckless driving. If you don't trust him with the car, do something about it. Don't wait until you get a call from the police.

Should I buy my son a car? He's wanted one ever since I can remember.

So have I, but no one ever handed me a brand-new car. Ordinarily, I say no to this question. However, there may be some circumstances in which you might *help* a kid buy a car, but never a new one. The circumstances would have to include above-average maturity demonstrated by the kid, along with a need over and above joy-riding.

How much should I let my kid drive the car?

I encourage you to negotiate a number of pleasure miles on a weekly basis. Or you might say, "You can have the car for four hours per week when we're not using it."

Should I let my kid drive the car to school?

If I had my way, every school district would have a law prohibiting *all students* from driving to school. Exceptions to this rule would be at the discretion of the principal. Taxpayers shell out a tremendous amount of money for school buses, and then parents turn around and pay outrageous prices for gasoline so that the car can go back and forth to school.

If I didn't let my daughter drive to school, she would throw a gigantic temper tantrum.

That's too bad.

I don't expect my son to support the car. I figure that as long as he treats it right, I'll let him drive it. What do you think?

I think he ought to pay something. He could pay part of the insurance, gas, upkeep, or something else. He also should be expected to clean it up occasionally. I have never liked this business of giving gifts to children just because they're young and cute. It is a disservice to the integrity of working for a living.

My son has had two speeding tickets in two months. Should I continue to let him drive?

I think you should suspend his driving privileges for one month before the state does it for much longer. You may also want to implement some version of a "snoopervision" program when he gets his driving privileges back.

I don't want my kid to have to work while she is young. I had to work and didn't take advantage of all the things I could have. I want my kid to enjoy sports, parties, and other extracurricular activities.

Take a hard look at what you're saying. You have been successful in part because you had to work for what you got. Now you want to deprive your kid of the same lesson because you don't want to see her suffer. If she gets all the fun now, she won't know how to work for her fun. I think adults should have more fun than kids, because it's tougher to be a grown-up than a teenager. Many of the adults I know worked hard while they were young, and now they are successful enough that they can permanently enjoy skiing, boating, tennis, golf, and other "extracurricular" activities.

It's tougher to be a grown-up than a kid? Come on, kids have it much tougher these days than I did when I was growing up.

I hear that same meaningless argument too often. If kids have it tougher in a more challenging world, then where does that put adults? It means we not only have to live in that *same* challenging world; we also have to help our kids learn responsibility when all they want to do is party and have fun. Kids have amazing ability to forget about their troubles while grown-ups stew and fret about how to solve them.

My kid wants lunch money to eat out during school. He says that school lunches are horrible. Do I give him the money?

No, but give him a choice. He can have the lunches at school or he can pack his own.

I found out that my daughter was skipping lunches and saving her lunch money for cigarettes. I know I can't stop her smoking, but I want her to eat right.

Tell her that you will check on her lunch attendance and if you find out that she is still not eating, you will force her to take her lunch.

But what if that only forces her to steal money?

Then you have a deeper problem and you probably need help figuring it out. Get some counseling, and don't give in to her blackmail.

My fourteen-year-old earns his own money and wants to buy an eight-hundred-dollar stereo set. I think that is too much, but he argues that he can spend his money any way he chooses. What do I do?

Strictly speaking, it is not *his* money, not as long as he lives off you and is a minor in the eyes of the law. It sounds as if this boy knows about his rights but hasn't learned about his responsibilities. If the boy ranks high on my responsibility scale, let him buy a set that costs about four or five hundred dollars.

My son says that the stereo set he bought with his money is his to play as loud as he wants whenever he wants to. What now?

Oh, really? If he doesn't wise up, tell him he can play it out in the street. Short of this, put the stereo in your closet for a week.

You say to take away a possession if a child abuses it. But when I take a toy away from my six-year-old, he finds another one in five minutes and forgets about the one I took away.

It sounds like your child has too many toys. If a child doesn't have to earn his things and protect them by responsibility, then it is very difficult to punish him by removing the goodies. If you want to punish him, you'll have to use something else, possibly a fine or some type of restriction of freedom. While you're doing that, try to reduce the number of toys (through damage or attrition).

My kid is fifteen and says that most jobs demand that you be sixteen. He doesn't work, because he's not old enough.

He can carry papers, mow lawns, babysit, rake leaves, and do other odd jobs around the home and the neighborhood. His age is an inconvenience, but I don't like to think it is an impossible barrier. Many states allow 15-year-olds to hold a job *if* they have a work permit.

My teenager earned several hundred dollars this summer and wants to buy some extra clothes, records, and decorations for her room. Do I let her spend it all?

No. Remind her that she will need some money for the long, chilly winter. Prompt her to make out a budget, using her savings for later expenditures. Then, whatever she has left can go for the things you mention.

How much should I expect my child to save for college?

You already know what I think about parents' penny-pinching pursuit of college-education money. I think kids should have to earn *at least* all leisure money plus some part of the tuition. Talk with him or her about your decision two or three years ahead of time.

All these programs sound good, but they take time. I thought you said your advice would save time.

You don't have to use all the programs I suggest. Pick out one or two that fit your specific situation and use them to teach your children responsibility. Once your child scores high on my responsibility scale, you'll have plenty of time to do other things.

The main thrust of my recommendations concerning work, money, and possessions is aimed at the trouble that can result from teenage irresponsibility. I have one more piece of advice that will give you clout with your kids during the second decade of their life. It may be the most powerful thing you can do to a teenager.

Absolutely out of the blue, when the kid least expects it—when he or she is talking on the phone, listening to records, studying, playing cards, or just sitting around watching TV—come up to him or her, hesitate for a second or two, to get his or her attention, and say, "You are very important to me. I love you more than you'll ever know."

Can you imagine his shock? He will be so dumbfounded, he won't answer. He may even blush and stammer. You need not wait for a response. If he wants to know whether or not you're sick, just tell him, "Oh, we have so many tough times around here, I just wanted to tell you something that is always on my mind."

This expression of unconditional love is akin to what you did when he was an infant. You are restating a warmth that is often difficult to remember. When you're faced with endless disciplinary headaches and you don't think you can stand the kid any longer, forget about discipline and let him know you still love him.

With love operating as a strong magnet pulling for respect and responsibility, the tough-minded suspension of driving privileges or the demand for more work and less pay gives hell-raising kids a clear picture of right and wrong. This distinction can be a godsend when embattled parents face rebellious teenagers who yell, "Responsibility is a bummer! I gotta swing. So get out of my way and let me do my thing."

15

Coping with Crises

*Principle #14. Exceptional circumstances or crises will not
excuse children from responsibility*

Life has a way of sneaking up on us and slapping our
hearts with sudden, unexpected pain. Death, disease, and
divorce are just three of the heartaches that insinuate themselves into our lives. When these situations affect or afflict our
children, the pain is twice as great. Rare is the person whose
heart doesn't bleed for a battered child or a kid who suffers
severe emotional trauma. Our first impulse is to reach out and
take the world off the kid's shoulders. We don't realize it, but
when we try to make the pain disappear, we make things
worse. That's why my down-to-earth advice for coping with
crises is reflected in the old-fashioned saying "When the going
gets tough, the tough get going."

This statement tells children to meet a crisis head-on. It
expresses a belief that some life is better than no life. It is a
testimony to the importance of survival under trying circum-

stances. Most of all, it is a defiance that confronts life's painful blows and retorts, "No matter what you do to me, I will get stronger because of it."

When a child faces a crisis, he or she must grow in strength no matter what the adversity. If an adult tries to make the world go away, it hurts, not helps, the child in crisis. It takes special fortitude and patience to help a child face a painful crisis without giving him or her sympathy, pity or other emotional outpourings that cripple instead of cure.

"What do you need from me?" "How can I help?" and "I'm here if you need me" are three offers of support that muster courage and can turn the crisis into a positive learning experience.

"You poor thing," "I feel so sorry for you," and "It's just not fair" are crippling comments that suggest that the child doesn't have the inner strength to meet the challenge. Expressing support encourages the child to respond to the crisis; expressing pity encourages the child to give up and to sink into self-pity and irresponsibility. Expecting a child to be strong and self-determined is the first step toward responsibility.

I will give you an overview of how my get-tough approach to discipline applies to crises. As you can tell from principle 14, I believe that children's responsibility is not excused simply because they encounter one of life's heartaches. I will outline five steps to follow in coping with crises and then answer questions about specific problems. I will suggest how you can maintain discipline and order while helping a child find the inner toughness to get going when the going gets tough.

Step One: Express and control emotions

When a crisis hits, emotions fly all over, bouncing us from pillar to post. Your first step should be to express and control these emotions, both in yourself and in the child. In a safe and acceptable environment, let go. If you must, scream, cry, and curse about life's inequities. Give yourself and the child the right to vent anger. If time doesn't permit such emotionalism, set aside another time for dealing with feelings.

If you don't express and control your emotions, they may get in the way of supporting the child and you will unintentionally stimulate dependency and self-pity.

Step Two: Think of alternatives

When a crisis hits, it's not unusual for your first reaction to be "There's only one way out of this." Finding a second, third, and even fourth course of action is the greatest gift you can give to the child in crisis. It provides you and the child with a feeling of freedom that can stimulate courage and self-determination.

When you have thought of every conceivable course of action, you have maximized your chances of finding the best thing to do. If you don't have time to consider all options calmly, or if your only option is to do nothing, then you must simply do your best with the freedom you have. You can increase your ability to select the best course of action by using the "decision-tree" process outlined in the appendix.

Step Three: Gather all possible information

In conjunction with thinking of all possible alternatives, make certain you are aware of all the information available pertaining to the crisis you face. If you're working to control your emotions while you search for the best course of action, you certainly won't have the time or energy to become aware of a piece of information that throws an entirely different light on the problem.

Step Four: Seek objective help

Don't be too proud to turn to a friend or counselor for guidance during a crisis. You need not run right out and grab the first person you see and tell him or her all your problems. Search for a person whom you know you can trust but who is not personally involved in the crisis. This person, probably a friend, will listen to you, help you search out all pertinent information, and assist you in selecting the best course of action.

Step Five: Help the child learn from the crisis

If you complete the first four steps, you will be prepared to help the child go through the same process. He or she will need help expressing and controlling emotions, making decisions, gathering all information available, as well as feeling support from loved ones. If you're able to remain strong, much of that support can come from you.

Guide the child in finding the inner strength to meet the challenge. With a loving heart and a firm hand, help him or her to get tough. When the child says, "Make the world go away," you can answer, "I can't, Honey. But if you let me, I'll help you learn how to live with it."

These steps will be modified depending upon the nature of the crisis. Sometimes you will have more time for reflection and emotional outpouring; other times you'll have to take immediate action. Often, your search for objectivity will have to wait and your gathering of information will have to be done quickly. No matter what the sequence or timing of the first four steps, never forget about step five: Helping the child get tough is your first priority.

I'm recently divorced and am worried about my thirteen-year-old. He was physically abused by his father. He was beaten, slapped in the face regularly, and one time he suffered a broken arm. I know I can never undo the emotional pain, but how do I help him with his depression?

If the boy is truly down, he most likely is repressing anger, frustration, and feelings of rejection. He could be experiencing hundreds of feelings as he is confused by thousands of thoughts. It would not be surprising if he was withdrawing from discovering who he is and where he belongs in this world. The best way for this boy to learn a lifelong lesson from such a painful experience is to have professional counseling. Seek out a counselor known to work well with teenagers and be willing to go with the kid at first. You might also want to examine why you stayed with a man who was so abusive. Above all, make certain he's not subjected to further abuse, but don't express pity for him. Both will have a damaging effect.

When I was young, my mother and I got into horrible fights. As far back as I can remember, she slapped me whenever I did the least little thing wrong. Now I'm about to have my first child and have read that even though I don't want to, there is a good chance I will abuse my child. I'm scared to death.

Though some of the pain you endured will always be with you and will rear its ugly head when you least expect it—for instance, during frustrating times with a small baby— you can control it. You must discover your free will and say, "I *will* not permit the frustration to build to that point."

I encourage you to redouble your efforts to be an effective disciplinarian. Nothing diffuses frustration better than a child who does as he or she is told. Likewise, nothing adds to frustration quicker than a child who continues in disruption as a parent continues to warn, cajole, and threaten.

It would be very easy for you to go to the opposite extreme and say, "I'm going to give my child all the nurturance that I never had. I'm going to have so much patience you won't believe it." If you act on this, you set yourself up for failure. Just because you went through hell, don't try to put your child in heaven.

If you try to be superhuman, you'll only add more frustration which could result in an emotional explosion, during which you'll go to the opposite extreme and hurt your child unintentionally. This, of course, would stimulate tremendous guilt, from which you'd try to escape by increasing your nurturance. You can see how this could easily become a vicious cycle.

If you use a strong will and effective discipline, you won't pass on the tendency toward abuse, which often is handed down from generation to generation like a family curse.

I've had terrific guilt trips about not leaving my alcoholic husband sooner. When he was drunk, he physically and emotionally abused not only me but also my two kids. Now that I have them by myself, they are rowdy, disrespectful, and beyond my control. I can't be tough with them when their problems are my fault. I'm trapped again.

You're only trapped by your guilt. Though it may be true that your reluctance to leave subjected them to abuse, you need not continue the abuse by letting them use past pain to excuse present disruption. It only makes matters worse.

Keep in mind that some of their disruption may be *unrelated* to the past; it may be their way of making the world conform to their wishes. They may be using your guilt and their rebellion to act out normal impulses. You should rediscover effective discipline and have round-table discussions, with or without a counselor, aimed at regaining your clout.

It sounds as though you've changed. And since it's easier for kids to change than it is for adults, you have every right and responsibility to expect your children to shape up. If you can't forget the guilt, you'd better talk to a counselor yourself.

My wife is a good woman. She gets frustrated easily and takes it out on the kids. The other night, my sixteen-year-old daughter hit my wife on the arm. I understand why she did it, but I can't let her get by with it. What should I do?

First of all, look at whether or not you are compensating for your wife's temper by overprotecting the girl. You could be trying to make up for the abuse. If your wife is as uptight as you say, she needs to talk to a counselor. Since you are part of the marriage and family, you should go with her.

If your daughter recognizes that she overreacted and is apologetic, cut one hour off her curfew. If she is sassy and belligerent, ground her for two nights. It's probably a good idea that the girl talk with the counselor as part of a family session.

But what if my wife won't talk with anyone?

Then you should talk to a counselor about what to do next.

I'm a teacher and a parent and have some students with learning disabilities in my classroom. I know how to discipline a normal child, but how do I discipline an abnormal child?

First, get rid of the notion that children with learning disabilities are "abnormal." They're not. They have special problems affecting certain areas of problem-solving. As such, they are different from the other students, not "abnormal." Second, try to discipline the LD students the same way you do the others. You may have to cut down the number of minutes for "time-out" because of impaired attention span. Or you may have to be more specific when you inform some of them of the rules—making lists, repetition, etc. Hence, try to alter your procedures quantitatively, not qualitatively.

What do I do with kids who make fun of disabled children?

You try to explain the nature of the disability, and if they persist in their nasty remarks, you punish them.

How do I explain learning disability to my other children? I barely understand it myself.

Rely on more experienced parents to guide you in this difficult task. Talk with some of these people and find out how they explained it. When I explain learning disabilities, I use the idea of a "short circuit in one of the wires in the computer that sits on top of his shoulders." I even draw pictures of the brain, depicting it as a machine with hundreds of wires. Then I explain that for some unknown reason, some of these wires got crossed. I encourage all involved, including the disabled kid, to compensate for the short circuit by learning how to use other wires to make up for the ones that don't work right. This approach takes the stigma away from learning disabilities as it provides for a method of remediation.

I just learned that my son has above-average intelligence but still has a learning disability. It took me a long time to understand how the two could possibly go together. Now I get terribly frustrated with him when he forgets his duties, is sloppy at the dinner table, and does other strange things. Then I feel guilty for being angry. Now what?

Learning-disabled children are frustrating—those with strong natural intelligence even more so. Just about the time you start counting on them to be "typical," they hit you with some ridiculous behavior.

Take special effort to separate your unconditional love for the child from your conditional responses, many of which will be laden with frustration and disappointment. You can use this distinction to control your guilt at getting angry. You're mad at the behavior, not at the child. I encourage you to join a group of parents of LDs so that you can share your thoughts, feelings, and solutions to everyday problems.

My trouble is that my husband and I have accepted our daughter's disability, but her grandparents have not. They spoil the daughter worse than they do any other grandchild. They do things for her that she must learn to do for herself. After spending a couple of days with her grandparents, I have to retrain my daughter.

Many grandparents are natural sympathizers. It's traditional that Grandma and Grandpa get to spoil the grandchildren. It usually doesn't hurt that much. You just have to teach the kids not to expect the same thing from you. In the case of a disabled child, grandparents should be encouraged to limit their spoiling her to what they would do if the child were not disabled. Let your parents know how they are hurting your daughter. If they love her, they will back off and be willing to conform to your wishes.

My son has a learning disability and is a real handful. The problem is with my bright daughter, who is two years younger than the boy. She is embarrassed by the boy's antics and gets angry when he acts strange around her friends. I don't want her suffering from the problem. They are both teenagers.

Your daughter will have to learn not to be intimidated by her brother's antics. She will have to be a little tougher than most teenagers. She will have to face that fact that her individuality is not defined by what other people think of her brother's behavior. If people judge her by what her brother does, then they aren't worth her time. Share with her how you've learned that lesson.

My four-year-old broke his leg and had to spend five weeks in the hospital in traction. He drove everyone nuts with his crying, demands, and temper fits. I was so worried and embarrassed, I didn't have time to know what to do. Now I wonder if he will be scarred because of the problems he had and the way I reacted.

It sounds as if your son had to grow up rather quickly. Being in a hospital in traction is enough to drive anyone up a wall, especially an active little kid. Forget your embarrassment and any possible guilt. Use the experience to help your son get tough.

My five-year-old daughter went through a similar experience, and I didn't know what to do. How should I respond to temper fits when a kid is going through a crisis?

The same way you would if he or she was having a temper fit around the home. The best thing to do when confronted with a temper fit is to ignore it; take the audience away. I've counseled pediatric nurses to avoid cajoling and oversympathizing with children who are going through a medical crisis; it only adds to the frustration that already exists. I remember that the person who was most effective in handling these cases was an older nurse who simply went about her business, giving shots, taking temperatures, and doing some other unpleasant things without undue delay. She told the children to open up and take their medicine in a soft but firm tone. She would come back later and play with them, showing them that she wasn't the bad lady they thought she was.

My son is twelve years old and has been a juvenile diabetic for two years. Recently, he has started cheating on his diet. What should I do?

I will assume that you have expert medical care. The most powerful thing you can do with a juvenile diabetic is to let him know that his proper diet is a family affair. If you care for him, watch his charts, help him with food exchanges, create new sugarless treats, and keep a watchful eye on his insulin and urine tests, he will care more. I am a big supporter of summer camps for kids with diabetes. See if there is one in your area.

My fifteen-year-old was hospitalized for three weeks after being in an accident with a friend who had been drinking. He's recovered well. Do I punish him now, or just forget about it?

I suggest one week of restricted freedom. Then I would recommend a five-week probation period during which you "snoopervise" his riding in cars. Let him know that he'd better avoid bad drivers or he won't get his freedom.

Isn't that a little strong? The boy learned his lesson by being hurt.

I'm not certain kids learn from accidents. Though many do, you can't take the chance. This boy can't afford any more accidents; he's already had his lucky turn. Next time, his error might be fatal.

My oldest boy was killed in a car wreck last year. I've decided that my youngest boy won't be allowed to drive until he graduates from high school. He says I'm overreacting, but I just can't go through another tragedy.

If you can rise above your pain, then you have to ask yourself, "Am I judging my son's behavior based on observations or prejudices caused by a past trauma?" If you really want to avert future disaster, demand that your son exhibit above-average driving skills, and then you can have more faith that he will be safe. You might be forcing him to sneak around, which could result in another accident. It might make you feel better if you implement a program of "snoopervision" for several months. Just explain the program to your kid before you do it.

My twelve-year-old was arrested for vandalism. He was stealing ornaments from car hoods. We have to go see a juvenile officer, and I'm not sure what I should do.

There are several suggestions I have for you. First, dedicate yourself to making this crisis worthwhile by turning it into a valuable lesson for the boy. Second, don't tell the kid not to worry. He broke the law and should worry. Third, don't give the police the idea that you've given up parenthood just because your kid made a mistake. Stay in control by letting the officer know that you appreciate his help in solving *your son's problem.* Fourth, make certain the boy receives a punishment—restriction of freedom, suspension of privileges—from you. And follow the other steps outlined in the discussion of rip-offs.

Why should I do all these things? Seeing the police officer should be enough punishment. It was when I was young.

I'll bet the reason it was enough for you is that you were afraid of what your parents, not the police, would do to you. Most police warn, threaten, and promise a punishment "next time." Over the past twenty years, "next time" has come to mean only more threats. Kids are discovering that juvenile officers are shaking their fingers and that nothing else is happening. As I said before, kids are becoming less and less fearful of getting caught, because they are not being punished when they do get caught. The justice system is losing its clout with kids because it's all bark and no bite.

My kid was jailed, charged with burglary. This is the first time he's been in trouble. He is sixteen and not a bad kid. What should I do? Maybe I ought to leave him in jail to think about it.

No, don't leave him in jail. Put up the necessary bail, retain a lawyer, avoid any guilt trips, and put him on strict, homebound probation. Refrain from interrogation, but let the boy talk to you if he wants to. Likewise, let him know that you will deal with him after the court gets finished with him. Until then, give him your support.

You're contradicting yourself. You just said that police officers don't have any bite, and now you are telling us to protect the kid from the law. What gives?

I'm not telling you to protect the kid from the law. I'm suggesting you protect the kid from the way the law is *adminis-*

tered. Most juvenile-justice systems do not have the ability, knowledge, or personnel to execute a program of effective discipline for first offenders. If you keep a close eye on the procedures and make certain the kid's rights are not violated, you can execute your own punishment so that the kid learns a lesson.

Good heavens, you're tough. Must we treat our kids with such regimentation? Do you want our homes to become like West Point?

Better West Point than Woodstock.

My fourteen-year-old daughter was arrested for shoplifting and thrown into a detention cell. She's never been in trouble before. I think the police went too far. What can I do to make amends to my daughter?

The best thing you can do is to help her stay away from the juvenile-justice system forever. Your story only supports my contention that we don't handle first offenders well. Be careful not to show the girl pity; she'll only use it to feel justified in seeking revenge, which will mean more contacts with the police. Give her a realistic penalty, and don't forget to include some form of restitution to the store she ripped off.

My seventeen-year-old has been in a lot of trouble. He's horribly disruptive around home, has been kicked out of school and warned too many times. Now he's been arrested for stealing a stereo from a friend's apartment. He claims that the stereo is his. What do I do?

Make sure the boy is placed in solitary confinement for his own protection, and leave him in jail for a while. Then talk with him about shaping up. Tell him that you will get him out of jail on bail provided that he comes home, minds the rules, attends family-counseling sessions with you and your husband, and doesn't get in any more trouble. Also, tell him that if he doesn't follow through on these matters, you will revoke the bail money and let the court punish him any way it sees fit.

Isn't that giving up on the boy?

If you can separate your love from your intolerance for disruption, you can continue to give him your best shot of love and discipline and at the same time totally reject his deviant behavior.

My fifteen-year-old daughter was arrested for shoplifting and then given a warning and sent home. We grounded her for a month. One night I heard her talking on the phone to her best friend, giggling about getting caught and bragging about all the times she wasn't. Should I pretend I didn't hear that?

Absolutely not! Let her know exactly what you heard and that you obviously didn't use the right punishment. Change the grounding to two weeks, but include no phone, no friends, no TV, and no stereo during the grounding.

You haven't mentioned the importance of communication with kids who get caught. Don't they need to talk about why they rip off and to understand that it is wrong?

I bet that most kids already know that. I've dealt with many kids who've stolen something and who, when confronted, said, "I know it was wrong." When asked why they did it, they typically replied, "I thought it would be fun." Keep in mind that morality isn't instilled in a child's head simply because parents tell them the difference between right and wrong. They must *behave* correctly.

As for communication, remember what I said earlier: Parents don't start communication; kids do. If your kid wants to talk about it, give him or her an opening and then wait. If they talk, great. If they don't, you'll have to wait longer.

My eighteen-year-old daughter was raped by some kid two weeks after she started college. She's home now and won't talk about it to anyone. I'm worried about her.

Rape can be a living death for the victim. It has to be one of the ugliest of all crimes. Make her go to talk with someone about the incident. If she absolutely refuses to cooperate, seek out someone to help you deal with your daughter's withdrawal. Above all, let your daughter know that you will *not* let the issue drop until she talks to someone.

Our sixteen-year-old daughter is pregnant. I still haven't recovered from the shock. My husband says she should have an abortion; I want her to give the baby up for adoption; and she wants to marry her boy friend, who is eighteen. Which way do we turn?

First, you should recover enough to discuss the issue rationally. You need reliable information about the three alternatives you present, and you won't get that information if you argue back and forth. Talk with an abortion clinic, your priest, minister, or rabbi, if you have one, and anyone else who can give you objectivity. In the last analysis, your daughter should be allowed to make the decision.

But I strongly disapprove of abortion and will not allow a minor to have one.

Check the laws in your state and see how much control you have over your child in this matter. You may need to talk to a lawyer in addition to the people I referred to.

Our family doctor called me recently and told me that my seventeen-year-old had a venereal disease. I almost fainted. I hesitated to tell her until it came out during a horrible argument. She is better now, but still hasn't forgiven me. What should I have done?

Asked your family doctor to tell the girl. After all, it's her body and her responsibility. You and the doctor made a mistake by not telling her immediately. Admit your error, and from now on, focus on her general level of responsibility, not on her sexual morality.

I'm divorced, and my ex-wife is remarried. My nine-year-old son says he doesn't like his stepfather, because the man makes fun of him. What can I do?

You have the painful reality of having divorced your wife but not your son. It's probably harder for you to live with than it is for your kid. About the only thing you can do is help your son make the best of a situation that he sees as bad. Before giving him too much compassion, realize that the boy may be taking the natural frustration of missing you and turning it into a reason to be manipulative. He may be stretching reality with his assessment of your ex's new husband.

You can help clear up the matter by refraining from giving your son anything extra; that is, over and above what you would give him if he were living with you. If you make a big deal out of his natural reaction, you could be adding fuel to the fires of rebellion.

But what if I find out that he's right?

Confront your ex-wife and her husband and see if you can talk it out. If that fails, take the problem to an attorney and see if you can force a resolution in court.

My ex-husband is trying to buy off his guilt by giving our two children everything they want. They think Dad is a great guy. They think I'm just an old meany. How can I stop this?

Unless you and your ex communicate better than you used to, you can't. You can, however, remind the kids that they only see one side of their father—the good guy—whereas you show them the good, the bad, and the ugly. Let your ex-husband have the kids for three weeks during the summer. That should be long enough for him to become a disciplinarian. Then maybe the kids will look upon you differently.

My nineteen-year-old is a bright kid. I was stunned when he flunked out of college in his first semester. I don't know whether to disown him or let him stay home forever. What now?

It's understandable that you would have two opposite reactions when thus shocked. The best thing you can do is to ask your son what his plans are. Don't support him unless he moves steadily toward a goal of eventual independence. Keep in mind that many successful people flunked out of something at one time or another. The boy needs to hear "Pull yourself up by your own bootstraps."

We can all look forward to a crisis. Each of our lives will be touched with unexpected sadness and pain. We are all afflicted with a "condition," whether it be a passing sickness or the hellish experience of losing someone we love. Grief is as much a part of life as happiness is.

Discipline must not be thrown out the window when life dumps rain on our parade. In fact, when life gets tough, we need law and order more than ever. If we can't remain in control of ourselves and our children, then we might as well shut our eyes to reality and fall in line with those who find solace in feeling sorry for themselves.

Self-pity, or "mental thumb-sucking," is the first step toward the final resignation of our will. And with death hanging so close by all of us, there's no sense in helping it along. Life is more precious than that.

16

The Blind Spots of Loving

Principle #15. Parents will remain alert to the blind spots of loving, which can diminish their effectiveness

The last thirty years or so of "enlightenment" have taken a negative toll. In acquiring new knowledge, we've lost sight of much of the old. I think it's a mistake. We've moved away from the commonsense principles used by our forebears to make us a people who had the courage, knowledge, and determination to make the best of what we had. We're so busy looking ahead that we've forgotten what it took to bring us to the present.

Instead of preparing our kids for the harsh realities of life, we've succumbed to the notion that we must protect them from the school of hard knocks. We've slipped into the assumption that once the "good life" is attained, it doesn't have to be maintained. What's worse, we're passing that notion on to our children. They in turn leave home expecting the good life to be handed to them and are ill-prepared to handle the rejection, failure, and disappointment that are ever present.

I hope I've persuaded you to exercise your power, to stay in control of your children, and to wean them slowly toward self-control. I trust that you have a better understanding of how to turn the reins of control over to your kids, giving or taking slack in the control rope depending on their behavior.

If you've studied carefully and know the limits of your power, and you reduce your tendency to nurturance as you increase the lessons of nature, you will still make mistakes. Many of these mistakes can be traced to erroneous assumptions and myths concerning the parenting role. These misconceptions usually result from emotional involvement coupled with misleading advice. I call these pitfalls the "blind spots of loving."

The attachment of the heart that is expressed in unconditional love makes you vulnerable. As long as you choose to love, no amount of expertness in discipline will protect you from being the target of childish manipulation. It comes with the territory. Children will feel safe with your love and see how far they can push you. Sometimes they will get away with something they shouldn't simply because you are blinded by your love. I don't blame kids for trying to manipulate, and I don't blame parents for falling victim to the con job. I suggest you be aware of the blind spots and learn how to cope with them.

I would like to summarize some of the blind spots I see occurring most often. You will notice that most of these are covered elsewhere in the book in much more detail. These are the things that can cause you to scratch your head in bewilderment and say, "I don't know what's going on."

Parents should not feel guilt

Nothing stimulates parental confusion and erodes parental authority more than guilt. Yet parents feel guilt about possible errors more than any other emotion. Guilt is another way of saying "I *made* my child do what he did." I'm sorry to inform you that no parent (or other human being, for that matter) is so powerful that he can *make* a person do something. Don't forget about free will and the choice process.

Parents are not responsible for their children's behavior

In concert with the folly of feeling guilt is the notion that parents are to blame when children misbehave. When a child acts irresponsibly, nobody or nothing got inside his or her brain, ripped out the free will, and took control of his or her actions. When a kid misbehaves, parents are not to blame; the child is. If you really love your child, help him or her face this unsavory bit of life.

Parents should not try to be their child's best friend

It is highly unlikely that any parent who considers discipline a top priority and who wishes to teach his or her children right from wrong will be a child's "best friend." Children need parents to be organizers, evaluators, judges, planners, scrutinizers, and supervisors. Children can find best friends in other places. If you aren't the child's parent, then he or she will have to find someone else to fill that special role.

Parents cannot teach values

When you teach your child your morality, you first must explain so that he or she understands. Then you must enforce your explanations with rewards and punishments, thereby putting the morality into action. Once the child knows how to *act* on his or her understanding of right and wrong, he or she will evolve a value system that is uniquely his or hers. You cannot teach your children values. They must discover those on their own. Values, by definition, are habits that have grown up and been accepted or rejected by the individual.

Communication is not most important

Parents have been led to believe that open, honest communication is *most* important to a child's health and well-being. This is not true. Though communication is essential to productive parent-child interaction, it is not more important than discipline. If you want to stimulate good communication with your children, first teach them to behave themselves, and then they will have the security and self-confidence necessary to approach you with difficult subjects.

Children, not parents, initiate communication

If you're turning gray trying to make your children talk with you, forget it. You don't initiate communication; children do. They will let you know when they want to share feelings, thoughts, problems. All you can do is remain alert to the signs of children's wanting to talk. You can help this process by asking questions occasionally and shutting your mouth and opening your ears when the kid begins to answer.

Talk does not teach right from wrong

Though talk may be the first step in instilling a sense of morality in children, it does not teach them right from wrong. Without action, children will not learn what to *do* and what not to *do*.

Keep explanations separate from punishment

Once you've said no or taken punitive action against your child, he or she will be in no mood for an explanation of why you did what you did. If you think you must give the child an explanation for punishment, do it *before* the actual punishment. Or, better yet, wait until the child gets over the punishment and then explain your actions.

Discipline does not mar the child's unconscious

When you punish a child or exercise your authority over him or her, you don't damage the child's mind. If anything "damages" a child, it is a permissive attitude that allows the child to engage freely in disruption. Don't be afraid to discipline your children; it may eventually save their lives.

Some fear is necessary

The development of a rational sense of fear is necessary for children's survival. In fact, a fear of real danger is necessary for all of us. When children fear life's dangers and learn how better to survive, they come to respect the parent (or other authority figure) who taught them such a valuable lesson.

Manipulative behavior doesn't indicate sickness

Even though your children's "con jobs" can drive you goofy, remember that some degree of defiance and manipulation is healthy. It shows spunk and security. Manipulative behavior indicates the child is testing the limits of confinement. Be content when you see it; *but do something about it.*

Keep your goals limited

Don't try to be all things to your children at all times. Take time for yourself and pursue your needs and wants. Keep your eye on four or five crucial responsible behaviors. For most children, these behaviors include getting acceptable grades, using respectful language, maintaining household chores, observing curfew, and protecting their privileges. It's good to remember that responsibility is contagious, but so is sloppiness.

Children don't want to grow up

Generally speaking, children don't want to grow up. However, they want to grow older so that they can enjoy more freedom and privileges. Put yourself in their place. If you were enjoying the good life with lots of privileges and not many responsibilities, would you want to grow up, become an adult, and carry the weight of maturity?

Punishment is limited in disciplinary value

Punishment teaches a child only what *not* to do; it does not teach a child what to do. You must work in a system of rewards and "warm fuzzies" in order to shape positive behavior. That's why I insist that discipline requires positive as well as negative lessons.

Parents are supervisors and have power

Like it or not, when you accept parenthood, you also accept a supervisory role, which includes power. Children assume a subordinate role and expect parents to exercise the power of supervisors. If parents fail to be supervisors, children do not learn how to deal with power and authority.

Equality cannot exist in disciplinary issues

Disciplining a child for his or her own good often involves doing something to the child that he or she will not like. When you discipline—when you exercise power—your action will necessarily seem "unfair," especially if it is negative. Thus, when you assume the supervisory role, it is impossible to exercise power and equality at the same time. Keep your eye on just rewards and punishments and forget about being fair.

Parents do play favorites

Many parents experience considerable guilt because they think they might or do play favorites with one child over another. I recommend that you recognize the reality of favoritism. However, playing favorites does not occur because you have more love for one child than for another. As I've said before, love is unconditional and boundless and therefore cannot be a part of favoritism. What does stimulate favoritism is behavior that is better or more acceptable than other behavior. If a child picks up his or her room, gets good grades, and generally minds your rules and regulations, then you will favor him or her when it comes time to dish out special recognition or privileges.

Remind your children of this reality and encourage them to behave in such a way that you can show them favoritism.

Refuse to argue with your children

Arguing takes two people. When you argue with your children, you admit that you are losing your clout. Parents who freely discuss all sides of an issue need not "lower" themselves into debating who's in charge. If you argue, you tell the child that you aren't willing to back up your words with action.

"Everybody" is a ghost of peer pressure

Peer pressure works directly against individual choice. As such, it is essentially negative, even when it results in positive change. Do not permit yourself to be persuaded by arguments about what "everybody" is doing. Rather, continually turn the conversation back to why the child wishes to do a certain thing. Through the development of individuality, you can help your children cope with this very real ghost.

There's no such thing as

. . . a child's excuse. When a child makes a mistake, he or she should be expected to explain how it happened. However, it is wrong to let the child assume that an explanation is the same as an excuse. It is not. Children explain; parents excuse.

. . . a child's room. Children are given temporary custody of a place in *your* home. Provided they follow the morality established by you, you permit them to maintain a certain degree of privacy. If they violate your rules, you can seize custody of *your* room.

. . . a second warning. When you warn a child, you have made a threat of punishment for continued disruption. If you warn a second time, you are saying that you didn't mean it the first time you said it.

If you have gone wacky trying to be fair, engaging in end-less arguments, giving second and third warnings as you have taken responsibility for your children's actions, you should be getting fed up. I hope you're ready to say "I've had it with permissiveness; I'm going to get tough."

Now your only problem is finding the proper balance of toughness and nurturance to fit your personality. My princi-ples and recommendations provide ample guidance. But, for Heaven's sake, don't try to parent the way I would, even if you totally agree with every bit of my advice. I must remind you that I still have many failures, even as a professional.

A short story demonstrates my point.

I am proud of my ability to get kids involved in counseling. Frightened or easily embarrassed kids like my humor, goofy mannerisms, my Mickey Mouse phone and watch. Smart alecks are impressed by my street-wise, tough-talking mouth, which sits atop my six foot five, 225-pound frame. I have a style to fit every kid. They love me or hate me, but never are indifferent. Well, almost never.

Recently, the concerned parents of a fifteen-year-old boy spoke with me about their son. Todd was doing poorly in school and becoming increasingly unruly at home. They wanted me to talk to him and see if I could find out what was troubling him.

After an hour of productive conversation, I felt that we had established excellent rapport. I tentatively concluded that Todd was suffering from many normal teenage traumas plus a lack of involvement with his father. The problems didn't seem too difficult. I figured four or five sessions with Todd and two or three with his parents and everything would be okay.

However, when I next spoke with Todd's mother, she gave me some shocking news. She said, "Todd doesn't want to see you anymore. He doesn't think you can help him."

I was flabbergasted. "Why?" I asked.

Her answer still rings in my ears. "He thinks you're boring!"

I hung up the phone and had an immediate identity crisis. *"Me? Boring? I don't believe it!"*

I sat back in my chair and stared at the wall. Finally, my

eyes were drawn to the top of the desk. There sat Mickey Mouse, with that bright yellow receiver in his right hand and a timeless smile of happiness on his face. His cheery mood lifted my spirits. I suddenly decided what had gone wrong. I think I spoke out loud. "Mickey, it's all your fault. You blew it!"

Mickey took my best shot without moving a muscle. Inside my head, I heard his reply.

"Hey, listen, Dr. Dan, I know more about kids than anyone, even you. After all, I have more than fifty years of experience with every type of kid imaginable. And, believe me, some of those kids were murder."

I sat still. I've always been impressed with Mickey's wisdom.

He continued. "Don't be discouraged. You're not the first person to have trouble reaching kids. You should have seen Minnie one time. She had so much trouble with my nephews, you wouldn't believe it. So, have faith, Dr. Dan. Nobody said it would be easy."

Mickey concluded his remarks with a piece of advice that is as durable as Mickey Mouse himself. He noted, "If you love them enough, you gotta be tough."

Appendix:
Disciplinary Procedures

"Discipline" means "to teach." We learn to do what we *do*, not what we *say*. Thus, discipline demands action. You can't exercise your authority by talking; you must act. As I've indicated before, you can plant the seeds of morality only by talking. It takes disciplinary action to make the words flower into moral behavior.

This collection of disciplinary procedures is action-oriented. Since you must teach right from wrong by use of rewards and punishments, I've included positive as well as negative procedures. Each outline gives you a title, description, recommended ages for which it should be used, examples of application, and precautions. I've added a brief note concerning the risk in each procedure. This is to alert you that disciplinary procedures (especially strong punishments) can cause rebellion, revenge, guilt, and other harmful side-effects. Thus, when the risk is moderate or severe, pay strict attention to the precautions.

Following is a list of the procedures outlined in this appendix. The procedures are arranged alphabetically throughout the appendix, for reference purposes.

Decision Tree	Responsibility Checklist
Family Counseling	Restitution
Fines	Restraint
Ignoring	Restriction of Freedom
Incentives	Role Reversal
Modeling	"Snoopervision"
Natural Consequences	Spanking
Ostracism	Startling
Outside Reinforcement	Study Sessions
Physical Movement	Suspension of Privileges
Premack Principle	Time-out
Probation at Home	Work Details
Removal	

TITLE: Decision Tree

DESCRIPTION: A pictorial method of explaining the complicated process of making a choice. Adults as well as children can use the decision tree to sort out options and alternatives, thereby unifying the decision-making process. As a disciplinary procedure, the decision tree teaches patience, thoughtfulness, planning, and self-control. It can be applied to most situations. (See illustrations on pages 188, 189, and 190.)

AGES: All

EXAMPLES OF APPLICATION

Your fourteen-year-old can use the decision tree to figure out what to do with the school bully.

Your five-year-old can draw a decision tree to figure out which toy to buy with his savings.

Guide your eighteen-year-old in using the decision tree to make choices about college, marriage, sexual activity, and what to do about friends who lie.

You use a decision tree to figure out which disciplinary procedure to employ in dealing with a recalcitrant child.

PRECAUTIONS: The younger the child, the more you should supervise the procedure so that frustration won't develop. Help the young child limit the number of alternatives to four or five. Remind the child that doing nothing is *an* alternative, but it is rarely the *final* one.

RISK: None

TITLE: Family Counseling

DESCRIPTION: The searching out and consultation with a professional who has had experience and training in family matters. Seeking counseling is not an admission of guilt or failure; it is a recognition that exercising authority and running a family are extremely difficult. As with all complicated problems, seeking family counseling is simply a matter of getting a second or third opinion. Don't be afraid to "shop" for a reputable counselor by talking with friends and acquaintances or to change counselors if you're not receiving the help you desire.

AGES: All

EXAMPLES OF APPLICATION

Seek counseling when you've tried all avenues of discipline and are confused.

Seek counseling for yourself to see how much you might be adding to disciplinary problems.

Seek counseling before trying some strong disciplinary procedures that have severe side-effects.

Seek counseling when you think you have a teenager who is heading for big trouble.

PRECAUTIONS: Induce, cajole—do anything you can to get the kid to go with you. Let him or her know that everybody is part of the problem. If he or she won't go, you go and seek help on how to get him or her involved. Your family is more important than any stigma other people might place on you. Don't let your kid think that he or she is "crazy."

RISK: None

TITLE: Fines

DESCRIPTION: Levying monetary penalties for misbehavior. The amount of the fine is determined by the severity of the transgression, the number of times it occurs, and the child's age and ability to earn money. Fines can be imposed whenever the authority figure notices the transgression, and the money should be collected immediately, using the Premack principle and work details if necessary. Put fines in a special piggy bank and use them for family outings.

AGES: All children who appreciate the value of money

EXAMPLES OF APPLICATION

A five-year-old is fined a nickel for teasing his three-year-old sister.

A seven-year-old is fined a dime for spitting peas out during dinner.

A fourteen-year-old is fined a quarter for leaving his stereo on.

A sixteen-year-old, who has a job, is fined three dollars for leaving the bathroom a mess the second morning in a row.

PRECAUTIONS: Fining won't work if children don't appreciate the value of money. Be careful not to levy an unjust fine or a fine that the kid can't possibly pay. Fining works best when you collect the money immediately. You don't have to fine yourself for the same transgression, but it helps reduce the gap between you and your children.

RISK: Mild, in that some parents might use money as the *only* disciplinary procedure and forget about "warm fuzzies" and modeling.

TITLE: Ignoring

DESCRIPTION: The purposeful avoidance of any response to a disruption or negative behavior. Ignoring looks like no action, but it is a very difficult action to take. You have to work hard to do nothing. It is an action that takes the audience away from a disruptive child.

AGES: All

EXAMPLES OF APPLICATION

You don't respond to your fourteen-year-old who complains that a ten-o'clock curfew is unfair.

Your six-year-old asks for more candy; you say No once and then ignore further protestations.

You ignore a three-year-old who rolls on the floor and cries because you said it was bedtime.

PRECAUTIONS: Ignoring is hard to do. Once you start to ignore, carry through until positive behavior begins. If ignoring doesn't work or you're too angry to ignore, or if the child threatens to damage himself or something (one) else, take action other than blowing up. Don't ignore if you're eventually going to have a temper tantrum of your own.

RISK: None, if you can outlast the disruption.

TITLE: Incentives

DESCRIPTION: Establishing a positive payment as a goal for the child to work toward. An incentive can be money, extra privileges, a new toy, or some "goodie" that the child finds acceptable. The older a child, the longer he or she should work before getting the payoff.

AGES: All

EXAMPLES OF APPLICATION

Your child can earn a candy bar by helping you shop for the best prices on canned goods.

A sixth-grader can earn money toward the purchase of a BB gun by bringing home a B in a difficult subject.

A freshman in high school can earn a night out during the week by helping her brother with homework.

A seventeen-year-old can have the car an extra night for washing and waxing it.

PRECAUTIONS: Make certain the child earns the payoff with good behavior, not by stopping bad behavior. The former is an incentive; the latter, a bribe. The payoff must be something the child wants. Ask the child to help you determine a realistic incentive. You should balance the "earn, earn, earn" orientation of incentives by expressing your unconditional love regularly.

RISK: Very mild, in that some parents might use incentives to "buy off" a child rather than spend time with that child.

TITLE: Modeling

DESCRIPTION: Authority figure exhibits the behavior that he or she wishes of the child. You also demonstrate actively what you want the child to do in specific situations.

AGES: All

EXAMPLES OF APPLICATION

You pull your hand away from the figurines on the coffee table after looking and pointing at them. Then you have your one-year-old repeat what you did.

Fine yourself for cursing after imposing the same rule on your children.

Admit your mistakes to your children when you make them.

Drive carefully.

Don't throw litter out the window.

Control your drinking.

PRECAUTIONS: You can never model decent behavior too often. The only precaution is that the more you demonstrate negative behavior, the harder it will be for you to enforce your rules and regulations. I believe that rank has its privileges, but the more you exercise this right, the higher the price you have to pay.

RISK: None

TITLE: Natural Consequences

DESCRIPTION: An incidental but important disciplinary procedure in which the authority figure uses the logic of an infraction to dictate the consequences. Used positively as well as negatively, natural consequences are powerful teaching tools.

AGES: All

EXAMPLES OF APPLICATION

If a kid takes two dollars from your wallet, he or she will be penalized financially.

Abuse of the phone results in loss of phone privileges.

Curfew violations result in some loss of freedom.

Demonstrating an excellent control of temper results in an extra evening out.

Leaving the car a mess results in loss of driving privileges.

Cooking dinner without being asked results in a special treat at a favorite restaurant.

PRECAUTIONS: When employing natural consequences, let the action do the talking. If you say too much, you could add insult to injury. If you use the procedure positively, it will gain clout when used negatively.

RISK: None, as long as not done vindictively.

TITLE: Ostracism

DESCRIPTION: The purposeful exclusion of a disruptive child from part of the family activity. Ostracism is an active form of ignoring in which the child gets the message "If you continue to be disruptive, you will be excluded from being part of the family for a certain period of time." Ostracism can range from having the child eat in another part of the house, away from the family, to ignoring a teenager until he or she expresses a desire to belong to the family.

AGES: 12 and over

EXAMPLES OF APPLICATION

A twelve-year-old is ostracized from the family for two hours for flagrant irresponsibility regarding daily chores.

A thirteen-year-old is not permitted to eat with the family, because he refuses to learn how to cooperate with his younger brother.

A seventeen-year-old is not permitted to eat, do laundry, or take part in any family activities, because he will not quit smoking marijuana.

PRECAUTIONS: Because ostracism strikes at the heart of belonging and is a last-ditch effort, *it should be done with professional consultation*. When used in extreme forms, it *must* be done with consultation. It is the strongest thing you can do to a child within the confines of your home.

RISK: Severe. Pay close attention to the precautions.

TITLE: Outside Reinforcement

DESCRIPTION: Seeking the help of an agency, group, or individual outside your family that can lend support to your discipline. In seeking outside reinforcement, you are simply admitting that you need help, *not* that you've given up on your family. Outside reinforcement should occur in conjunction with family counseling.

AGES: All

EXAMPLES OF APPLICATION

You talk with the local diabetes foundation to help you with dietary regulation for your juvenile diabetic.

You talk with the local juvenile officer in finding a new way to enforce your "no drugs" rule.

You join Parents Anonymous to discuss your problems of being a single parent.

You talk with family-planning counselors about pregnancy when you think your teenage daughter is sexually active.

PRECAUTIONS: If at all possible, let your children know you are seeking the outside reinforcement and invite them to tell the people their side of the story. Remind the agency or group that you are asking for their assistance; you don't want them to take control away from you. As with family counseling, recognize that your family's welfare is more important than any possible social stigma.

RISK: Mild, in that some might see your request for help as abdication of your authority.

TITLE: Physical Movement

DESCRIPTION: This procedure is so simple many parents forget all about it. "Physical movement" means that after giving a directive, you simply enforce it by going to the child and making him or her do as you ask.

AGES: Infancy through 10

EXAMPLES OF APPLICATION

You sit your child down after he or she fails to do so when told to.

You go out into the yard and pull the child down from the swing set after he or she doesn't comply with your directive.

You grab your eight-year-old by the arm and take him through the steps of taking out the garbage, reminding him, "The next time I have to do this, you will be fined a quarter."

You grab your eight-month-old daughter's hand and gently force her to put the knickknack down when told to do so.

PRECAUTIONS: Use physical movement after one warning. If you wait too long, you will be too angry to be gentle.

RISK: Very mild if done immediately.

TITLE: Premack Principle

DESCRIPTION: A simple procedure, developed by a researcher named Premack, in which an authority figure stops all activity until children comply with the last directive. In effect, the Premack is another way of calling a time-out, much as a referee might do. You don't call "Time in" until the problem has been resolved.

AGES: All

EXAMPLES OF APPLICATION

You tell your six-year-old that he will not eat supper until his nickel fine has been paid or worked off.

You prohibit your sixteen-year-old daughter from leaving on a date until her room is cleaned up.

You say, "No phone calls, visitors, snacks, TV, playing with toys, or any other fun until you two kids complete a decision tree on how you will stop fighting."

PRECAUTIONS: Don't back away from your directive when complaints fill the air. If you stick to the Premack, you won't have to explain why you're doing it. Above all, enforce the procedure.

RISK: Mild. Only problem is that you may suspend Premack before all jobs are completed.

TITLE: Probation at Home

DESCRIPTION: A procedure permitting parents to impose tighter controls on all behavior for a specified period of time. In effect, the parents become "probation officers," evaluating behavior in the broad category of responsibility. The child is placed on a "short rope," so to speak, and is regularly warned that any infraction of the rules will result in a stronger penalty than ordinarily would be imposed.

AGES: 11 and over

EXAMPLES OF APPLICATION

You place your twelve-year-old on probation for driving the car around the block during your absence.

You place your fifteen-year-old on probation after grounding him for one week for coming home drunk.

You put your seventeen-year-old on probation for one month after he resumes his driving privileges, which had been suspended.

PRECAUTIONS: Set a period of time for the probation, not to exceed two months. The probation should be more general than "snoopervision" and should come *after* you have penalized the child. Be careful to avoid harassing the child during probation.

RISK: Moderate, because of the possibility of harassment.

TITLE: Removal

DESCRIPTION: Removing a child by order or bodily from a disruptive situation. This is a stop-gap measure, intended to cool off tempers. Some other disciplinary procedure probably should occur after tempers have calmed. Authority figures should not be afraid to apply this action to themselves when their tempers are out of control. The kids characterize removal as "Walking it off." Grandma would say, "Count to ten before you speak."

AGES: All

EXAMPLES OF APPLICATION

Mom walks into her bathroom and splashes cold water on her face instead of losing her temper at a whining child.

A six-year-old is told to go to his room to cool off when arguing with his brother.

A teenager walks down to the park and back, thinking over the reality that life isn't fair.

Mom uses physical force to take a five-year-old to his room to stop his tantrum.

PRECAUTIONS: If you use this procedure too often and/or don't implement another procedure after cooling off, you are copping out instead of coping. Be *very* careful in using physical force to remove a child from disruption. If you're not in control of your temper, you won't be able to be gentle while being firm.

RISK: Moderate to severe if bodily contact is involved; otherwise, mild.

TITLE: Responsibility Checklist

DESCRIPTION: A paper-and-pencil method of measuring a child's daily responsibilities, added up over a week's time. Daily check-off of household jobs occurs as the child is supervised in the completion of his or her assignments. Incentives and/or punishments are tied to percentage of tasks completed.

AGES: 2 or 3 through teens

EXAMPLE OF APPLICATION

Responsibilities	Days of Week
Take out garbage	Sa Su M Tu W Th F
Clean up room	
Help with dishes	
Feed dog	

Place checkmark when you agree task has been completed. Determine percentage of achievement on Friday evening and make rewards/punishments last for one week based on that percentage. For example:

Below 50%	Third-degree grounding
50–60%	Second-degree grounding
60–70%	First-degree grounding
70–80%	One dollar earned
80–90%	Two dollars earned
90% +	Three dollars earned

PRECAUTIONS: Supervise the task completion according to *your* convenience. The first week of implementation, give more explanation and some leeway, but remind children that leeway will end. You may wish to skip the punishment part and work on incentive only.

RISK: None, provided all parties agree as to definitions of such words as "clean," "help," and "straighten."

TITLE: Restitution

DESCRIPTION: A pay-back process for offenses such as theft, vandalism, lying, cheating, or any other "rip-off" in which a victim is involved. Restitution is given to the injured party by the child as a lesson that a rip-off insults another. Not only does the child have to pay for the act itself; he or she also owes the victim compensation for the insult. Restitution, therefore, could be called an "insult penalty."

AGES: All who can understand "Making up for what you did"

EXAMPLES OF APPLICATION

Your seven-year-old has not only to pay back the dollar he stole from your purse but also to complete a one-hour work detail to make restitution for the theft.

You impose a third-degree restriction on your ten-year-old for eight days; four days' pay for cheating on a math test, the remaining four for the insult to your morality concerning cheating.

Your fourteen-year-old is caught vandalizing the park. He must work one week to pay for damages to the park and an additional week before restitution is complete.

PRECAUTIONS: You'll be angry if your kid pulls a dumb stunt. An insult penalty doesn't have to be harsh or long-lasting to get the message across. Once again, avoid put-downs; let your actions do the talking.

RISK: Mild. Restitution is one procedure that calls for a thorough explanation, especially during teenage years.

TITLE: Restraint

DESCRIPTION: The firm but gentle physical restraining of a child who continues disruption when told to cease. It may often be used in conjunction with removal and should be followed by some other procedure.

AGES: 1 through 12; cease using when someone might get hurt

EXAMPLES OF APPLICATION

Child refuses to stand in the corner and you must hold him or her there until he or she "decides" to stay put. Grab the child by the shoulders from behind and hold.

Restraining an older brother who won't stop hitting his younger brother.

Restraining a two-year-old whose tantrum is so bad he or she can't be reasoned with and won't leave voluntarily. You will probably need to remove bodily as well.

PRECAUTIONS: Be very careful not to squeeze the child too tightly. If you must use restraint, do it before you reach a boiling point.

RISK: The risk moves toward severe the madder you get. Tempers can result in not-so-gentle restraint.

TITLE: Restriction of Freedom (Grounding)

DESCRIPTION: Authority prohibits the child from coming and going from the room, house, or yard in the usual fashion. This act of restriction is called "grounding" by most parents. The procedure typically is tied to the suspension of privileges, since some privileges are automatically suspended when grounding occurs. Restriction works best when used in degrees that depend upon the nature and frequency of disruption.

AGES: School age

EXAMPLES OF APPLICATION

Here are five suggested degrees of grounding:
First degree: Child is restricted to your yard after dinner for one week because he crossed the street without permission.

Second degree: Same child is restricted to your yard all the time for one week because he crossed the street again.

Third degree: You restrict a child to the house for one week for picking a fight with a smaller child.

Fourth degree: You ground your child in his room after dinner because she watched TV after that privilege was suspended.

Fifth degree: You confine your child to his room all the time (except school, work, eating, bathroom) because he drove the car around the neighborhood while you were gone.

PRECAUTIONS: Grounding will not work on those children who don't care to run around. If it doesn't, use something else. Don't exceed two weeks for any grounding, and keep the fifth degree (which is actually a way of implementing "jail" at home) to no more than two days. Fourth- and fifth-degree grounding should be reserved for serious violations. Also, if the child is confined to his or her room, make certain the toys—stereo, TV, radio—are removed first.

RISK: Minimal in first three degrees; moderate to severe at degrees four and five. Reduce risk by encouraging child to "pay his time."

TITLE: Role Reversal

DESCRIPTION: A role-playing technique that calls for the participants to switch roles; one assumes the role of the person one is confronting. This procedure is best used when two kids are mad at each other and the authority figure has time to carry out the procedure. It's an excellent technique for resolving sibling fights and teaching empathy.

AGES: Any who can act out a role

EXAMPLES OF APPLICATION

Make your twelve- and fourteen-year-olds switch roles and continue their fight over which TV program to watch.

YOU switch roles with your lazy sixteen-year-old daughter and see how she feels when she has to clean up after you.

When your fifteen-year-old daughter makes fun of her nine-year-old brother, have her switch roles and make her shut up while her brother insults her.

PRECAUTIONS: Avoid any needless insults and suspend the procedure if it doesn't work quickly. Role reversal takes time; don't try to use it between getting supper and cleaning up after the dog. Allow at least ten minutes and then encourage the participants to discuss the procedure. This can be an excellent time to stimulate communication between parent and child.

RISK: None, if pointless insults are avoided.

TITLE: "Snoopervision"

DESCRIPTION: Extremely close supervision. It is a willful violation of a child's privacy during which an authority figure scrutinizes behavior while looking for the slightest indication of disruption. "Snoopervision" concentrates on behavior that ordinarily would not be evaluated. It is employed when the child violates the right to privacy and that violation could lead to serious consequences. "Snoopervision" is most effective when the child is told *what* will happen, but not *when* or *where*.

AGES: In most cases, teenagers

EXAMPLES OF APPLICATION

Searching a teenager's drawers and closet after discovering that he or she uses drugs.

Following a teenage driver after he or she has had a reckless-driving charge.

Walking into a child's classroom unannounced (teacher and principal know) after learning that he or she is not responsive to classroom discipline.

PRECAUTIONS: Limit the number of days of "snoopervision." If it doesn't have an effect in two weeks, something else should be tried. It should be carried out matter-of-factly, without ridicule.

RISK: Severe. Children value their privacy. You should violate it only when the child has persisted in behavior that could lead to danger.

TITLE: Spanking

DESCRIPTION: Three or four swats with your hand or a paddle on the child's buttock or the hands. The hits should be immediate and sharp but not hard enough to cause physical injury. Spanking should be reserved for those situations in which the child's behavior is placing him or her in imminent physical danger. If you can't spank a child so as to interrupt dangerous behavior, then you probably shouldn't spank at all.

AGES: 1 through 6

EXAMPLES OF APPLICATION

A two-year-old is spanked on the hand for reaching toward a hot stove.

Your three-year-old is spanked for running recklessly into the street.

You spank your four-year-old for persistently climbing into a precarious perch on the swing set.

You spank a five-year-old for teasing a mean dog.

PRECAUTIONS: Spanking too often dulls the child to physical pain. In turn, he or she can become more disruptive and more indifferent to spanking. Spanking a child too often can also result in too much fear, which erodes authority. Try to find other disciplinary procedures for children above the ages of five or six. Never hit a child in the face.

RISK: Moderate, when precautions are followed.

TITLE: Startling

DESCRIPTION: The use of some action that immediately interrupts the child's behavior in such a way that he or she is shocked. Startling should be used only when a child has "lost control," cannot be reached quickly, or when authority wishes to get his or her attention abruptly. Many things can startle children; the value depends upon the child's age and how often the authority uses the startling technique.

AGES: All

EXAMPLES OF APPLICATION

Your eighteen-month-old is about to pull the dog's hair, and you clap your hands loudly.

Your three-year-old is pulling the baby's arm out of the socket and you scream, "Stop it!"

Your four-year-old is in a tantrum beyond control and you throw a little water from a cup into his face.

Your ten-year-old is swiping his sister's dessert and you growl harshly.

PRECAUTIONS: Most parents don't realize it, but if they don't yell or scream too often, such loud vocalization has positive shock value. Of course, you must follow up startling with another disciplinary procedure. If you do, eventually the shock itself will be sufficient. This is how the "evil eye" gains clout.

RISK: Mild if not done too often. Moderate to severe if water is used. Startling must be used in atmosphere of positive support.

TITLE: Study Sessions

DESCRIPTION: The imposition of quiet time during which child is expected to study. These sessions can be put into effect at times when the children are most apt to be able to concentrate and can be used even though there is no "official homework." Just because schools don't give homework is no reason that parents can't.

AGES: School age

EXAMPLES OF APPLICATION

A study session of one hour is imposed immediately after school for the young children.

A study session of two hours, from seven to nine P.M., is imposed on high-school students.

A study session of two hours is imposed on Saturday morning for children who have done poor work during the week.

PRECAUTIONS: Do not be sidetracked by arguments that the teacher assigned no homework or that other kids don't have to study. If you get positive cooperation, be willing to suspend the session upon occasion. Let children know that their main job when young is to learn as well as they possibly can.

RISK: None, except for the complaints you will encounter.

TITLE: Suspension of Privileges

DESCRIPTION: This is probably the most thorough punishment technique used by parents. Privileges that are usually suspended include TV-watching, snacks, having a friend over, phone calls, listening to music, driving the car, and playing with toys. Since privileges go hand in hand with freedom, suspend privileges in degrees—phone calls for an hour, then two, then all evening, etc. Selection of the privileges to be suspended depends upon what is important to the child, the nature of the disruption, and the frequency of the problem.

AGES: All who can appreciate the privileges

EXAMPLES OF APPLICATION

You suspend Saturday-morning cartoons for a five-year-old who left the TV on when he went outside to play.

You take away phone privileges after supper for a fourteen-year-old who uses disrespectful language toward you.

You suspend friends' visits, phone calls, and stereo privileges because your sixteen-year-old ran up forty dollars' worth of phone bills.

You take away all games for one week because your nine-year-old cheated his younger brother.

PRECAUTIONS: Finding the balance between too much and too little punishment is difficult. Use the idea of natural consequences to help you. If you want to give a strong punishment, take more privileges away for a shorter period. The quicker a punishment is over, the better.

RISK: Minimal if precautions are followed.

TITLE: Time-Out

DESCRIPTION: Placing a child in a situation in which inactivity and boredom can be maximized. One of the best time-out measures is standing a child in a corner. The child is placed in the corner, given a "sentence" of so-many minutes, and told, "You are not free until you pay me ten minutes without any noise or movement." If the child grumbles, jumps around, or creates a disturbance, the time starts over again, no matter how close to the end he or she was. Use a kitchen timer and say, "Freedom returns when the bell rings." Keep a close eye that the sentence is served. Start with the number of minutes of the child's age.

AGES: 2 through 12

EXAMPLES OF APPLICATION

Stand a three-year-old in the corner for three minutes for not picking up toys when he was told to.

A five-year-old gets ten minutes in the corner when returning from a shopping trip for causing disruption during the trip. (You double the sentence when public disruption is involved.)

Stand an eight-year-old in the corner for eight minutes after he makes fun of a five-year-old who had to stand in the corner.

PRECAUTIONS: Make certain you follow through! If you don't, you lose a very effective disciplinary procedure. You can increase the length of the sentence after the effectiveness wears off.

RISK: Possibly the *most effective yet mild* disciplinary procedure.

TITLE: Work Details

DESCRIPTION: The assignment of work tasks in and around the home that are above and beyond daily responsibilities. There are several uses of work details; among these are earning extra money, working off a fine, helping with a special project with no hint of reward or punishment, and making restitution.

AGES: 4 and over

EXAMPLES OF APPLICATION

You contract with your thirteen-year-old to clean the basement and garage and wash windows in order for him or her to earn spending money.

You assign a three-hour work detail as a punishment for a child who came home two hours late.

You tell your ten-year-old that he alone must do the dishes in order to work off the fifty-cent fine he received for playing with his food during dinner.

PRECAUTIONS: Justice must play an important role in the determination of the work assignment. It might be easy to overdo the extent of the assignment if you're angry. Figure out a schedule for converting work into value using such things as the current minimum-wage law, the age of the child, and the difficulty of the task assigned. Don't forget to ask the child what he or she thinks would be just.

RISK: Minimal to moderate, in that you might overdo the assignment.

Index